Organizations
Working
Together

Volume 191 Sage Libr

RECENT VOLUMES IN . . .
SAGE LIBRARY OF SOCIAL RESEARCH

Organizations Working Together

Catherine Alter
Jerald Hage

Sage Library of Social Research 191

SAGE Publications
International Educational and Professional Publisher
Newbury Park   London   New Delhi

For information address:

 SAGE Publications, Inc.
2455 Teller Road
Newbury Park, California 91320

SAGE Publications Ltd.
6 Bonhill Street
London EC2A 4PU
United Kingdom

SAGE Publications India Pvt. Ltd.
M-32 Market
Greater Kailash I
New Delhi 110 048 India

Printed in the United States of America

Library of Congress Cataloging-in-Publication Data

Alter, Catherine.
    Organizations working together / Catherine Alter, Jerald Hage.
        p. cm.—(Sage library of social research: 191)
    Includes bibliographical references and index.
    ISBN 0-8039-4826-3.—ISBN 0-8039-4827-1 (pbk.)
    1. Strategic alliances (Business)   2. Interorganizational
relations. I. Hage, Jerald, 1932-   . II. Title.   III. Series:
Sage library of social research : v. 191.
HD69.S8A45   1993
338.8—dc20   92-27125
                                                                   CIP

95 96 10 9 8 7 6 5 4 3

Sage Production Editor: Judith L. Hunter

Contents

ONE

Interorganizational Networks: A New Institution

Just as free markets are being hailed as the salvation of Eastern Europe, the Soviet Union, Latin America, and other parts of the world, evidence is mounting that institutions other than markets are coordinating and controlling the economies of Western Europe, the United States, Japan, and elsewhere in advanced industrialized countries. In an analysis of a century of American industry, Campbell, Hollingsworth, and Lindberg, in *The Governance of the American Economy* (1991), demonstrate that markets are not the only way prices are coordinated. A wide variety of institutional arrangements—joint ventures, associations, promotional networks, obligational networks—are being used to coordinate activities across organizational boundaries. In a companion volume in press, edited by Hollingsworth, Schmitter, and Streeck, a number of contributors provide similar evidence in a series of analyses of contemporary industrial sectors in Western Europe, North America, and Japan. This body of research suggests that, because interorganizational networks produce superior economic performance and quality, there is a movement away from large, vertically integrated firms.

The thesis of this book is that new mechanisms for coordinating and controlling different sectors of the economy are emerging, and it is the systemic network that offers the greatest competitive advantages in a global economy. Our central argument is that systemic networks—clusters of organizations that

1

make decisions jointly and integrate their efforts to produce a product or service—adjust more rapidly to changing technologies and market conditions, develop new products and services in a shorter time period, and provide more creative solutions in the process.

This book is about organizations that are linked together—clusters of single corporations, firms, private voluntary organizations, and government agencies. These networks of organizations may choose to exchange or pool their resources, or they may decide to work together toward some common and mutually agreed upon end, or they may collaboratively produce a product or service. This phenomenon, we believe, is not new but is increasing in frequency. There are visible and important reasons why interorganizational networks are multiplying, and that is the focus of this chapter. Before examining theories about the antecedents of interorganizational formation, let us describe this new institution.

Until recently, U.S. corporations adopted organizational structures that were large and centralized and relied on vertical control and communication mechanisms (Aldrich & Mueller, 1982; Chandler, 1977), or what Campbell et al. (1991) called hierarchies. Corporate strategy was to eliminate competitors to gain control over their buyers or suppliers, and the methods were merger, price war, and large advertising budgets. American and European industry sometimes formed cartels, a special kind of network, to control prices and production, but generally this was not an effective strategy because of competitive pressures and the desire to maximize profit (Campbell et al., p. 186). Profit-making organizations' primary objective, of course, was to gain maximum leverage over needed resources by besting rivals by whatever means were at hand.

Today, however, many companies are developing structures that are smaller, decentralized, and based on strategies of cooperation and horizontal relationships. Campbell et al. suggest that the movement toward "flexible production systems" has led to a variety of obligational networks, bound together by subcontracts and cooperative contracts among small firms, and strategic alliances and joint ventures among large and small firms (Kogut, Shan, & Walker, 1990; Powell & Brantley, in press). Examples are to be found in auto, aerospace, bio-tech, chemical, information and computer technology, and new materials industries, and it is not an accident that these sectors are in the forefront of this institutional evolution (Pollack, 1992a). This is an organizational movement in the direction opposite to that predicted by transactional cost analysis (Williamson, 1975), where concerns about small numbers and cheating predominated. Instead of firms attempting to control their environment via vertical integration, they are selling parts of their business and accomplishing through voluntary alliances what formerly was achieved through combat. Let us examine one brief example of what we will call a symbiotic joint venture.

In 1924 Corning glass entered its first joint venture, to make cartons for glass production. Later, in 1941, a handshake between the Corning CEO and Dr. Willard Dow formed Dow-Corning. Today, Corning calls itself a "global network," and has partnerships or joint ventures with 15 companies in 13 counties. Says current CEO James R. Houghton:

... we use the concept of the network in a broad way: A network is an interrelated group of businesses with a wide range of ownership structures. Although diverse, these businesses are closely linked (Houghton, 1989, p. 3).

Corning executives are clear about the reasons they have chosen a network structure: Speed. Companies, they say, do not have the luxury today of nurturing a product through many years of invention, development, manufacturing, and marketing. Because foreign firms have diversity of expertise and strategic market information that Corning could never obtain on its own, partnerships are a fast way of expanding into new markets. Interorganizational alliances provide the flexibility that is needed to take advantage of new market opportunities.

The other impetus for network formation for Corning is associated with the competitiveness of foreign markets. Because success is so difficult, Corning believes that the only strategy is to produce quality—to meet or exceed the

Continued

continued from previous page

requirements of the customer. They find, however, that a focus on quality has internal as well as external benefits. Again, Mr. Houghton:

Each year when quality teams from all parts of the world converge at our headquarters, we have people from different businesses discussing their experiences, communicating ideas and sharing a common bond. By focusing on quality we have developed a common language so that workers at an American glass plant can, at a basic level, understand the efforts and ambitions of a Corning laboratory technician working at a factory in France (Houghton, 1989, p. 3).

Corning executives believe their network is still "work in progress," but that in spite of the learning they must do to improve its operation, it will give them the flexibility and strength to prosper.

NETWORKS OF ALLIANCES

Today, United States corporations have formed more than 2,000 alliances in Europe alone (Kraar, 1989), and 12,000 worldwide in just the last decade (Work, 1988). Most of these joint ventures are concentrated in areas where either product development costs are quite high or speed of product development must be fast (Berg & Hoekman, 1988; Hladik, 1988; Moxon, Roehl, & Truitt, 1988). Counting just international joint ventures—those between the United States, Europe, and Japan—the following patterns can be seen (Pollack, 1992a). In 1989, there were 198 joint ventures across national borders between bio-tech firms, almost a doubling in 5 years; 115 in new materials with a similar rate of increase; 445 in information technology, about a 30% increase in 5 years; 103 between the major chemical companies, also about a 30% increase; and only 34 joint ventures in aviation, but ones that involve the companies in complex joint product development arrangements.

One very illustrative example among aircraft manufacturers is Airbus Industrie, a consortium involving four governments—France, West Germany, United Kingdom, and Spain—and their respective companies, Aerospatiale, Deutsche Airbus, British Aerospace, and CASA. Another illustration is Boeing-Japan, which includes the American firm Boeing with two Japanese consortia—Japan Aircraft Development Corporation and Japan Aircraft Corporation—as well as three Japanese heavy industry companies—Mitsubishi, Kawasaki, and Fuji Heavy Industries. On the engine side there are also two joint ventures: CFM International, which combines General Electric with Snecma, a French company; and International Aero Engines, which combines Pratt and Whitney (a U.S. firm), Rolls Royce (a U.K. firm), Japan Aero Engines, Motoren-und-Turbinen-Union (a German firm), and Fiat (an Italian firm) (Moxon, Roehl, & Truitt, 1988).

The most dramatic development of international joint ventures, however, has been in the automotive industry, which has seen the number jump from 26 to 79. Where there formerly were bitter rivalries, now there are working relationships. For example, Ford currently builds minivans with Nissan at a Ford plant in Ohio, assembles Mazda's Mercury Tracers in Mexico, has a working agreement with Mazda to build Ford Probes in Michigan, and merged their operation in Brazil and Argentina with Volkswagen (Kraar, 1989). Since we assume that profit-making firms want to maximize profits, this behavior, particularly since it represents an about-face from the previous century (Chandler, 1977), begs for an explanation.

Firms are creating joint ventures with other firms (including their competitors) when launching new products, rather than expanding their own operations. One illustration is in the biotech industry, where small bio-tech firms form cooperative relationships with large pharmaceutical companies to produce, store, and market large quantities of biological products (Powell & Brantley, in press). How quickly this industry transformed itself is reported in a paper by Kogut, Shan and Walker (1990). Bilateral partnerships, of which there were only 46 in the period prior to 1984, were formed with such rapidity that by 1988 there was a total of 296 joint ventures.

In an exhaustive study of 126 new bio-tech firms founded with a product orientation toward human bio-tech (e.g. therapeutics, diagnostics, or both) and having more than 10 employees, Powell and Brantley (in press) found 765 interorganizational agreements. Most of these joint ventures are within the United States, and the total represents four times the number identified in the international studies (Hergert & Morris, 1988; Pollack, 1992a). Powell and Brantley focused on the relationships between these many small firms (only a few of which had more than 500 employees prior to 1990) and their large partners, such as Hoffman-LaRoche (18 joint ventures with small biotech firms), DuPont (12 joint ventures), and Bristol-Meyers Squibb (10 joint ventures), and public sector research organizations, such as the National Institutes of Health (48 joint ventures), with the National Cancer Institute alone having 11. Large universities such as Stanford, Harvard, Johns Hopkins, and several medical schools were also found to have four or more agreements with small high-tech firms.

Nor are these kinds of collaborative relationships limited to just large bio-tech firms. Hakansson (1990), in a study of 123 small Swedish firms, found that two-thirds of them allocated more than 30% of their development work to collaborative relationships. The bulk of these relationships involved either suppliers or customers, and they replaced the kind of vertical integration found in large firms. These relationships tended to be stable and usually not formalized by contract, indicating that a considerable amount of trust had developed.

More recently, relationships have developed between firms that are in the same product market niche. These relationships between former competitors are a very interesting institutional change. In some cases, successful large firms have disaggregated themselves into multiple small firms, which then develop their own separate relationships with other organizations (Eccles & White, 1988). This means, of course, that large firms, by decentralizing their operations, can have a wider reach without the problems associated with comparable size. The downsizing of established business firms via the establishment of joint ventures is an important trend. Corning Glass Works is, of course, the veteran alliance builder, but it is not unique.

Systemic Production Networks in Manufacturing

Joint ventures and strategic alliances are bilateral relationships with formal controls or informal cooperative agreements (Berg & Hoekman, 1988; Powell & Brantley, in press). As important as these mechanisms are, they represent only a partial movement toward the focus of this book, systemic interorganizational networks—multilateral arrangements among diverse organizations that band together to produce a single product.

An excellent example of this new kind of institutional arrangement is found in the Japanese automobile industry (Womack, Jones, & Roos, 1990, pp. 148-182). Rather than manufacture the whole car themselves and practice extensive vertical integration, Toyota and other Japanese car manufacturers purchase many parts from suppliers. Suppliers, who provide a particular component, also have suppliers who, in turn, also have suppliers. What makes these first, second, and third source suppliers a network, as distinct from a production chain, is that they engage in joint design and problem solving. The Japanese call these vertical *Keiretsu*, or system line.

The car assembler targets a total price, a price that allows a reasonable profit for both the assembler and the suppliers. To achieve this profit, the assembler and supplier work together to lower the cost of each part. For this system to be effective, both the primary supplier and the assembler must share a great deal of information about production costs and profits, participate together in designing the component parts, and work with the engineers of the secondary suppliers.

Joint design of a car and its components, however, is perhaps not the most telling aspect of how these systemic networks coordinate activities. Assemblers and suppliers must engage in a great deal of joint problem solving relative to both quality and quality control. In the United States automobile industry, defective parts are typically rejected. In Japan, defective parts become an occasion for joint problem solving within the network and an opportunity for an innovative solution.

Another distinctive characteristic of production networks is that prices are jointly set and cost savings are jointly shared between manufacturers and suppliers. The consequence of the Japanese network is that suppliers have economic incentives to continue cost reductions, while at the same time not only maintaining but also continuing to improve quality. By contrast, American automobile manufacturers set prices that encourage suppliers to cut corners on quality. This results in defective parts that cause delays in production, forcing American manufacturers to maintain large inventories, which in turn drives up costs. Paradoxically, Japanese car manufacturers, with no inventories, have far fewer production delays than do the Americans (Womack et al., 1990).

The price of component parts in a Japanese supplier network shifts across the life of the product cycle, steadily declining. This ensures suppliers with both a constant stream of profits and economies of scale. As a consequence, there is no incentive to block innovation. By contrast, American automobile manufacturers attempt to maximize each production run, and suppliers therefore do not expect profits until several years after the start of production. Economic downturns injure American suppliers more frequently than their Japanese counterparts, and their incentive to innovate is lost.

Thus we have described long-term relationships between organizations involved together in the production of a product. Problem solving occurs across organizational boundaries, team decision making predominates, and prices are set jointly and not within a single hierarchy of power and authority. The resulting performance advantages are higher quality, faster problem solving, and thus greater flexibility. The joint design of a product and its components, and the sharing of information about production costs, ensure parts of high quality that work the first time. Thus there is little or no time lost in production and there are shorter production cycles. Indicators of network production processes are shown in Table 1.1.

Table 1.1 compares measures of Japanese network production methods with American and European production methods (adapted from Womack et al., 1990). The indicators concerning supplier performance and involvement show that one-half of engineering time is borne by the suppliers in Japan, as opposed to 14% in the United States. Assemblers design 81% of the parts in the United States, but only 30% in Japan. Lead time in the United States for dies is three times greater, and the number of defective parts is 40% higher.

The amount of time in staff hours required to produce a new product is the best unobtrusive measure of adaptive efficiency in manufacturing. (This is a different definition of the term than that used by North [1990], who uses the concept of adaptive efficiency to mean changes in the institutional rules.) In a detailed study, Clark (as reported in Womack et al., 1990, p. 111) found it took the Japanese an average of 1.7 million hours of engineering and 46 months to deliver a new model. The Americans and Europeans, by contrast, took 3 million hours of engineering and 60 months. Networks allow the Japanese to shorten the production process

Table 1.1 Cross Regional Comparisons of Suppliers

	Japanese Japan	Japanese American	American America	All Europe
Supplier Performance: [1]				
Die change times (minutes)	7.90	21.40	114.30	123.70
Lead time for new dies (weeks)	11.10	19.30	34.50	40.00
Job classifications	2.9	3.4	9.5	5.1
Machines per worker	7.4	4.1	2.5	2.7
Inventory levels (days)	1.50	4.00	8.10	16.30
Number of daily JIT deliveries	7.90	1.60	1.60	0.70
Parts defects (per car)[2]	.24	na	.33	.62
Supplier Involvement in Design:[3]				
Engineering carried out by				
suppliers (% total hours)	51.00	na	14.00	35.00
Supplier propriety parts (%)	8.00	na	3.00	7.00
Black box parts (%)	62.00	na	16.00	39.00
Assembler designed parts (%)	30.00	na	81.00	54.00
Supplier/Assembler Relations:[4]				
Number of suppliers per				
assembly plant	170.00	238.00	509.00	442.00
Inventory levels (days, for 8 parts)	0.20	1.60	2.90	2.00
Proportion of parts delivered				
just-in-time (%)	45.00	35.40	14.80	7.90
Proportion of parts single sourced	12.10	98.00	69.30	32.90

SOURCE: Reprinted with the permission of Rawson Associates, an imprint of Macmillan Publishing Company from *The Machine That Changed the World* by James P. Womack, Daniel T. Jones, and Daniel Roos. Copyright © 1990 James P. Womack, Daniel T. Jones, Daniel Roos, and Donna Sammons Carpenter.
[1] From a matched sample of 54 supplier plants in Japan (18), America (10 American-owned and 8 Japanese-owned), and Europe (18) (Nishiguchi, 1989, Chapter 7, pp. 313-347).
[2] Calculated from the 1988 J.D. Power Initial Quality Survey.
[3] From the survey of 29 product development projects (Clark, Fujimoto, & Chew, 1987, p. 741; Fujimoto, 1989, Table 7.1).
[4] From the IMVP *World Assembly Plant Survey*, 1990.

and reduce costs, which enables them to create more innovative designs. One indicator of decline in American competitiveness is the ratio of the product design cycle in East Asia vis-à-vis North America and Europe, and what is true in manufacturing is true in many other sectors (MIT Commission, 1989).

One lesson to draw from this example is that American manufacturers should consider disaggregating their organizations, establishing networks, and jointly designing their products with others. To be successful, managers must lean how to coordinate prices and production across organizational boundaries. If American managers learn more about systemic networks and how to manage them, then there is hope that American competitiveness will improve.

Parallels in the Public Sector

Oddly, what is becoming true in manufacturing has been true in the public sector for some time. Although the private-for-profit and public not-for-profit are thought to be worlds apart, they share many characteristics. The movement away from vertical integration is one similarity, although it has been given different names. Perhaps the most dramatic example is the deinstitutionalization movement that closed state mental hospitals and returned mentally ill patients to local communities, in the hope that the quality of care would improve and costs would be reduced. Similarly, states have stimulated many attempts to coordinate the services provided by independent providers at the local level, just as there has been the attempt to stimulate product development in industry by using industrial consortia.

This movement began during the late 1960s, when the federal government experimented with decentralizing control of human service delivery. These efforts sprang from sincere doubts about the capability of the U.S. government to deliver effective human services to its citizens in their homes and communities. Because of our federal structure of categorically divided program responsibility and its vertical funding channels through federal, regional, state, and local agencies, it was recognized that services were fragmented, often duplicative, yet inaccessible due to conflicting eligibility requirements. Led by Elliot Richardson, then Secretary of the Department of Health, Education and Welfare, federal bureaucrats experimented in giving some control of programs to service providers. The strategies of reform were known as services coordination and integration, and included a wide range of programs such as Community Action, Community Mental Health Centers (CMHCs), Model Cities, Comprehensive Health Planning, and Service Integration Programs (Agranoff & Pattakos, 1979; Warren, 1973). They employed a number of different approaches, such as consolidation of funding streams, comprehensive community planning, functional specialization among organizations, joint programs and collocation, and task integration (DeWitt, 1977).

The first evaluations of these programs were disappointing (Aiken, Dewar, DiTomaso, Hage, & Zeitz, 1975; Morris & Lescohier, 1978), and by the mid-1970s the reform movement had ceased, even though many knew that interorganizational coordination would indeed develop slowly and at an irregular pace if given the chance (Agranoff & Pattakos, 1979; DeWitt, 1977). National attention turned to the Vietnam war, and human services improvement was forgotten.

But the need for services coordination at the community level continued to increase unabated because new client populations and new services proliferated at a steady pace. One example of service innovation created as the result of new knowledge is found in medicine, where more effective methods of controlling pain were found, which led to new thinking about palliative care for terminally ill patients, which became the foundation of the international hospice movement. Within a decade of the creation of St. James Hospice in London, even moderate-size communities in the United States were developing hospice care systems. To do so, it was necessary to integrate services and treatment provided by private physicians, hospitals, home nursing services, volunteer organizations, mental health programs, and the clergy (Alter, 1988a). Interagency hospice care programs are only one example of how invention and new knowledge have increased, not decreased, the pressure and urgency for interorganizational coordination. *The influence of new knowledge and new technologies on interorganizational structures and the need for new ways of coordinating complex human services will be a constant theme of this book.*

Pressure was put on communities to develop systematic approaches to service delivery. Certainly the most visible example during the 1980s was the deinstitutionalization movement, because substituting community-based care for institutional care requires a wide range of concrete medical and psychosocial services that must be available on a 24-hour basis, a mode of care requiring very high levels of coordination. Both governmental and private funding agencies insisted with increasing frequency that grantees establish interagency coordinating committees and councils.

Now, in the early 1990s, only two decades after Richardson proposed services integration, we find both considerable change in the delivery of services in many communities in the United States and renewed interest in the problem of getting service organizations to work together. As a result of technological and political change, there is more coordination among agencies in programs serving the mentally ill (Broskowski, 1981; Turner & Tenoor, 1978), the terminally ill (Alter, 1988c), the elderly (Alter, 1988a), and juveniles (Alter, 1988b; Dryfoos, 1991). These developments are interesting, given the prediction that cooperative behavior between competing agencies is unlikely (Pfeffer & Salancik, 1978). Why are agencies now more cooperative than they appeared to be some two decades ago? What changes in society explain this evolution? Has change been influenced primarily by federal initiatives or are there broader societal determinants?

The Theoretical Problem

From our viewpoint, it is these cooperative behaviors—the growing number of partnerships, alliances, joint ventures, consortia, obligational and systemic networks—that represent a stunning evolutionary change in institutional forms of governance (Aldrich & Mueller, 1982). As an example of how important these have become in the business world, a wide range of articles have appeared recently on the strategy of cooperative behavior and the need to form strategic alliances (Contractor & Lorange, 1988; Jarillo, 1988; Mowery, 1988; Nohria & Eccles, in press; Sydow, 1991). These interorganizational networks of product development, manufacture, and delivery of human services raise a number of interesting questions about various assumptions of rational organizational behavior. Again, we find ourselves asking: Why should firms or agencies cooperate? What changes in the society are producing this shift in strategy and behavior?

We propose to answer these questions by developing a theory about cooperative behavior between organizations and the conditions that produce effective coordination in this new institutional form. New theory about interorganizational networks and delivery systems, applicable to both nonprofit and profit sectors, is timely for a number of reasons. The emergence of organizational networks and systems—for the development of commercial applications for superconductor technology (Hilts, 1989; Richards, 1989), the treatment of sexually abused children, the manufacture of automobiles and trucks (Womack et al., 1990)—are significant developments for both practical and theoretical reasons.

We believe the theoretical importance of interorganizational networks is quite obvious. We predict that they are the future institution. We anticipate, and it is the reason we write this book, that this new institutional form will increasingly replace both markets and hierarchies as a governance mechanism (Williamson, 1975, 1985), and that networks are as fundamentally different as were the multidivisional corporation (Chandler, 1962) and its predecessor the large bureaucracy (Aldrich & Mueller, 1982; Chandler, 1977; Weber, 1946). For organizational theorists, they pose a number of intellectual challenges. Conventional wisdom assumed that public organizations would always attempt to maximize autonomy (Aldrich, 1979; Benson, 1975; Gouldner, 1959; Hall, 1990; Whetten, 1981); however, by the mid-1980s this assumption was challenged by Lincoln and McBride (1985), and more recently in the strategic management literature (Jarillo, 1988; Nielsen, 1988). They were thought not to resemble private organizations that, by definition, always attempt to maximize profit (Scherer, 1980); again, an assumption that has been challenged by the concept of satisficing (March & Simon, 1958) and our example of Japanese lean production networks. Conventional wisdom may need revision. How is it that what was in the 1960s thought to be impossible, or at the least impractical or ineffective, has now become everyday reality? What does this imply for the development of organizational theory? These questions are the focus for the remainder of this chapter.

ANTECEDENTS OF COOPERATIVE BEHAVIOR

There have been a number of fundamental changes occurring in the United States and other advanced post-industrial societies that not only make more complex organizational forms a distinct practical possibility, but also are a stimulant to their development. These changes reflect long-term shifts in markets, economic policies, culture, and levels of knowledge and education, and these changes have accelerated in the past three decades.

The Shift From Efficiency for Quantity to Efficiency for Flexibility and Innovativeness

The central argument in transaction cost analysis (Coase, 1937; Williamson, 1975) was that if one institutional governance mechanism is more efficient than another in reducing the costs of exchange, that is, the costs of information search and enforcement of contracts, then there is a tendency toward that form. This argument can be used to explain the shift from markets with small firms to large corporations that dominate their industrial sectors. Examples of this process are provided in the analysis of the meat packing, railroad, telecommunications, and steel industries in Campbell et al.'s, *The Governance of the American Economy* (1991) and in Chandler's *The Visible Hand* (1977).

The problem with this approach is that it does not explain the current movement away from vertical integration, unless we recognize that there are different kinds of efficiencies. One type of efficiency is associated with large-scale standardized products, or what Hollingsworth referred to as "Fordism" (1991). Another type, however, is associated with quality, flexibility, and innovativeness. If a firm must adjust rapidly to new market conditions and produce a new product in a short time period, then a network does this more efficiently than a large vertically integrated company. General Motors, the company that was most vertically integrated, has long production runs and was more efficient, but only as long as consumer tastes and demands remained constant. Toyota, with its systemic network of suppliers, is able to more rapidly adjust to shifting demands such as fuel-efficient cars, convertibles, and air bags.

The fact that there are different types of efficiencies has not been made clear in discussions of the governance of the private sector (see Hage, 1984, for an exception), but again the issue is similar in both public and private sectors. The deinstitutionalization of mental patients, for example, was accomplished in part to provide improved individualization of care. Thus, in both sectors, networks become the means to accomplish efficiently the customization of products and the individualization of services.

The Integration of Economic and Political Objectives

One naive contemporary belief is that economics and politics do not mix, that markets are apolitical. On the contrary, the governments of many counties adopt industrial policies, which, in order to be implemented, require partnerships between state agencies and private corporations.

The Japanese central state, for example, brought together their shipbuilding companies during the 1970s and facilitated agreement on whole series of production and price reductions so that the decline of the industry would be orderly (Strath, in press). In consumer electronics (Cawson, in press), the French central state is supporting Thompson's global strategy of remaining a world player in the manufacturing of television sets. In the United States, the American central state has taken the lead in research and development needed for the military and for eradication of selected diseases such as AIDS (Hollingsworth, 1991, p. 64). It is this investment in medical research that has given rise to the bio-tech industry. Powell and Brantley (in press) report that 50 of more than 700 bio-tech joint ventures involve the National Institutes of Health, and another 28 involve universities supported by government funding. When the state promotes research that produces products, Hollingsworth labels the relationships a promotional network, a network involving all of the competitors. The special role of the Japanese central state in the encouragement of sunrise industries and in the coordination of various industrial sectors is well known, and summed up in the phrase "Japan, Inc." This type of state involvement in economic organizations is the major theme of *The Governance of the American Economy* (Campbell et al., 1991) and *Comparing Capitalist Economies* (Hollingsworth et al., in press).

There is also a large and growing literature on the role of the state in the health and welfare market. In many advanced industrial states, the central state controls and coordinates the delivery of health care (Hollingsworth, Hage, & Hanneman, 1990), social security (Hage, Hanneman, & Gargan, 1989), and education (Garnier, Hage, & Fuller, 1989; Hage, Garnier, & Fuller, 1988). In a broad overarching thesis, De Swaan (1988) documents this general pattern of collectivization of poverty, welfare, and education. Economic and political considerations are so enmeshed in the development of national health and welfare policy that it is quite impossible to separate them in the public sector (Morris & Lescohier, 1978; Wildavsky, 1979).

The Importance of a Culture of Trust

A key feature of the transaction cost framework is the assumption that the relationships between participants in markets is inherently based on distrust (Williamson, 1975). Buyers are supposedly afraid that when they purchase from a single source and there are no competitors, the supplier will take advantage of the situation and maximize profit.

We have already observed, however, that sharing of profits is basic in the Japanese automobile industry. We might ask, therefore, if there are cultural aspects to the development of networks. Clearly, the Japanese have a long tradition of building cooperative relationships, an inheritance of their rice culture. The principles of cooperation and long-term alliances are the cultural values that support the obligational networks and joint capital investments in Japan. These social ties and capital links create and reinforce Japanese supplier/buyer relationships.

It would be wrong, however, to assume that these conditions exist only in the East because of Asian culture. We have observed that obligational networks in the United States have been generated in microcultures at the local level. One of the best examples is Silicon Valley's semiconductor industry (Delbecq & Weiss, 1988; Rogers & Larsen, 1984). There is a culture of accommodation, if not trust. People move from one company to the next, following projects. Capital is easily raised to start new ventures. Social ties and capital links create a complex of overlapping cooperative relationships and a culture of trust. What is true of Silicon Valley is also true of many local communities today where many organizations, public and private, cooperate together to accomplish public good. Over time, relationships develop and trust builds (Bradach & Eccles, 1989). This culture can also be found in Europe; for example, in cooperative contracting in specific industrial areas—northern Italy, southern Sweden, and western Denmark (Hollingsworth, 1991, p. 59). Missing from this analysis is an evolutionary explanation about why more people within organizations are willing to engage in the risky behavior of participating in a joint venture, strategic alliance, or production network. One answer is that a new culture is developing, the culture of cooperation.

We believe that networks have been especially important at the local level in the United States where the effectiveness of weak ties has been recognized for some time (Granovetter, 1973, 1985; Mathiesen, 1971). Clearly, we all witness the strength of cooperation in Silicon Valley of California, in the N.I.H. strip along Route 270 in Maryland, and in the research triangle in North Carolina. Indeed, we suggest that concentration of research and development helps foster a local climate of trust, and for this reason the interorganizational structures in these localities are the wave of the future.

Increasing Levels of Education and Cognitive Complexity

While there are legitimate concerns about educational achievement in some areas of the public educational system, it is a fact that the proportion of students entering college has been about 60% and the proportion graduating from college about 30%, but both are now rising steadily (U.S. Abstract of Statistics, 1989). We are gradually moving toward a system of mass higher education.

This trend has many implications. We can anticipate that future graduates will be more knowledgeable than those of the 1970s, and the constant improvement in pedagogy will mean that graduates of the 1990s will be even better prepared to handle the complexities of everyday life. Graduates of the future, taught analytic and problem-solving skills, will be better able to conceptualize multivariate causal models. They will be capable of thinking abstractly and tolerating cognitive dissonance, and will be able to move conceptually through hierarchical levels. Learning computer skills will enable all college educated professionals to collect, store, retrieve, and analyze vast amounts of information. Tom Peters and Robert Waterman conveyed this idea when they quoted F. Scott Fitzgerald in their book *In Search of Excellence*: "The test of a first-rate intelligence is the ability to hold two opposed ideas in mind at the same time and still retain the ability to function" (1982, p. 89).

Higher education is not the only way in which people develop complex cognitive processes. Travel, television, books, movies, and other forms of entertainment expose us to alternative perspectives on the world and its problems. The phenomenal expansion of the travel industry and the growth of the popular media, especially the specialized magazine and book markets, are well known (Toffler, 1981). These varied experiences and sources of new knowledge are leading to more complex cognitive structures, thereby making it much more likely that more complex institutional forms can function effectively (Hage & Powers, 1992).

What is the evidence for this assertion, given the present concern about illiteracy and the quality of education? For one, political analysts have been confounded by the more complex voting choices of the public today, in contrast to the past when people typically voted straight party tickets. The proportion of independent voters, which has been steadily rising for the past three decades, is another piece of evidence. It is not unusual for an individual today to take a conservative position on national defense but a liberal one on abortion, and prefer conservative economics but be liberal on environmental issues. The simplistic categories of conservative and liberal, Democrat and Republican, no longer have a great deal of meaning because they do not reflect our more complex view of the world.

Another indicator of more complex cognitive structures is the rise of the consumer protection movement. Thanks to groups such as Nader's Raiders, many consumers now conceptualize the relationships among products, the environment, and social welfare. We now judge a car not only for the status it brings us, but also for its gasoline mileage, emissions level, safety, and operating costs—and it is a symbol of our competitive status vis-à-vis the Japanese. Further, products and services are increasingly evaluated for their quality, which in itself is an indication of more complex thinking. In short, we now demand that products and services be environmentally nonintrusive, safe, and made by companies that evidence a social conscience. This is a far cry from the simple ways in which consumers evaluated products in the 1950s. A comparison of *Consumer Reports* from the early 1950s and the 1990s makes readily apparent both the considerable increase in the number of criteria used to evaluate products and the complex analytical techniques needed to apply them. The success of the magazine is itself a testimony to this change in evaluation of products and services.

Still a third indication of more complex cognitive structures is the rapid increase in the number of interracial and intercultural marriages and adoptions. In the United States there has been a tenfold increase in these marriages between 1970 and 1980 (100,000 per year in 1980), and it is now estimated that 5% of all children born in the United States are interracial. This type of change is possible only when we are accepting of differences, treasure diversity, and are future focused rather than being trapped by the past.

We need to be able read symbolic communication to understand and use the constant role redefinitions produced by technological change. Symbolic communication provides a way of handling the role redefinition problems found in dual-career marriages, in interracial or intercultural marriages, and in interorganizational network systems. Increased education and exposure to a variety of cultures vicariously via the media, or directly via travel, or even more directly through significant others such as spouses or friends, allows us to develop the ability to read symbolic communication and to handle the negotiations of differential expectations.

Complex cognitive structures make it more possible for individuals to conceptualize networks and to implement them. Herbert Simon (Nielsen, 1988) argued that the biggest barrier for the development of cooperative behavior is the traditional micro interorganizational market framework that explicitly assumes a zero-sum competitive system. Cognitive complexity enables individuals to break out of an egoistic orientation and enter into partnerships with others to achieve larger, collective, and mutually benefiting goals. In post-industrial society there is a need for these more creative minds; people who can tolerate ambiguity and paradox, problem solve at different levels of intra- and interorganizational structures, manage rapid technological change, and solve its complicated problems (Hage & Powers, 1992; Peters & Waterman, 1982).

The Growth in Knowledge and the Shift to New Technologies

A major stimulant to network development is the growth in knowledge, produced by steadily increasing investments in research and the rapid technological changes that result. Hladik (1988) observes that many of the 334 United States/foreign joint ventures she studied involved product development. Berg and Hoekman (1988) made the same point about some 500 joint ventures involving companies in the Netherlands. Moxon, Roehl, and Truitt (1988) found this to be true in the civilian aviation industry, and it is also relevant in a large number of the joint ventures in bio-tech (Powell & Brantley, in press). Finally, Hergert and Morris's (1988) analysis of the 829 international collaborative agreements found that almost two-thirds were formed for the purpose of product development.

Technological change is being fueled not only by the faster-than-inflation increases in both business and government investment in nonmilitary research, but also by rapid increases in the expenditures of Britain, France, Germany, and Japan in research and development. In the aggregate, these four countries have quadrupled their investments in constant dollars and have passed the United States' expenditures during the past decade, a period which also saw American expenditures in constant dollars double (National Science Foundation, 1989).

New knowledge has led to the creation of new occupations as well as new organizations. In manufacturing there has been a proliferation of small high-tech companies, creation of new profit centers in large high-tech companies, and thousands of joint ventures to take advantage of the many new products being developed. Bio-technology (Kogut, Shan & Walker, 1990; Powell & Brantley, in press), as we have already suggested, is the paradigmatic case. In the nonprofit sector, halfway houses, rape crisis centers, and hospices all exist today because new knowledge has created new treatments and, therefore, new programs and occupations.

Rapid rates of technological change have made the strategies of horizontal and vertical integration a liability for many business firms because they cannot respond fast enough to change. As a consequence, large firms divest themselves of large parts of their businesses. This same force makes smaller units more effective because they can act more quickly and with more latitude than large bureaucracies or the single authority chain. Many business firms are creating profit centers within their divisions, and public and private bureaucracies are decoupling their departments so that they can operate more adaptively in a rapidly changing environment (Weick, 1976).

Below, when we discuss the theoretical implications of research on interorganizational network systems, we explain why decentralization is a more effective strategy. For now we merely note that the rise of large businesses in the United States, as Chandler (1977) so brilliantly demonstrated, is predicated on large and stable demand: Both markets and organizational hierarchies as mechanisms of coordination require relatively high rates of stability for success. The more that new products with shorter and shorter product lives dominate our markets, large organizations will find themselves increasingly at a disadvantage because they are unable to adjust rapidly to market conditions (Hage, 1988).

Parallel to the growth in knowledge is the development of new technologies that allow for increased customization of products and individualization of services. Piore and Sabel (1986) emphasized flexible manufacturing as a second industrial divide that is changing the world. The classic laws of supply and demand assumed that consumers always have time to become aware of the relative advantages and disadvantages of various new products and that producers have time to react as these new niches open. As the rate of technological and product change speeds up, however, the tasks required for production and marketing have to be accomplished in shorter and shorter cycles. Today, in even fairly stable sectors, cycles are becoming significantly shorter, making long-range planning more difficult (Berg & Hoekman, 1988).

Given this rate of technological change, it is not difficult to understand why small size with interorganizational alliances, as opposed to large size via merger, is seen as providing a strategic advantage by both profit-making corporations and nonprofit agencies alike (Hladik, 1988; Laage-Hellman, 1989). Although cooperation may take many forms, the impetus for joint ventures and network formation is found both in the growth in knowledge and in the quickening pace of technological change. Since consumers are more discriminating, more educated, and have higher expectations of products or services, organizations must make larger investments in research and production in order to produce quality. In order to lower costs and risks, organizations wish to spread the costs and risks to others (Contractor & Lorange, 1988). By forming cooperative relationships, they share equally in the costs and benefits of market research and development and quickly gain expertise in other needed areas, as is illustrated in the example of Corning Glass (Hladik, 1988; Moxon et al., 1988; Powell, 1990).

THEORIES OF INTERORGANIZATIONAL
NETWORK FORMATION

A number of new theories have been developed in sociology that are of use to managers, administrators, professionals, and scientists who must work in interorganizational networks. It should not be surprising that at the same time some new interorganizational institutions are developing, there are also new theoretical developments, even if these new insights do not immediately appear to be relevant or related. We would argue that the emergence of interorganizational production networks is going to alter the theoretical landscape, necessitating the construction of not only new theory but also a synthesis of existing paradigms and perspectives. It is with this objective that we write this book, to begin the task of constructing a synthesis about institutional theory and governance mechanisms. In building our theory we have drawn on three major perspectives— interorganizational relations theory, population-ecology theory, and rational choice theory. Our synthesis can then be compared with transaction cost analysis as a competing paradigm. As we touch upon each of these theoretical perspectives and/or paradigms, we indicate how interorganizational analysis can open new vistas within them, a theme to which we return in the last chapter. The combination of these various perspectives enhances understanding of our model of systemic interorganizational networks and constitutes the beginning of the synthesis of these various theories into a larger paradigm of institutional governance.

Theories of Interorganizational Relations

Our knowledge about interorganizational networks in the public sector stems from a series of studies that focused on the relationships between organizations (Aiken & Hage, 1968; Boje & Whetten, 1981; Hall, Clark, Giordano, Johnson, & Van Roekel, 1977; Lincoln, 1985; Van de Ven & Ferry, 1980; for reviews, see Morrissey, Hall, & Lindsey, 1982; Rogers & Whetten, 1982; Whetten, 1981). Their emphasis on dyadic relationships has been so strong that this specialty has been called IOR (interorganizational relationships). Only recently have theorists started to distinguish between forms that are based on dyadic relationships and those composed of three or more organizations (Morrissey, Tausig, & Lindsey, 1984; Van de Ven & Ferry, 1980). When all relationships between multiple partners are aggregated, then the focus of inquiry is the network.

Much of this early work focused on the problem of centrality or conflict in client exchange networks and looked at specific variables that are antecedents to dyadic relationships. For example, an article by Aiken and Hage (1968) presented findings concerning the sharing of resources by two agencies, a phenomenon that parallels joint ventures, strategic alliances, and obligational linkages in the private sector some two decades later. They argued that an emphasis on innovation, coupled with a constraint on resources, forced unwilling public agencies into joint programs. In turn, the major driving impetus was the structural complexity of the agency.

In what is almost a replication of the work by Aiken and Hage (1968), 20 years later Kogut and Singh (1988) found that the factors affecting whether a firm would choose to acquire another or enter into a joint agreement in order to penetrate the American market were determined by the firm's small size, product differentiation, and diversification of product. Each of these variables led to the choice of joint ventures as the best alternative, and both differentiation and diversification were associated with high product innovation and complexity. In this study, however, industrial R&D was only weakly associated with the choice of joint venture, once they controlled for size.

Books and articles have recently appeared about alliances, joint ventures, obligational networks, and promotional networks in the private corporate sector (Contractor & Lorange, 1988; Mowery, 1988; Nohria & Eccles, in press). We have already cited the work of Campbell et al. (1991) and Hollingsworth et al. (in press). Each of these works is beginning to develop a theory about the creation of different kinds of networks.

Some insights are contained in a book edited by Contractor and Lorange (1988). Buckley and Casson (1988), in "A Theory of Cooperation in International Business," argue that the level of trust that develops between joint venture partners is a function of the motives of the partners. Further, they state that research and development is likely to lead to the sharing of information and the building of trust, while joint marketing ventures are more likely to create distrust and cheating behavior.

From our perspective, the most interesting new ideas are contained in several different studies by a research group in Sweden (Hakansson, 1990; Hallen, Johanson, & Mohamed, 1987), who found that sharing of technical, organizational, commercial, or market information leads to adaptiveness, and it is this success that builds trust. In a comparative study of 27 Swedish and 25 British firms, industrial marketers (more than one per firm) were asked about their most important relationships with customers in France, Germany, Italy, Sweden, and the United Kingdom (Hallen et al., 1987). Independent of the very strong relationship between adaptation and information exchange, the Swedish researchers found that need influenced both adaptation and information exchange strongly, while production complexity had a somewhat weaker relationship. In other words, there are a set of variables that encourage people to share information and to adapt, and these facilitate the building of a relationship but, in turn, there are situational factors that also influence whether this process will occur.

In another chapter in Contractor and Lorange, Killing (1988) argued that successful alliances require a balance between the task scope of the alliance and organizational complexity. If the scope involves many activities, many products and markets, then interorganizational complexity must be increased. This is accomplished by higher frequency of interaction, a reduction in routinization, and the right combination of skills in each partner. This set of concepts bears a remarkable resemblance to the ideas that we shall advance in Chapters Four and Seven. While these are useful insights, they do not provide an explicit theory of interorganizational network formation.

Population-Ecology Theory of Organizations

A macro perspective on organizations, known as population-ecology, emerged during the late 1970s (Aldrich, 1979; Carroll, 1984, 1988; Hannan & Freeman, 1977, 1989). This perspective attempted both to explain the growth and decline of distinct kinds of organizations (called populations) across time and to predict their survival or extinction rates. And here is where population-ecology theory is most useful. Our central argument is that interorganizational network systems represent a distinctive and even revolutionary institutional form that applies across a wide range of sectors and that represents a strategy of adaptation and survival.

The thesis of population-ecology is a simple one. As variations in the environment occur, new populations of organizations emerge to take advantage of these opportunities, and other populations decline and disappear. The bulk of the empirical work using population ecology (for reviews, see Carroll, 1984, 1988), has focused on birth and death rates of various populations of organizations such as newspapers, labor unions, wineries, and industrial plants, and in most instances the analyses have been rigorous and have involved hazard rate analysis. Most of this empirical work, however, has dealt only with single organizations and not with cooperative and enduring relationships between organizations. Although Aldrich (1979) coined the term *action sets* for coalitions of organizations, he referred only to temporary arrangements, not to the kind of long-term institutional arrangements that we describe as interorganizational network systems in Chapter Two. He did describe boundary-spanners, however, an important concept for understanding how interorganizational networks emerge, but he did not develop a theory applicable to them.

One of the central insights of population-ecology is the idea of specialists versus generalists (Carroll, 1985; Hannan & Freeman, 1989). But the degree of niche specialization has so far only been related to the probability of survival and not to the probability of creating joint ventures and systemic networks. Yet, there is growing empirical evidence that small firms, especially those with diverse products, are more likely to develop collaborative relationships (Kogut & Singh, 1988) and joint ventures (Pollack, 1992a; Powell and Brantley, in press).

It is strange that contemporary population-ecological research (Carroll, 1988) has not studied joint ventures and the several ways they impact on survival, because the concept of symbiotic relationships is an old one in the ecological literature (Hawley, 1950, 1968). Symbiotic relationships are usually, but not always, the essence of joint ventures and systemic networks. We shall use this idea as one of our important dimensions in the typology to be presented in the next chapter. Harrigan (1988) found that ventures involving complementary assets were more successful. The same is implied in the linkages between small bio-tech firms and large pharmaceutical companies (Powell & Brantley, in press).

The work of Astley and Fombrun (1983), however, is very useful for building a theory of interorganizational networks. They observed that organizations adopt a wide range of collective strategies to manage their environments. They postulated four kinds of collective strategies: agglomerate, confederate, conjugate, and organic. The agglomerate strategy occurs in those markets where there are many small organizations that have low levels of interaction, but make concerted demands upon political elites to regulate the business of large scale competitors. Confederate strategies are attempts by organizations in concentrated industries to achieve, by concerted action, organizational goals that they could not achieve on their own. In this mode, organizations form trade associations to pressure their government into adopting policies favorable to their business, or they form cartels and/or engage in price-fixing schemes to increase their profits beyond the level that they could achieve on their own. Conjugate strategies, such as joint ventures or interlocking directorates, represent the efforts of organizations from different economic sectors to share resources or information in order to improve their organizational outputs. These kinds of associations are of interest to us because they represent the movement toward collective action intended to achieve a supra-organizational goal. Organic strategies, which represent the most mature interorganizational network, go beyond symbiotic relationships to include chains of organizations working together to achieve a common output.

How important some of these strategies are in different business sectors is illustrated in an article by Nielsen (1988). Ocean Spray Cranberries, Inc., was founded by independent farmers who agreed to market their product together by pooling their resources. In Astley and Fombrun's terms, this was an agglomerate strategy. Another major example of mutually beneficial cooperation are the many relations between the bio-tech and chemical/drug industries, examples of conjugate strategies because the firms are in different economic sectors. Typically, the bio-tech firm has a new product but not the production or marketing capacity. Cooperation does not always guarantee success, however. Nielsen provides a number of examples where it occurred in a declining market, and where cooperation allowed for an orderly decline.

The focus on the evolution of organizational forms provided by population-ecology is useful for understanding interorganizational networks. These theorists suggest that there are three stages in the evolution of organizational forms, produced by particular combinations of technology, structure, and coordination mechanisms (Aldrich & Mueller, 1982), and they speculate that a new form emerged in the 1970s. We believe not only that there is a new organizational form called the organic, as evidenced by small high-tech companies and profit centers (Burns & Stalker, 1961; Hage, 1980, 1988), but also that there is a new institutional form called the interorganizational network, which itself has multiple forms—obligational, promotional, and systemic networks.

Perhaps the major limitation to date of most population-ecology theory is its implied assumption that selection or survival depends on efficiency as the prime utility. The general framework suggested by Aldrich (1979) leaves open the question of which utilities are selecting what organizational populations and forms. Although the bulk of his theory deals with organizations, these ideas can be generalized quite easily to the level of network as alternative institutional arrangements. Within each of these kinds of institutions there are both populations (the specific level) and forms (the general level). (For a definition of the difference between populations and forms, see Aldrich & Mueller, 1982.)

We suggested above that people in post-industrial societies have more complex cognitive structures and this is reflected in their political attitudes, in their consumer behavior, and in their emotional preferences. Population-ecology theory has failed to recognize the implications of these changes, and has remained with the implicit assumption that efficiency or productivity is the single most important utility. While it is true that both governmental bureaucracies and large corporations became dominant because of their greater economies of scale (Chandler, 1977; Hage, 1980), this is not the prevailing "taste" or preference of consumers today (Peters & Waterman, 1982).

The critical theoretical insight is that the utilities selecting this new institutional form are flexibility, or innovation, and customization. One of our basic assumptions is that these utilities, rather than efficiency, are the ones by which successful institutions such as interorganizational networks are being selected. In other words, it is not quantity relative to price that is important to most clients or customers; rather, it is customized service, innovative products/services, and adaptive efficiency.

One major explanation for the emergence of the interorganizational network form using the population-ecology approach is that there is more cooperative behavior between public agencies and private-for-profit firms because there has been a change in the nature of the utilities from quantity to quality, from mass-produced products to customized products, and from custodial services to individualized treatment services. These shifts reflect changes in the cognitive structure of college-educated populations; they do not represent the values of everyone in society. These shifts have led to the growth in new populations of organizations and the demise of large-scale bureaucracies (Hage, Collins, Hull, & Teachman, 1991).

Our second explanation for the new form is the explosion in knowledge and the concomitant changes in the speed of technological change. A continuing theme that runs through much of the business literature is the need for flexibility, speed, and adaptiveness. Organizational forms, such as large-scale bureaucracies, do not have this adaptive and flexible capacity. More fundamental is the need for complex arrangements that can integrate diverse and disparate pieces of new knowledge. This is one reason why businesses are now developing joint ventures; they allow the combination of different kinds of expertise. Our third explanation is that research and development creates highly specialized niches, even for large generalist firms and agencies where they need access to different and even new competencies. These are usually complementary and as a consequence the relationship can be seen as symbiotic, as we have already argued. But the key point is that highly specialized niches reduce the extent of competition, the kind that exists even between generalists. We tend not to think of the scope of competition as declining across time, but the process of specialization and especially of customization has this consequence.

Thus, there is a paradox. At the same time that growth in knowledge and rapid technological change are creating pressures for smaller and more flexible units—small high-tech companies and their counterparts in the public sector (called decoupled units by Weick, 1976)—the units are recombining into more complex forms called interorganizational networks. This is not to say these are the only causes of interorganizational networks; there are other explanations, ones found in different theoretical perspectives and paradigms. The key point is that population-ecology theory will not be predictive until it builds in a specification of the utilities upon which populations of organizations and of other kinds of institutions are being selected. Once this is done, it then becomes a powerful perspective. And as this is done, population-ecology theory can be merged with other new perspectives, in particular rational choice theory.

Competition Versus Cooperation: Rational Choice Theory

We began this chapter with the question: Why is it that organizations, by nature and necessity concerned with their own prosperity and survival, share resources and work with other organizations, especially if the others are competitors? In particular, all the current theory in transaction cost analysis focuses on the problem of distrust or, conversely, the issue of cooperation.

For a long time social scientists assumed that without a strong central authority to mandate cooperation, all individuals and organizations would, in pursuit of self-interest, war against each other. Thus Thomas Hobbes conceptualized the "Leviathan," the state that guarantees a safe and predictable life in exchange for obedience from its citizens. While we believe that some institutions, such as courts and law enforcement agencies, do emerge for this reason, we do not believe Hobbesian theory explains the origin of interorganizational networks.

We start our theoretical journey with the concept of cooperation because we believe that for too long the Hobbesian conceptualization has caused the question of social order to be posed in the wrong way. Rather than ask what prevents individuals and organizations from waging war against all others and then arguing that the state and other institutions such as markets emerge to regulate conflict, we propose to ask why individuals and organizations cooperate even when it might not be in their immediate self-interest to do so. In other words, it is cooperation that is the most significant concept when trying to understand the nature of social order. This has not always been the case when studying organizations, where the focus has usually been on control.

Neoclassical market theory is so well known that it needs little discussion. This paradigm views social order as an outcome of the interaction of selfish individuals sharing no common ends or values. By following their own interests, individuals unintentionally and spontaneously establish self-reproducing institutions and thereby attain order. This process has been used to explain the emergence of the major institutions of our time, such as states (North, 1981) and markets (Polanyi, 1944). The notion is that institutions evolve by invisible-hand mechanisms that are endogenous and therefore not observable, and are maintained by self-sustaining and voluntary participation that no one has an incentive to change, for by doing so he or she would only be made worse off. In this view, social order is seen to flow naturally out of an institutional nexus that is the unintended consequence of purposive self-interested action (Hechter, 1989). Cooperation is, therefore, the most important and most successful tie that binds and is the basis of institutional order, according to invisible-hand theory.

This hypothesis has been tested in the laboratory, and theory has been developed based on the concept of reciprocal altruism (Axelrod & Hamilton, 1984). Game theorists have shown that individuals who cooperate at every turn and do not defect unless another does so first will, in the long run, be better off than those who do not cooperate. In computer tournaments using the prisoner's dilemma game, the most successful strategy has been shown to be Anatol Rapoport's TIT-FOR-TAT, in which the second player moves in cooperation with the first player's choices until the first player makes a noncooperative move, at which point the second player also changes to a noncooperative action. Further, Axelrod (1984) has shown that TIT-FOR-TAT has a clear evolutionary advantage when it is known that payoffs are positively related to survival. Buckley and Casson (in Contractor & Lorange, 1988) apply this set of ideas to explain why firms remain in collaborative ventures. The partners do so not only because they recognize the long-term advantages, but also because they know that if one cheats, the other may retaliate by a similar act of cheating. In this way a form of social control emerges.

While the idea of reciprocity is an important concept in understanding interorganizational networks, game theory based on two-person interactions is probably not very useful. Aside from the ecological problem of having to generalize from individuals to organizations, there is the obvious problem that in interorganizational contexts organizational behavior is often hidden and caused by the actions of many people. Nevertheless, the basic idea of TIT-FOR-TAT—that the benefits of cooperation are not fixed and are not the results of a zero-sum game—is a useful heuristic on which to base principles of network management, an idea we will return to in Chapter Eight.

There is currently a resurgence of interest in rational choice theory, especially among sociologists (Boudon, 1986; Coleman, in press; Hechter, 1987), and there is a journal on this topic. Among other themes, this literature attempts to understand why people join forces and cooperate. Like the advocates of invisible-hand theories, these writers believe that social order is attained through the action of autonomous self-interested individuals. Unlike invisible-hand theorists, however, rational choice theorists do not believe that social equilibrium is attained spontaneously. Their pessimism stems from the belief that co-operation is difficult to sustain among self-interested actors who are bound to pursue selfish ends, rather than altruistic ones, and who are able therefore to "free ride" (Olson, 1965). They argue that self-centered individuals cannot realistically hope to obtain social order. How then, if this is the case, does social order, based on voluntary relationships and not coercion, ever develop? Hechter (1989) offers the answer shown in Figure 1.1.

Group solidarity is held to be a function of two independent elements: the extensiveness of the normative obligations that individuals assume by virtue of their membership in a given group, and the extent to which they actually comply with these normative obligations. The greater the average proportion of each member's private resources contributed to collective ends, the greater the solidarity of the group. Members act in ways that are consistent with collective standards of conduct because they are obligated rather than compensated. In other words, people give up private resources to gain access to collective ones. When individuals conform to group regulations, they do so because they gain something they can obtain only as members of the group. This theory, then, explains variation in members' willingness to comply with corporate rules: When the extensive-ness of the obligation or the probability of complying with these obligations is high, solidarity will be high, and vice versa. The emphasis of this model is on the costs and benefits of joining collectives, and the potential loss of autonomy is one of the costs that actors must bear to achieve the group good.

Interorganizational networks are not, of course, groups of individuals, but task institutions developed to achieve certain self-interest and/or supra-organizational objectives. Rational choice theorists, however, have argued that groups can be conceived of as if they were individual actors (Boudon, 1986). Thus organizational units might be analyzed from this perspec-tive, but to do so requires a broad understanding of the costs and benefits of interorganizational cooperation as opposed to individual relationships.

From our perspective, however, rational choice theory has a major limitation—it does not encompass the concept of collec-tive or public good. We believe that the growth of knowledge has led to a recognition that problems are more complex and that cooperation is perhaps the only alternative for solving them. The solution of a complex problem is the joint good. For business organizations it may be expertise about marketing in another country which requires a joint venture. For service organizations it is the necessity of providing multi-problem clients with a multiservice intervention plan. We do not mean to imply that all interagency cooperative behavior is altruistic. Indeed, our thesis is that both economics and ethics are driving forces, and we subscribe to Etzioni's framework in *The Moral Dimension* (1988). There are both self-interest and moral commitments involved in the rational choices of private and public organizations, desires to gain more resources and to accomplish exemplary goals.

There is clear evidence today that some individuals will strive to achieve collective goals even when they do not benefit themselves. Several decades ago Hage (1974) found that doctors would support an educational program that would reduce their authority and status within the hospital if it would improve patient care. Not all physicians felt this way, however: It was the doctors with higher levels of education and more specialized practices who adopted this altruistic perspective. More recently in a series of laboratory experiments, Dawes (1991) has found that if strangers are allowed to talk to one another in a variation of the prisoner's dilemma game, they are more likely to take the collective perspective than to maximize their own self-interest. Marwell and Oliver (1984) had similar findings; namely, many people are oriented toward achieving joint goods even when they personally do not benefit. We believe that this is an expression of the moral dimension of human activity.

In an extensive study of the membership in 35 collective action organizations, Knoke (1988) found that not only were public goods or moral commitments able to attract members, but also that those who joined were much more willing to donate more time and money when the organizations' objectives were altruistic. In contract, when collective action organizations followed the logic of Mancur Olson's arguments (1965) that people will "free-ride" if not given individual incentives, their efforts tended to attract people who were much more likely to be apathetic. Knoke observes: "These patterns are consistent with evidence from several case studies and experiments suggesting that equity concerns, fairness principles, and altruistic norms regarding the well-being of others (non-members) are exceptional

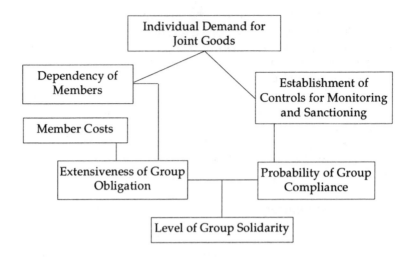

Figure 1.1 Model of Group Solidarity

SOURCE: Adapted from *Principles of Group Solidarity* by M. Hechter (1987). Berkeley: University of California Press. Used with permission.

powerful social forces shaping the collective-action decisions of individuals" (p. 326). If this were not the case, individuals would not form social action organizations, such as the Committee for Creative Nonviolence, to help the homeless or join demonstrations to eliminate abortion. Indeed, the latter organizations and their counterparts, the organizations that support free choice, have extraordinarily motivated individuals who are willing to make large personal sacrifices for their cause.

Another limitation of the rational choice framework is that it ignores trust and its consequences for the willingness of groups to collaborate. Trust also impacts on the need for controls to monitor and sanction because it increases the probability of group compliance. As there is more trust there is less need to ensure compliance. The problem with the rational choice model and its particular formulation of group solidarity (see Figure 1.1) is that it does not explore concrete changes in society that would explain the movement towards greater group solidarity.

Just as rational choice theorists have not made room for moral commitments, they have ignored the pernicious costs of interorganizational conflict (Alter, 1990; Benson, 1975; Hall et al., 1977). The current swing in societal values toward punishment rather than treatment, for example, causes dysfunctional relationships between social work agencies and police departments, and increases the conflict between their professionals. Concerns about interorganizational conflict are likely to decrease, however, as members of the interorganizational network gain information about each other. As individuals interact in these situations they learn more about each other, develop trust, and invent techniques for managing disharmonies between themselves (Laage-Hellman, 1989; Lawrence & Lorsch, 1967; Walton & Dutton, 1969).

The Calculus of Interorganizational Cooperation

Interorganizational cooperation has both costs and benefits that need to be clearly understood. Table 1.2 describes this calculus of network cooperation. It is not meant to be an exhaustive list, but a summary of the many costs and benefits of interorganizational cooperation that have been identified in the literature. Each item in Table 1.2 has a quid pro quo. This does not mean there is necessarily a potentially equal loss or gain in each area, but that as a whole organizations must calculate that the benefits outweigh the losses before they will concert their efforts with others. For example, a perceived loss of autonomy may be offset by the ability of the firm or agency to specialize, and with more specialization there is less likelihood of direct competition.

Table 1.2 shows a very wide range of motivators and risks associated with cooperative relationships. Depending on the circumstances, different writers focus on certain aspects of this calculus. Powell and Brantley (in press), quite correctly, place a much greater emphasis on the opportunities to rapidly gain access to information and expertise, thus creating the capability for new products. Others tend to emphasize the economics and risks of product development (Contractor & Lorange, 1988; Hergert & Morris, 1988; Moxon et al., 1988). All agree, however, that it is the opportunity to create new market niches, in an area in which there is a great deal of specialization, that lessens the costs and increases the benefits of cooperation.

For example, in a study of 520 Dutch joint ventures, Berg and Hoekman (1988) emphasize that one of the major advantages

Table 1.2 Calculus of Interorganizational Collaboration

Costs	Benefits
Loss of technological superiority (Hladik, 1988; Pollack, 1992a); risk of losing competitive position (Moxon et al., 1988).	Opportunities to learn and to adapt (Hakansson, 1990; Laage-Hellman, 1989), develop competencies (Hladik, 1988), or jointly develop new products (Hergert & Morris, 1988; Powell, 1990; Powell & Brantley, in press).
Loss of resources—time, money, information, raw material, legitimacy, status, etc. (Benson, 1975; Litwak & Hylton, 1962).	Gain of resources—time, money, information, raw material, legitimacy, status, etc. (Litwak & Hylton, 1962; Nielsen, 1988); utilization of unused plant capacity (Hergert & Morris, 1988; Moxon et al., 1988).
Being linked with failure; sharing the costs of failing such as loss of reputation, status, and financial position.	Sharing the cost of product development (Contractor & Lorange, 1988; Hergert & Morris, 1988) and associated risks (such as failure to develop new products quickly enough and with enough quality), risks associated with commercial acceptance, and risks associated with size of market share (Hladik, 1988).
Loss of autonomy (Gouldner, 1959; Hladik, 1988) and ability to unilaterally control outcomes (Gray & Hay, 1986); goal displacement (Beder, 1984); loss of control (Moxon et al., 1988).	Gain of influence over domain (Alinsky, 1971); ability to penetrate new markets (Harrigan, 1986); competitive positioning and access to foreign markets (Contractor & Lorange, 1988; Hladik, 1988; Kogut & Singh, 1988); need for global products (Hergert & Morris, 1988).
Loss of stability, certainty, and known time-tested technology; feelings of dislocation (Beder, 1984).	Ability to manage uncertainty (Trist, 1983), solve invisible (Aldrich, 1979) and complex problems (Hage, 1988); ability to specialize or diversify (Alter, 1988b); ability to fend off competitors (Sosin, 1985).
Conflict over domain, goals, methods (DiStefano, 1984; Hladik, 1988; Pfeffer & Salancik, 1978; Schmit & Kochan, 1972).	Gain of mutual support, group synergy, and harmonious working relationships.

Delays in solutions due to problems in coordination (Moxon et al., 1988).	Rapid responses to changing market demands; less delay in use of new technologies (Berg & Hoekman, 1988; Moxon et al., 1988).
Government intrusion, regulation, and so on.	Gaining acceptance from foreign governments for participation in the country (Contractor & Lorange, 1988; Hladik, 1988).

of early product development is the long period of product monopoly and the resulting large share of the market. However, they also report that there are a number of risks inherent in attempting to introduce products too soon.

In a study of 420 international joint ventures between the United States and foreign firms, Hladik (1988) noted that the costs of developing new products were about $1.5 billion for a new aircraft engine and $1 billion for a telecommunications system. General Motors and Toyota shared the cost of developing a new small car, which cost them $2.5 billion.

Risks or uncertainty become greater when the companies attempt to establish a presence in a foreign market, even one they know well, (Kogut & Singh, 1988). They must hire managers and workers and adapt their products to local markets. These have high costs attached to them, making the alternative of finding a partner attractive. Indeed, it is this sharing of risks that pushes the evolutionary process in the direction of cooperation. One agency or firm can independently develop a new product, market it in a new country, handle a new client population with complex problems, and so on, and the uncertainties of success become its sole responsibility. Cooperation spreads these risks but, on the other hand, creates the potential for also having to share the consequences of failure.

The acquisition of resources and the sharing of risk are benefits that often covary. For example, when the government participates in commercial or military product development, private and public firms both gain resources and spread their risks. One of the more interesting developments is the increase in governmental participation in the public and private sector because of concerns over the loss of key industries. This blurs the distinction between public and private, and makes government involvement another and separable component of the cost-benefit calculation. Frequently, governmental intervention changes a dyadic or triadic joint venture into what we label a systemic network. Another common theme in the business literature (Kogut & Singh, 1988), and one reason why much of the current research in schools of management concentrates on international joint ventures, is the cost of entering a new country with its separate culture, tastes, patterns of distribution, and risks of market acceptance. Further, some governments make collaboration the price of admission. Hladik (1988) observed that the only way in which American firms can enter China is with the participation of a Chinese firm. This process, however, works in reverse as well. Boeing has so dominated commercial aviation that the Japanese sought a joint venture with the firm as the only way they could become competitive in the market. As Moxon, Roehl, and Truitt (1988) observed, however, this particular partnership has been a complex one. On one hand, Boeing risks losing its technologies to the Japanese; on the other, Boeing might be able to eliminate a potential competitor. Thus, the calculation of costs and benefits can be extremely complicated and sophisticated.

Theories of Interorganizational Collaboration: A Synthesis

To develop a synthesis of theories about cooperation we drawn on the existing literature on interorganizational relationships (Aiken & Hage, 1968; Berg & Hoekman, 1988; Campbell et al., 1991; Hakansson, 1990; Hakansson & Johanson, 1988; Hallen et al., 1987; Hladik, 1988; Hollingsworth et al., in press; Kogut & Singh, 1988; Laage-Hellman, 1989; Moxon et al., 1988; Powell & Brantley, in press; Snehota, 1990), population-ecology, and on the theory of group solidarity. In Figure 1.2 we have placed the four variables—need for expertise, need for funds and sharing of risks, willingness to collaborate, and need for adaptive efficiency.

The business literature that examines collaborative relationships between large businesses has stressed the need for funds and risk sharing (Moxon et al., 1988), while the literature on successful ventures has noted the need for competencies (Harrigan, 1988). These two variables summarize a large number of potential benefits listed in Table 1.2. For example, the need for expertise

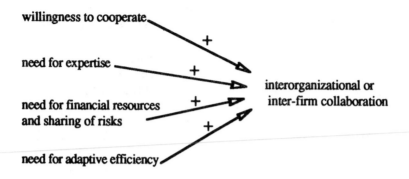

Figure 1.2 A Synthesis of Theories of Interorganizational Collaboration

involves opportunities to learn and the ability to penetrate new markets, to manage uncertainty, and to have rapid responses to changing market demands and technological opportunities. The need for funds implies not only the gaining of resources and increased influence over domain, but also the sharing of the costs and risks of product or service development. We believe these are the two major forces tilting organizations toward collaboration of one kind or another.

Not listed in Table 1.2 are two conditions that must exist for interorganizational collaboration to occur. The first is the willingness to collaborate, which is the most basic condition and affects even the perception of the costs and benefits. Willingness starts, of course, from an awareness and understanding of other organizations' needs and the perception that they are in some way compatible with one's own. Likewise, organizational members must be aware that collaboration will result in what we call adaptive efficiency. In the example of Corning at the beginning of this chapter, Mr. Houghton stressed the advantages of his global network as speed, flexibility, and quality. Similarly, in the discussion of the Japanese automobile production system, we indicated that the Japanese were more efficient in rapidly developing new products than the American automobile industry. If we define adaptive efficiency as the length of time needed to develop a new product, times the amount of effort, then the Japanese are three times as efficient in their adaptiveness as the Americans. Effectiveness is a separate question, but the steadily increasing market share of the Japanese indicates that they are quickly developing successful products. Each of these prior conditions is necessary, but not sufficient by itself. Each must be present to create the pressure to enter collaborative relationships or to move to higher levels of collaboration. In the next chapter, we will describe some 12 forms of interorganizational collaboration that differ in the amount of cooperation they require. The combination of these four variables provides the needed push.

Transaction Cost Analysis

This brings us to a consideration of the structures and mechanisms of social order: What are the mechanisms of social control? How are they selected? These questions have been the topic of study among economists for centuries. The most recent answers posited by institutional economists, that hierarchies are more efficient (Williamson, 1975, 1985), focus on too narrow a set of issues. We believe there are many other performance objectives driving the selection of governance mechanisms today, although efficiency has remained a primary one.

We have already suggested that the concept of efficiency must be altered. Large vertically and horizontally integrated firms are efficient when the product is standardized, is produced in high volume, and can remain unchanged over a long time period. In the previous section, however, we argued that the rapid growth in R&D, technological change, and shifts in consumer preferences have altered the way in which efficiency should be defined. The firms that survive today are those that adjust rapidly to shifts in technology and markets and can innovate quickly and produce quality products at the same time—what we would call adaptive efficiency.

Rapid adjustment often requires firms to sell parts of their organizations and to develop long-term relationships with single source suppliers. Williamson (1975) argues that when there are a few buyers or sellers, or what he calls small numbers, there is less control because there is a greater probability that individuals will renege on their contracts. He does recognize that the propensity for opportunism is a consequence of the frequency of exchange. In general, however, the world is moving in the opposite direction from the one his theory predicted. The highly specialized niches have relatively few suppliers and customers, especially when providing customized goods and services. Yet, it is precisely in these situations that we see the emergence of new institutional forms such as joint ventures and systemic networks, as described in the beginning of this chapter.

Another limitation of transaction cost analysis is the idea that managers and administrators calculate the pros and cons of one or another institutional arrangement. Perhaps some decisions are highly rational, but as Etzioni (1988) has recently argued, conscious calculation is the exception and not the rule. Instead, factors other than performance often lead to the selection of particular governance mechanisms, one of these factors being complex technology and another being the commitment to help, or what Etzioni has called the moral dimension. In our discussion of rational choice theory, we cited a number of empirical findings suggesting that not all people will make self-interested choices; some will consider various kinds of collective goals and public goods.

Furthermore, in our discussion above of cooperation we provided a number of examples—Silicon Valley, rice cultures, small American towns—where special circumstances created a willingness among people to engage in cooperative behavior. These examples, and a vast literature, have also demonstrated how research and development enterprises build cooperative relationships because they encourage exchanges of information. Finally, the theory of Aiken and Hage (1968) concerning joint human service programs in the public sector is still relevant. It points to the strategy of innovation that requires collaboration, and recognizes that this rational choice is dictated by the complexity of the agencies' structure. Similarly, increasing cognitive complexity of individuals leads people to perceive the costs of cheating and the greater benefits to be achieved by long-term cooperative behavior. These shifts, from egoistic short-sighted behavior to mutually beneficial long-term collaboration, are also rational choices.

Despite all of these motives, Williamson (1975), following upon the work of Coase (1937), posed the same question that interests us. What are the range of choices, and when are particular ones selected? The next chapter takes up this question and presents a typology of institutional options and growth.

CONCLUSION

During the past two decades enormous changes have occurred in both the private and public sectors. Large-scale vertically integrated firms have been downsized and broken into separate companies that then coalesce into obligational and systemic networks. Government services have been decentralized to the local level so that services are provided by small agencies which must be coordinated in various ways. The state has become increasingly involved in facilitating coordination in both sectors, and in a variety of ways.

The social forces that are producing these changes include shifts in consumer preferences away from standardized products produced at low cost, toward products that are innovative and of high quality. The growth in knowledge, especially through research and development, has generated rapid technological change and product innovation. In some areas and countries a culture of cooperation and of trust has facilitated the emergence of various kinds of networks. In some sectors of the economy and in different ways, the central state has become concerned about coordination and has attempted to act as a facilitator. Finally, rising levels of education among consumers force shifts in utilities, and at the same time a greater willingness on the part of firms to take risks produces cooperative behavior.

Our theory of systemic networks is relevant to these new intellectual traditions: population-ecology theory, rational choice theory, and theories of cooperation. We have argued that four factors are necessary for the development of collaboration between firms and agencies: the willingness to collaborate, the need for expertise, the need for funds, and the need for adaptive efficiency. In turn these four variables are affected by the culture of trust, the complexity of the task, the existence of highly specialized niches, and the emergence of small units—whether as separate organizations or within large-scale organizations. It is the combination of small size, high specialization, and complexity of task that best describes the current competitive situation in the private sector and the existing reality for the public sector. These explain why there is an evolutionary bias toward collaboration.

But we also do not want to argue that the pace of evolution toward joint ventures and interorganizational networks moves with equal speed. What differentiates countries and areas within them is the culture of trust that exists. Thus the Japanese private sector is ahead of the typical American business firm because of its historical conditions. These same conditions exist paradoxically in the public services sector in the United States, which, unlike the European system, has engaged in specialization for some time. Local conditions in other countries have also lead to various kinds of network relationships.

Our theory also explains why there are differences in the evolution toward interorganizational relationships of one kind or another. The small size of the firm or agency and the specialization of the niche vary considerably. Large firms, and especially generalist ones, are not as motivated to move in the direction of collaboration for these reasons. But even here, as the complexity of their tasks increases, large organizations are compelled by the force of circumstances to collaborate. Similarly, complex tasks are usually costly, creating not only the need for more resources but also the need for some hedge against inherent risks.

We have provided a wide variety of examples of collaboration in this chapter: joint ventures, strategic alliances, and systemic networks. But what precisely is collaboration? Many terms are used today without careful definition, so now we turn to descriptions of different forms of interorganizational collaboration and how they relate to the theory we have just suggested.

TWO

A Typology of Cooperative Interorganizational Relationships and Networks

There are many names given to interorganizational relationships—trade associations, cartels, cooperatives, joint ventures, interlocking directorates, strategic alliances; there are so many they cause confusion. To make matters worse, different authors combine these terms in different ways. Williamson (1975), for example, described transaction costs in economic exchanges, and focused on the circumstances under which vertical or horizontal (hierarchical) integration is a viable alternative to a market. This is turn inspired the work of Hollingsworth and his colleagues (Campbell et al., 1991; Hollingsworth et al., in press) and Grandori and Soda (1991). The Hollingsworth typology emphasized promotional and obligational networks, while Grandori and Soda were interested in distinguishing equity and non-equity networks, contracts and non-contracts. The typology found in the population-ecology perspective was still another approach that stressed the importance of competitive versus collective strategies (Astley & Fombrun, 1983). Similar, but less theoretical, was the classification of Kanter (1989), who was interested in different kinds of alliances.

Deciding whether markets or hierarchies are more efficient is of little relevance to the question we pose in this book, because both pure markets and pure hierarchies do not require significant levels of cooperation between organizations. The transaction cost analysis framework starts with a model of competition as the basis for markets and is concerned with which types of contractual relationships are the most efficient.

Our interest is not hierarchies, but interorganizational networks—public, private, and "partnerships" between the two. We want to know which network forms are the most flexible and innovative, and which are most capable of producing quality and adapting efficiently. Consistent with the arguments and empirical evidence of Johanson and his research team at Uppsala University (Johanson & Mattsson, 1987), we believe there is considerable cooperation within markets, especially if one examines the exchange relationships between suppliers and customers. We also agree with the Swedish researchers (Hakansson & Johanson, 1988; Hallen, Johanson, & Mohamed, 1987; Laage-Hellman, 1989; Snehota, 1990) that the frequency with which complex multiorganizational networks are formed is increasing. At this point, therefore, it might be useful to suggest a new way of thinking about and categorizing networks.

Our theory of interorganizational cooperation must start with a description and definition of an interorganizational network. Organizations are not autonomous entities (Burns & Mauet, 1984; Johanson & Mattsson, 1987), entirely free to choose their own future. They are, instead, anchored in networks of interactions with other organizations that provide raw material or clients and/or serve as markets for products and services (Azumi & Hage, 1972; Grandori & Soda, 1991; Snehota, 1990; Yuchtman & Seashore, 1967). Sometimes these interactions involve as few as two or three organizations, but they can have hundreds of participants. They can be established formally or informally and can be ad hoc or enduring. Regardless of their characteristics, they are a stabilizing force in the life space of organizations (Trist, 1983). By insuring stability, networks reduce uncertainty (Thompson, 1967). In this sense, networking is a very necessary and successful strategy in today's fast changing technological world.

The noun *network* and the verb *networking* are currently popular buzzwords. Small businesses are exhorted to develop "flexible manufacturing networks" in order to be capable of "rapid response to changing technology and tastes" (Johns Hopkins University, 1989). Social activists, whether promoting animal rights or children's rights, are told to build networks in order to secure leadership and political influence. If the academic literature is complex, the popular literature on networking is vague and vacuous. One reason we wrote this book is to explore in some detail useful concepts and terms for researchers and practitioners.

Our definitions are, therefore, the following:

Networks constitute the basic social form that permits interorganizational interactions of exchange, concerted action, and joint production. Networks are unbounded or bounded clusters of organizations that, by definition, are nonhierarchical collectives of legally separate units.

Networking is the act of creating and/or maintaining a cluster of organizations for the purpose of exchanging, acting, or producing among the member organizations.

Boundary spanners are individuals who engage in networking tasks and employ methods of coordination and task integration across organizational boundaries (Aldrich, 1979; Katz & Kahn, 1966).

These definitions are similar to Trist's (1983, p. 279), but are broadened considerably. Many theorists have focused on the purpose of *exchange* (Cook, 1977; Levine & White, 1961); others have stressed the mutuality of relationships used for *goal setting and achievement* (Rogers & Whetten, 1982; Thompson, 1967). Our typology and developmental theory that follows integrate these two approaches with the explicit idea that networks can also behave as production systems (Hall et al., 1977; Mulford & Rogers, 1982; Van de Ven & Ferry, 1980).

DEVELOPING THE TYPOLOGY

There has not yet been sufficient theoretical work to develop an exhaustive taxonomy of populations of networks, in spite of the large number of studies of single populations such as newspapers (Carroll & Delacroix, 1982), wineries (Delacroix, Swaminathan, & Solt, 1989), unions (Hannan & Freeman, 1989), and many kinds of business organizations (see review by Carroll, 1988). This is all the more surprising since McKelvey (1982) and McKelvey and Aldrich (1983) suggested that this is the central problem in organizational theory. Young (1988) criticized population-ecology theory for not making clear conceptual distinctions between populations and, by extension, populations of interorganizational networks. Astley and Fombrun (1983) developed a useful typology, as noted above, but it does not easily encompass networks as production systems.

We suggest a solution to McKelvey's quest: a typology of interorganizational forms organized along three dimensions—competitive versus symbiotic cooperation, the number of organizations involved in collaboration, and the level of cooperation. These dimensions produce a classification scheme that allows us to include the most important type of network in post-industrial society—the systemic production network—and specify how it differs from the many other kinds of networks. In the process, we provide an important cognitive map—a periodic table of cooperation—that lays the foundation for a theory of systemic networks that is developed in Chapters Four through Seven.

Given the usefulness of population-ecology theory, we construct our typology based on the fundamental distinction between organizations that share the same resource pool and those that do not; that is, relationships that are competitive versus those that are symbiotic. This typology of forms for competitive cooperation is shown in Figure 2.1; the typology of forms for symbiotic cooperation is shown in Figure 2.2.

Three Dimensions

Our major dimension, borrowed from Astley and Fombrun (1983), categorizes interorganizational forms into those used for competitive cooperation by organizations in the same sector and those used for symbiotic cooperation by organizations in different industrial or service sectors. Competitors are organizations of the same kind (producing the same product or service), while symbiotic relationships occur among organizations that may have some similarities but operate in different sectors.

As Astley and Fombrun observed, this distinction, an old one in the human ecology literature, allows us to predict when inter-organizational cooperative behavior is more easily achieved. Understandably, if organizations are not direct competitors, interaction is likely to be intense and cooperative behavior more possible.

Once we make a distinction between competing and noncompeting organizations, we then divide the lateral dimension in terms of the number of organizations involved in the cooperative effort. The Hollingsworth typology (1991) separated obligational networks from promotional networks on the basis of whether they were bilateral or multilateral linkages. We agree that the number of member organizations is important, particularly because of Williamson's (1975, 1985, 1991) thesis that small numbers increase the potential for cheating. He believed that when the number of suppliers declines they are likely to try to maximize their profits. Historically, this belief is partially responsible for pushing firms toward vertical integration.

We do not include in our typology another concept from population-ecology theory, which is the ecological location of organizations. When small numbers of organizations are working together, it is true they usually occupy the same geographic location, facilitating cooperation because there are likely to be other ties, especially social ones, that control behavior (Granovetter, 1985). We do not include ecological distance as a dimension, however, because we believe it is more useful to distinguish between small and large numbers of organizations in a single sector or across sectors.

The vertical dimension of our typology is the extent of cooperation. This is the unique contribution of our theory, although there are earlier suggestions in the literature. Aldrich (1979) distinguished between exchanges of information and exchanges of resources. Hakansson and Johanson (1988) and Johanson and Mattsson (1987) went further, identifying a variety of bonds including technical, planning, knowledge, social, economic, and legal. Each of these bonds can become the basis of a dyadic, triadic, or multi-organizational network. Both of these theoretical approaches, however, start with an exchange perspective. In our typology, exchanges are only the beginning, not the end, of cooperative interorganizational behavior.

Cooperation, whether among competitors (in the same sector) or among diverse organizations (in different sectors), can range from simple exchanges of information or resources, to limited cooperation in accomplishing a functional purpose, to broad cooperation involving the production of a product or service. Broad cooperative efforts, as described in our extended example of Japanese auto production networks, are the major focus of this book.

Just as we created three levels of cooperative behavior, we could have subdivided the two lateral dimensions, since sectors differ in many characteristics. For instance, we could add the duration of collaboration. Aldrich (1979) first referred to action networks as temporary groupings of organizations, typically for short-term economic or political gain. Time indirectly enters each cell of our typology because same-sector relationships tend to be unstable as competitive pressures pull organizations apart; that is, joint ventures and cartels collapse because members cheat. For this reason, competitive joint ventures usually have explicit time frames written into their contracts (Womack et al., 1990).

These refinements, however, are not essential for comprehending the logic of our typology, which is based on several hypotheses. First, exchanges of information, money, political influence, and materials are relatively simple tasks that require relatively limited amounts of interorganizational cooperation; at the other end of the continuum, joint production is a complex process that requires high levels of interorganizational cooperation. Second, networks of organizations residing in different sectors generate more cooperation than organizations located in the same niche of the same sector. Third, networks composed of many members find it more difficult to cooperate than do dyadic or triadic linkages. It follows, then, that multiple member symbiotic production networks represent an opportunity for high levels of both cooperation and conflict. It is these characteristics that make symbiotic networks worthy of our attention. Just as there has been a proliferation of symbiotic joint ventures in the past decade (Hergert & Morris, 1988; Pollack 1992a; Powell & Brantley, in press), we argue (but cannot prove) that there has been a corresponding increase in systemic production networks as well.

Symbiotic relationships have the potential for much conflict. Just because we title our typology "cooperative interorganizational relationships and networks," we do not mean to imply there is an absence of conflict. Laage-Hellman (1989) reported that joint product development collapsed when one party either did not have the right technical competencies or demanded a disproportionate share of the profit. Pollack (1992b) reported that small firms are pulling out of research consortia in the United States in increasing numbers. It is clear, as we demonstrate in Chapter Six, that conflict and cooperation are simultaneous processes within interorganizational relationships and networks (Alter, 1990).

The three basic dimensions of cooperative interorganizational relationships—same niche/different niche or sector(s), limited/multiorganizational memberships, and extent of cooperation—allow us to identify many different types of institutional arrangements that are effective for accomplishing a wide range of tasks.

COMPETITIVE COOPERATION

Our typology of interorganizational networks among competitively cooperating organizations is shown in Figure 2.1. Each of the increasing levels of cooperation produces two types of networks depending on the number of organizational members. Within each of the six resulting cells we distinguish between the function of the relationship.

Limited Cooperation. Two or three competitors can easily develop joint agreements that pool data and share information; for example, the *Automotive News* publishes extensive data on production and sales, as do many other trade association publications. Informal information networks, for example, develop in places such as Silicon Valley (Rogers & Larsen, 1984), even though computer firms occupy the same niches.

The best examples of cooperation between competitors are exchanges of information. Universities provide a large number of examples, including Bitnet and Internet, inter-library loans, and special programs to recruit minority students. There are many intercollegiate associations in the Ivy League, the Big Ten—in fact, in all regional associations of universities.

Common today are the exchanges of information among professionals and researchers across organizational boundaries. Those who must work with complex and difficult problems are sometimes forced to seek information from counterparts in

Competitive Cooperation Among Same Sector Organizations

	Dyadic and Triadic **Obligational Linkages**	Multiorganizational/ Sector Wide **Obligational Networks**
Limited Cooperation: information	**Joint Agreements:** pooling and exchanging information.	**Communication Networks:** pooling and exchanging information, professional associations.
friendship	**Social Agreements:** interpersonal support, dispensing favors.	**Social Networks:** emotional support and seeking advantage.
materials	**Subcontracts:** procuring.	**Purchasing Networks:** procuring.

	Promotional Linkages	**Promotional Networks**
Moderate Cooperation: technological objectives	**Joint Ventures:** joint product development.	**Research Consortia:** collectively financed and managed R & D.
economic objectives	**Partnerships:** borrowing and investing; advertising and purchasing.	**Cooperatives:** centralized purchasing and marketing **Consolidated Campaigns:** fund raising.
political objectives	**Alliances:** lobbying.	**Trade Associations, Unions:** lobbying and achieving common goals.

	Production Linkages	**Production Networks**
Broad Cooperation: production	**Joint Ventures:** manufacturing.	**Cartels:** controlling a market niche.

Figure 2.1 A Typology of Cooperative Interorganizational Networks

other organizations, even competitors—and stable information channels can develop. Conventions and trade shows increase the probability that exchange networks will develop, as do personal computers and electronic mailboxes and bulletin boards. Information sharing can even be mandated by law or encouraged by federal funding, as with the formalized information networks available so that professionals have timely access to the latest medical knowledge.

Sometimes the most important exchanges are not concrete, but intrinsic things of value such as friendship, trust, and loyalty (Mathiesen, 1971). An interesting public sector parallel is the networks of mutual support in human services where worker burnout is a constant problem. Good illustrations can be found in child protective services.

> During the 1980s child welfare services became almost exclusively focused on child protection. All the media attention given to this newly discovered social problem, coupled with severe economic problems in many cities, caused reports (and confirmed cases) of child abuse to triple. Caseloads averaged 85 to 100 per worker, turnover became 50% per year, and child protection agencies found it increasingly difficult to hire adequately prepared workers. In spite of these conditions, a core of veteran line staff stayed in child protection. They have been able to do so because of their personal networks—workers from private and public agencies who provide one another with emotional support, as well as information and referrals as needed by their clients. These networks seldom if ever meet as a whole, but telephone communication is intense and small groups of workers gather occasionally for breakfast, lunch, and at professional meetings.

Exchange networks composed of competitors have other characteristics in common. Members may conclude joint agreements out of individual need rather than collective need. Their creative energy is self-interest; members "do their own thing," while at the same time taking advantage of the benefits derived from their interdependence. They do not integrate what they do with others and thus can maintain themselves without collective governance because they do not require high levels of mutual trust.

Increasingly, highly capital intensive organizations producing products or services that have complex and rapidly changing technologies are engaging in long-term stable relationships with other similar firms (Hollingsworth, 1991). Instead of vertical integration, organizations today may specialize within the same sector by means of formal exchange relationships such as subcontracts. The following example is of special interest because it illustrates the development of a division of labor between competitors and the process by which market sub-niches are created.

> California Steel now buys basic steel from a joint venture owned by Brazilian, Japanese, and Italian interests that is located in Brazil. California Steel no longer produces steel itself, but finishes steel products. Each firm achieves gains in efficiency with this specialization within the same sector (Nielsen, 1988, p. 482).

In health care a very common form of subcontracting can occur between a HMO (Health Maintenance Organization) and a hospital (Hollingsworth & Hollingsworth, 1987). The former purchases at a flat rate the hospital's facilities, including operating rooms, intensive care units, and regular hospital beds. The HMO also negotiates contracts for expensive tests such as PET or CAT scans, stress tests, and the like. Although in some areas HMOs and hospitals might be competitors, in Boston, as described by Nielsen (1988, p. 482), they occupy different niches in the health care sector, with HMOs focused on primary care and hospitals on tertiary care.

We know of no parallel form through which subcontracting occurs among a large number of competitors. The reason is that multiparty contracts are very rare, and the likelihood that an organization would have to purchase raw materials from a large number of competitors seems remote.

Moderate Cooperation. The types of networks listed in Figure 2.1 as requiring moderate levels of cooperation are only illustrative and certainly not exhaustive, and are chosen to illustrate different functional purposes and the correlation between multiple functions and the need for increasing amounts of cooperation. For example, when subcontracting is the only purpose, then individuals are trading resources in order to meet only their own production processes. In joint ventures and cooperatives, however, they trade organizational resources, but also use their own participation as a means of achieving additional purposes. Through joint ventures, organizations can borrow, invest, purchase, advertise, and market. They can share technological expertise or jointly purchase expensive equipment. And through various forms of alliances they can strive to get legislation passed or rules changed that will benefit them all, a practice North (1990) labeled adaptive efficiency.

Joint product development, needing moderate levels of cooperation between two or three same-sector organizations, is becoming a standard practice. In one of the largest known databases on international joint agreements established by INSEAD in France for the years 1975 to 1986, joint product development accounted for 38% of 839 agreements (Hergert & Morris, 1988). Similarly, the Powell and Brantley study (in press) of more than 700 bio-tech joint ventures found that approximately the same proportion were involved in product development.

An excellent example of joint product development between two similar firms is the case of Kabi.

Kabi in Sweden joined Genetech in the United States to develop a new bacterium that would stimulate human growth using recombinant DNA technology. At the time Kabi was the world leader, but could only produce limited supplies of the product. It took Genetech one year to develop the genetically modified bacterium. Kabi developed the production process and in 1985, only 7 years after the project started, the new hormone was approved for sale. According to the contract, worldwide production and marketing were divided into two parts: Genetech produces the product for the North American market, and Kabi has Europe. They continue to conduct joint research and exchange information (Laage-Hellman, 1989, pp. 15-16).

What is interesting about this illustration is that it appears to be between two competitors, but, given their highly specialized knowledge base, a natural division of labor in technical competence was possible and both benefited from this moderate level of collaboration. Even more interesting is that when Kabi decided to develop another product, Genetech demanded a greater proportion of the profits, so Kabi turned to another company with whom it shared the development costs and risks.

The parallel form involving multiple competitors is the research consortia established in the 1980s by the federal government. Examples include Micro Electronic and Computer Technology Corporation (1983), a Software Productivity Consortium (1985), the National Center for Manufacturing Science (1986), and Sematech (1987) (Richards, 1989). The objective of these efforts was to assist a specialized niche or an industry in improving the extent and quality of its research. To date, however, these consortia have not been very successful, except perhaps for the Community Clinical Oncology Program (CCOP) which is described below.

In the 1980s the National Cancer Institute (NCI) created Community Clinical Oncology Programs (CCOPs) to help in the search for a cure for cancer. Each CCOP consists of a cluster of hospitals, physicians, and support staff, which can range in size from a few physicians and one hospital to as many as 50 physicians and multiple hospitals. The objective of the networks is to link the development and evolution of protocols for cancer treatment and control with ongoing service organizations. The NCI provides overall direction, program management, and funding. The CCOPs find patients willing to accept experimental treatments and feed research outcome information to regional research bases. Currently there are 51 operating CCOPs in 31 states and 15 research bases. Together they involve 253 hospitals, 103 group practices, and 2,000 practicing physicians (Kaluzny, Morrissey, & McKinney, 1990).

There are larger goals that our government adopts, such as increasing American competitiveness, maintaining national security, or repairing the ozone layer. These colossal goals must of necessity involve many organizations that have specialized expertise needed by the effort. The success of CCOPs in comparison with the other research consortia is probably due in part to the fact that a wide-based consensus exists that a cure for cancer is a vital goal. In addition, it is probably easier to achieve moderate levels of cooperation among public sector organizations where the profit motive is absent. As a consensus grows that American competitiveness is rapidly declining, then interorganizational research consortia may perform better.

Joint or collective action in pursuit of economic objectives is a different matter: There are many partnerships among competitors. For example, in the development of large shopping malls it is not unusual for Sears, Montgomery Ward, and several national department stores to join together in institutional marketing, advertising, and further development. The frequency of these interorganizational relationships is unknown because they remain largely invisible, embedded in the infinite number of market interactions that comprise the daily routine of organizations.

When large numbers of small companies are involved in cooperative purchasing and marketing, the collective's activities are quite visible. Wine growers in France, Italy, Germany, Spain, and Chile have frequently taken advantage of economies of scale by jointly bottling and selling their products, as have the much larger prune and cranberry cooperatives in the United States. Similarly, Premier Hospitals Alliance provides centralized purchasing for a network of 44 large teaching hospitals (Zuckerman & Kaluzny, 1990). Other examples in health care are the University Hospital Consortium (51 medical centers) and Voluntary Hospitals of America (800 hospitals).

A particularly interesting example of moderate cooperation among competitors is the role of the McKesson Company, which centralizes information, technology, and linkages among independent drugstores and pharmaceutical manufacturers, distributors, retailers, and consumers (Zuckerman & Kaluzny, 1990). McKesson is close to a coordinated production system, but the independent drugstores still own and operate their own businesses. Two things make cooperation in this network comparatively easy. First, independent drugstores, even though they are competitors, have a common enemy—the drugstore chain. Second, they have local niches and thus are not in direct competition with one another. Again, as with the hospital example, knowing the ecological spread of the resource base is important in understanding how much collaboration is possible.

Another illustration of multiorganizational product development is reported by Nielsen (1988). Public television stations cooperatively develop programs: They vote on topics and pool resources in order to produce films such as "The Civil War."

Like the McKesson example, local National Public Network affiliates, although located in the same city, have specialized markets. Washington, DC, for example, has three public stations; one at Howard University targets African-American audiences, one in Baltimore caters to multicultural audiences, and one in Washington caters to middle- and upper middle-class white audiences. These collaborative efforts differ from cartels because the cooperation does not involve collaboration on all TV programs but only on a selected few.

Cooperation in pooling of resources for political ends is different from the pooling of funds for joint project development. There are many political alliances among competitors at the local level, which frequently have been studied by those interested in the problem of interest aggregation in communities (Laumann, Galaskiewicz, & Marsden, 1978). Similarly, there are many sector-wide trade associations, each seeking its own self-interest. As Aldrich and Mueller (1982) demonstrated, the growth in trade associations and lobbying activity by networks of competitor organizations has increased steadily since the 1930s, and is one further indicator that political goals are so difficult to achieve that organizations, even competitor organizations, are willing to work together.

Broad Cooperation. In some sectors, such as the automobile and aircraft industries, the costs and risks of product development are so high that competitors are forced to cooperate. For example, we have the case of NUMMI, the joint venture between General Motors and Toyota, where Toyota needed General Motors to lobby Congress and the administration to block import quotas, and General Motors needed Toyota's lean production technologies. This is an example of a mixed political and technological exchange, one that Kanter (1989) called opportunistic. Other interesting examples are the joint ventures of Texas Instruments-Hitachi and Corning-Ciba-Geigy (Zuckerman & Kaluzny, 1990).

Unfortunately, the many studies on joint ventures do not make distinctions between whether the parties in a joint venture are in the same industry and in the same technological niche. Nor do they usually distinguish the amount of cooperation involved, generally lumping together joint ventures involving marketing, those involving production, and those that involve only product development. However, because these joint venture counts sometimes specify industry (Pollack, 1992a), we can make some reasonable assumptions about those joint ventures that are intrasector and those that are between sectors. For example, many of the joint ventures in automobiles must be between competitors, although frequently they are located in specialized and limited niches, or niches where the company is weak.

Another example of broad cooperation from the human services is an invention of the last decade—special needs adoption networks.

Family service agencies in several states joined together and created the Special Needs Adoption Network. The purpose of the network is to locate, recruit, train, and otherwise assist persons wishing to adopt handicapped and minority children. The agencies jointly support a small central office and staff, and agency CEOs make up the network's steering committee. Through publicity campaigns, direct advertising, and direct appeals, the network locates potential adoptive parents and places their names in a centralized database. When the agencies obtain an adoptive child, they may search the database for a potentially good fit. Membership in the network is, of course, voluntary for these agencies, but because its services are so vital and the placing of special needs children so extraordinarily difficult, the network has not had problems securing the support it needs for its operations.

Finally, cartels require a high level of cooperation among multiple organizations in the same sector because they attempt not only to control prices but also to coordinate production so that supply is limited and prices are maintained. Cartels have formed in the smokestack industries, and among railroads and mining operators, where production costs are high and markets fluctuate (Campbell et al., 1991). A contemporary illustration is the Council of European Federations of Industrial Chemicals. Nielsen (1988) reported that in 1983, after conducting a worldwide market study, the Council concluded there was an excess supply of petrochemicals. To prevent destructive competition, they worked with the European Economic Community and were able to reduce production and production capacity. Cartels have historically been more successful in Europe and Japan than in the United States because their governments have been more tolerant (even instrumental), and because cheating has been less of a problem. On the other hand, OPEC has not been very successful, particularly because the OPEC counties are so numerous. The question of how the ecological context influences trust is an important theme in the development of cooperative behavior and one we will return in Chapter Eight.

One simple test for assessing the level of interorganizational cooperation among manufacturing and service organizations is to count the number of different managerial functions that are performed collaboratively, such as development, purchasing, marketing, distributing, and so on. In Chapters Four through Six we provide functional parallels in the public services sector: namely, intake, assessment, treatment, and follow-up. The more functions that are accomplished jointly, the broader the cooperation.

SYMBIOTIC COOPERATION

Since we are most interested in symbiotic cooperation, the balance of this book will focus on relationships and networks whose members are in different sectors. Over time, the number of niches within sectors is increasing because of the growth in knowledge in industrial sectors and in the public sector, most notably in the high-tech areas. These forms of interorganizational collaboration have received much less attention, but there is a small literature for each of the six cells in the typology shown in Figure 2.2.

We believe cooperation is both more intense and stable among organizations from different sectors. Because they bring complementary rather than similar technologies to the partnership or network, they are more likely to form symbiotic relationships. Absent of the natural antagonisms of competitors, symbiotic relationships tend to have a greater frequency of interaction (Astley & Fombrun, 1983). As frequency and intensity of communication increase, the level of cooperation tends to increase and the relationship may evolve into a permanent production partnership or system.

Limited Cooperation. Obligational linkages and networks across sectors are far more common than we realize (Snehota, 1990).

Symbiotic Cooperation Among Different Sector Organizations

	Dyadic and Triadic Obligational Linkages	Multiorganizational/ Sector Wide Obligational Networks
Limited Cooperation: products, services, clients	**Obligational Linkages:** creating preferred subcontracts/referral sources.	**Obligational Networks:** creating clusters of preferred subcontractors Client Referral Networks.
power	**Overlapping Board:** making self-interested decisions.	**Interlocking Directorates:** making self-interested decisions.
money	**Financing Linkages:** creating preferred borrowers.	**Financing Networks:** creating preferred borrowers. *Gurupu* (formerly *Zaibatsu):* facilitating exchanges of stock and capital.
human capital	**Employment Linkages:** creating employment fast tracks.	**Human Capital Networks:** educating and grooming professionals.

Figure 2.2 A Typology of Cooperative Interorganizational Relationships and Networks

The first category in Figure 2.2 was labeled "obligation" by Hollingsworth (1991), who focused on subcontracting as the most dominant linking function. Rather than juxtapose obligational networks and promotional networks as he did, we disentangle the two into two dimensions: the number of organizations involved and the level of cooperation. We therefore distinguish obligational linkages, such as subcontracting between two or three firms, from obligational networks, which involve large numbers of firms or agencies (Boje & Whetten, 1981; Lincoln, 1985). These are ex-

	Production Linkages	Production Networks
Broad Cooperation: production	Joint Ventures: producing a product or service.	Systemic Production Networks: collective production methods, community-based service delivery systems. Vertical *Keiretsu*: collective production systems.

	Promotional Linkages	Promotional Networks
Moderate Cooperation: technological objectives	financial objectives	supra-sector goal.
	Joint Ventures: sharing expertise and equipment; R&D.	Partnerships: joint lending and borrowing.
political objectives	Ad Hoc Alliances: achieving a	Research Consortia: developing and sharing innovative

Figure 2.2 (continued)

change relationships, and the medium can be products, services, clients, or money. Much of the research of Johanson's group at Uppsala University studied linkages between suppliers and customers, or customers and end-users. They found that when exchange of supplies and raw materials is preferential and stable over long time periods, then obligational networks exist.

Quite different are the larger obligational networks that have been the traditional focus of network analysis in sociology. The most illustrative example we can cite is the Japanese supplier associations. These are networks of small companies which surround a large company, tied together by a dense web of reciprocal exchanges.

> Japanese corporations, such as Hitachi and Matsushita (Sako, in press), are surrounded by a web of supplier companies that serve several functions. They facilitate the transfer of the parent company's technologies to those who need to use them, and they allow the creation of solutions to technical problems that have to be shared, but in confidence (Womack et al., 1990, pp. 151-152). Suppliers of the suppliers may also have their own associations which seem to arrange themselves in concentric circles. In Japan these clusters and subclusters are not hard to detect and the boundaries are clear because the linkages are multidimensional—the exchanges are informational and technological, as well as social.

These associations should not be confused with the *gurupu*, which are investment networks. For example, one *gurupu* might involve an automobile company, a bank, a steel plant, a trading company, a shipbuilding company, and a finance company, and is thus more akin to a diverse conglomerate cutting across many industrial sectors. Nor should these associations be confused with the vertical *keiretsu*, although they reinforce social control in them.

In the United States there has been an extensive analysis of interlocking directorates (Laumann & Pappi, 1976). While these may involve exchanges of money or investment patterns, more typically they exemplify exchanges of information and power across industrial sector lines.

People who have valuable knowledge and skills are also a medium of exchange; in other words, human capital. These forms of exchange are cross-sectoral because they typically involve public and private educational institutions, consulting firms, and commercial firms. For example, persons with MBA degrees move from graduate programs in business into major consulting firms such as Arthur D. Little or Booze Allen & Hamilton, and after several years move into executive positions with major corporations. In exchange, the graduate schools are heavily endowed by industries they serve. Columbia University's School of Journalism places young reporters with New York newspapers, the training ground for American newspapers, and in return receives financial and political support from the industry. In another example, Rosenbaum, Karija, Setheasten, and Maier (1990) described the employment networks involving high schools and commercial interests.

Moderate Cooperation. When obligational linkages and networks are maintained over time, and a level of interorganizational trust is established, then interorganizational structures may take on additional functions (Johanson & Mattsson, 1987). The Agency for Science and Research reported in 1985 that 20% of the firms it surveyed were linked with other firms, universities, and government laboratories through networks involving joint research projects, commissioned research, or other forms of information exchange, and it predicted that in 1990 this figure would rise to 26% (Aoki, 1988).

Product and market development are the most common function of technological partnerships. ASEH, the leading Swedish supplier of heavy electrical equipment, works with almost all of the Swedish steel companies, resulting in major innovations—for example, inductive stirring in electric arc furnaces and the ASEH-STORH power metallurgy process (Laage-Hellman, 1989). In the United States, a cross-sectoral example of cooperation for the purpose of technological development is the triad of giants including AT&T, Chemical Bank, and Time, Inc., who joined together for information technology development.

America has been successful in developing symbiotic research networks for military defense. These networks involve university-based scientists, units of federal government, manufacturing firms, and other corporations (both suppliers and users). They have produced, among many products, commercial semiconductors, integrated circuits, computers, nuclear power, microwave telecommunications, new materials such as fiber-reinforced plastics, titanium, and new methods of fabricating metals (Hollingsworth, 1991). A clear example of this type of cooperation across industrial sectors where different technical expertise leads to innovation is the case of supercomputers.

A new consortium has been formed in an effort to maintain the U.S. lead in basic research on superconductors. The founding members are AT&T, IBM, MIT, and Lincoln Lab

continued

continued from previous page

oratories, a separate government-funded lab at MIT. The consortium was founded on the recommendation of the White House Science Council, which predicted that without much collaboration, dominance will be lost as it has been with laser and videotape technologies. Ralph E. Gomory, IBM senior vice-president for science and technology, says that "the notion is the absolute sharing of information . . . and the companies will give up control of the work to the consortium." The participants each contribute the equivalent of 25 full-time professionals and facilities—estimated at a value of $10 million—to the work effort and relinquish control over them to managers to be named by the governing board of the consortium. Management of the consortium directs all the researchers as a team and is responsible for producing new electronic devices, circuits, and interconnections, and new materials to make them with. In return for their investments, the companies get help from university researchers in developing commercial products, and the universities and government labs get additional funds to add staff and students. They all share in any profits that derive from successful product development (Hilts, 1989).

Many federations, such as the National Association of Manufacturers (NAM), have political objectives; most broadly, they wish to influence government legislation. They are distinct from trade associations or labor unions because they span multiple sectors and are thus concerned with broad-based legislation that influences all companies or all workers, such as health insurance or Social Security or tariffs. For example, the passage of the Taft-Hartley Act in 1948, a pet project of the NAM and bitterly opposed by the labor unions, did limit the unions' power. Likewise, fund-raising organizations, such as United Way, combine the efforts of many organizations from both the nonprofit and profit-making sectors.

We are also all familiar with the many high-profile interorganizational networks that seek to solve societal problems such as environmental degradation and gun control, or that promote causes such as economic competitiveness or animal rights. We label these promotional networks. They can involve a limited number of organizations, in which case they are more correctly called a partnership, but more frequently they involve large numbers of companies, government agencies, universities, and local organizations. The function of these networks in most cases is to achieve a collective goal that could not be achieved by a single or limited number of organizations. Similarly, there are many national associations formed for financial purposes, such as local fund-raising, that involve organizations from all sectors in a community.

A very interesting obligational network crossing public/private lines is the Jane Addams Resource Corporation (JARC) in Chicago.

JARC conducted an economic analysis of their declining neighborhood on the Chicago's south side and found there were more than 60 marginally profitable small metalworking firms that employed more than 2,000 workers. JARC organized these companies and their suppliers and distributors into a consortium that gave them a scale of operation that enabled them to adjust to market conditions. JARC now serves as staff to the consortium, which provides cooperative purchasing, collective marketing, and staff training, and creates opportunities for below market rate financing and venture capital options. The consortium also serves as an advocate for members regarding industrial land use issues, offers relocation and expansion assistance, and links members with city and state economic development programs. Several years after the creation of the consortium, JARC bought an abandoned industrial property in the neighborhood and renovated it for use as incubation space (Alter, Deutelbaum, Dodd, Else, & Raheim, 1992).

This Jane Addams network, even though its basic function is exchange, is a promotional network because its goal is neighborhood revitalization through economic development. The most successful examples of both macro and micro economic development today are those that cross public and private sectors.

There are networks that pursue self-interest goals by means of political methods. Federated unions are a good example, because many local unions can be highly diverse and yet find common ground in pursuit of their individual agendas. *Promotional network* is a good term for these various forms of interorganizational cooperation, because it conveys the idea that the function and activity have limits, which are defined by the overlap of the interests, desires, and goals of diverse members.

The Corning Glass illustration in Chapter One is a good example of many symbiotic joint ventures, but others are found in the field of bio-tech, where the companies are small and idea rich, but cash poor. Typically, they lack the capacity for large-scale production, distribution, and marketing. Kogut et al. (1990) traced the growth in joint ventures and found that while the number of new bio-tech firms peaked in 1981, the number of joint ventures peaked 5 years later, reflecting their problems with product development, and 85% were still in force in 1988 when the study was completed.

The Powell and Brantley study identified more than 700 joint ventures between bio-tech companies, and a sizable number involved product development as well as production, marketing, and distribution, but we have no way of knowing the sequence in which these functions were developed. It is the coordination of production, however, that we view as the most problematic and most in need of theoretical understanding and research.

Broad Cooperation. Having described symbiotic interorganizational forms requiring limited and moderate levels of cooperation, we turn to the complex structure we believe is the most important in post-industrial society; namely, systemic production linkages and networks. They are distinctive because they require the broadest cooperation—informational, technical, financial, and political, as well as managerial. Systemic production networks, which require broad functional integration, constitute a distinct logical type and can be described in terms of their structures, processes, and performances that vary across categories.

Our typology allows us to juxtapose cartels on systemic production networks. They both involve members in exchanges of information, technology, and other resources. They both require members to arrive at goals and objectives by consensus, and to engage in joint effort to achieve them. But while they have characteristics in common, they also differ in several critical ways. Systemic networks produce products or services that could not be produced by any one participant alone. Collectively, therefore, they are innovative. This same parallel exists between competitive joint ventures and symbiotic partnerships; the latter are much more likely to lead to new products or services that could not have been produced by one partner.

Japanese auto production networks might be thought of as same sector competitor networks, but in reality they more closely resemble symbiotic networks. In very complex products such as cars and airplanes, the components come from different sectors, making collaboration across the production chain more possible. As the automobile becomes more technologically sophisticated, the easier this becomes. A dramatic example is the use of electronics in automobile manufacture. As this task complexity increases and spans different sectors, vertical integration becomes less and less successful.

Unlike a cartel, which involves all the members of the same niche in the same sector, systemic production networks typically are coordinated by one assembler who connects with organizations that build components in different niches, who in turn connect with organizations that obtain parts from other sectors. Toyota, Nissan, Honda, and Mitsubishi each have their own systemic production networks. This is complemented by the supplier associations, which we have already described.

Japanese auto production illustrates the difference between cartels and systemic production networks—the collaboration encompasses the entire design to market process. Further, this network has an important social element. Social bonds develop during many meetings and via the elaborate system of joint borrowing in the suppliers' associations. These social ties are the basis of trust and commitment that move beyond the mutual dependency in exchange relationships. We stress this difference because the economists start with the assumption that profit must also be maximized, which in turn creates a climate of distrust. We want to start with the assumption that mutual commitment and trust can exist, and then assess the degree to which interorganizational forms can maintain the sharing of profits.

The balance of this book is devoted to describing multiorganizational systemic networks, so we will not provide multiple examples here. One example will suffice.

> One outcome of the women's movement of the 1970s was a concern in many communities with the frequency of sexual assault and the fact that there was little or no deterrence—

continued

continued from previous page

seldom were offenders prosecuted and even more infrequently were they convicted. Community studies of this problem revealed that victims did not press for prosecution because they were terrorized, not only by their assailants but also by the system. They knew they would be questioned by a policeman, would have to undergo unpleasant physical examinations, and if their cases went to trial they would be put on the defensive and perhaps degraded once again. The Women's Group, an organization in a large city on the East Coast, decided to act. Using a variety of tactics, the Women's Group created a service delivery system for victims of domestic and sexual assault. There are six organizational members: the Women's Group (providing counseling, shelter, and advocacy), the city's police department, the state attorney's office, the county hospital, legal aid, and the community college's displaced homemaker program. After 5 years, the participating organizations have in place interagency protocols that govern the timing, scope, and sequence of their response to crises, and assign functions, roles, and tasks to each organization in the network. Over a 10-year period, the number of prosecutions for rape in this city has quadrupled and convictions have tripled.

PROCESSES OF NETWORK DEVELOPMENT

The growth of interorganizational collaboration is an ongoing process. The level of cooperation within both competing and symbiotic interorganizational networks is not only a classifying variable but also an indicator of evolution. The problem of how networks evolve across time is central to our thesis about the increasing variety of cooperative networks. In the previous chapter, we observed that the antecedents of cooperative behavior included the following factors: a shift in the kinds of efficiencies needed (firms and agencies have to be efficient while being flexible and innovative), including short product lives and rapid technological change; increasing integration of economic and political interests facilitated by state involvement; rising levels of education and our increasing cognitive complexity; and a growing culture of trust. At various places in this chapter we reiterated the relevance of one or another of these factors.

Each of the three dimensions of the typology suggest alternative starting points in the process of evolution, and they allow us to predict which forms are likely to remain "stuck," and which are likely to evolve into more highly cooperative networks. Most of the limited forms of cooperation between competitors, such as hospital alliances that purchase services or trade associations that market products, are unlikely to evolve into cartels or cooperatives that engage in joint advertising. On the other hand, linkages requiring moderate levels of cooperation between competitors, such as joint product development, might evolve into joint ventures because a new product represents a new market niche.

As we discuss the initial starting points and the scenarios of development, we want to describe some interesting cross-national differences. Much of the evidence suggests that in manufacturing the Japanese are far ahead of the United States in the use of systemic networks. Likewise, we suggest that cartels are more successful in Europe and Japan than in the United States because of our legal restrictions. We believe these hypotheses pose several interesting theoretical questions about the antecedents of cooperative behavior.

The difference between competitors and noncompetitors that we described in Figures 2.1 and 2.2 is a useful way to begin our analysis. The two dimensions of symbiotic versus competitive and few versus many organizations reflect, at a minimum, four starting points for evolution. We start with the first and hardest pathway of development, namely the gradual creation of interorganizational relationships between a few competitive organizations.

Development Sequence of Networks
of a Few Competitive Organizations

Competitive linkages are harder to establish because the fears about autonomy are much greater. If symbiotic joint ventures are more influenced by opportunities for mutual learning because of complementary competencies, competitive joint ventures are more likely to be created to offset the high costs and risks of product development.

As firms divest themselves of parts of their production process, they automatically create a need for collaboration, as in the California Steel example. Thus, the movement away from vertical integration in order to be more flexible and innovative is inevitably a movement towards interorganizational collaboration across the production chain (Hollingsworth, 1991).

Increasingly, large firms in the auto, aircraft, aerospace, computer, and other industries must provide capital, marketing, and research services to their suppliers. As products become more complex and change rapidly, large firms no longer know how best to produce their products without supplier collaboration. To keep up with changes in the market, large and small firms must learn from one another about new markets and new technologies. To facilitate this, middle-level management moves back and forth between suppliers and final assemblers. As a consequence, price considerations have become less important in shaping the relationships among suppliers and customers (Hyman & Streeck, 1988).

Another reason competitive organizations are willing to develop linkages is competitive pressure. Economic pressures, however, must be much greater for competitors than noncompetitors to force them into dependent or interdependent relationships. We see these pressures in the automobile and aircraft industries, where there are enormous capital requirements, large economies of scale, global markets, excess capacity, and thus, the need to share risks (Hergert & Morris, 1988) .

Another factor encouraging collaboration is the change in the way large-scale competitive organizations are structured. Organizations that have multiple products and services "decouple" them in various ways to reduce the risks associated with the loss of autonomy, and to increase the ability of their smaller units to enter into flexible collaborative relationships. Control, as in Corning's case, is maintained via "an interrelated group of organizations with a wide range of ownership structures," in spite of the absence of hierarchy (Houghton, 1989, p. 3).

One beauty of interorganizational collaboration is that it allows organizations to sidestep the problems associated with loss of autonomy by simultaneously keeping control of their core functions while establishing joint ventures for peripheral or tangential functions and tasks. This is one reason why joint ventures are proliferating and why the business literature has concentrated on them; they have become ubiquitous, even among competitors.

Development Sequence of Networks of Many Competitive Organizations

We did not find examples of competitors in the same niche of the same sector engaged in preferred exchanges of raw materials. This appears to be an impossibility. The closest approximation occurs among universities that allow students to take courses on the campuses of their competitors. What is interesting about this example is that the cooperation flows precisely from the establishment of education niches even at the undergraduate level, making limited cooperation possible. Exchanges of information, however, are quite common among competitors because everyone has something to gain.

The creation of promotional networks does occur between competitors, but some of these networks are more difficult to establish than others. The government frequently must be involved in the creation of research consortia and argue that there are national reasons before the competitors engage in this activity themselves. A few competitors might find it useful to develop products together, but consortia are avoided for a number of reasons, mainly fears about loss of technological edge. The creation of promotional networks to put pressure on the government is much easier because the goals are more tangential to the core business.

There is also the creation of cooperation between competitive organizations for the coordination of prices and production, as in OPEC. Cartels are inherently unstable, and the larger they are the more likely someone is to cheat. Clearly, this factor of size is one reason why cartels are not very successful in the United States. We might also add that in Europe and Japan, where the elites are more integrated because of their common educational backgrounds, there is a higher level of trust among them, making cartels more feasible. Then, too, the European and Japanese governments frequently take the initiative to control production (Hollingsworth et al., in press).

Development Sequence of Networks of a Few Symbiotic Organizations

Organizations develop trading relationships today because they must (Cook, 1977). For many years it was thought that the least preferred strategy for organizational survival was one that required organizations to surrender autonomy (Benson, 1975; Pfeffer & Salancik, 1978). This is no longer the case. Today many recognize that linkages are a means by which organizations can assure a steady flow of resources (Kramer & Grossman, 1987) and enhance their chances of survival (Astley & Fombrun, 1983; Wiewel & Hunter, 1985). Further, once within an exchange relationship, organizations become party to symbiotic relationships marked by reduced competition (Warren, Rose, & Bergunder, 1974) and boundary defense (Potuchek, 1986).

An important characteristic of an exchange network is the emergence of boundary spanners (Aldrich, 1979). This does not always occur, of course, but as the volume of patterned exchanges increases, boundary spanners are likely to appear to negotiate the transaction and to resolve problems. And as the complexity of the exchange increases, as in major procurement and subcontracting, boundary spanners are needed to manage large amounts of information and intricate detail. The reason Japanese sales personnel visit their customers each day is to handle this information flow and to build social bonds.

Once boundary spanners exist, social bonds are created and interdependencies are recognized, and the stage is set for the evolution of the obligational linkage. When partners in a dyad or triad adjust their behavior in a network, it builds trust and cooperation (Johanson & Mattsson, 1987). Gouldner (1960) observed and explained the norm of reciprocity; we want to understand its origins. Johanson and Mattsson (1987) suggested that as organizational members learn through the relationship to do things better, and then modify their work procedures, they create mutual rewards that are self-reinforcing. In turn, of course, this process generates mutual dependency and interdependency. In this way, reciprocity is established, and the relationship deepens as learning continues and adaptiveness speeds up. Further, this learning improves the bottom line and is therefore rewarding both socially and economically (Etzioni, 1988).

Once this adaptation occurs, then the stage is set for joint product development if there an opportunity and there are complementary competencies. Successful product development leads naturally to the creation of a joint production venture, but again only if there are complementary competencies.

Development Sequence of Networks of Many Symbiotic Organizations

Another way of summarizing the development of symbiotic organizations is the three-stage model of network formation, shown in Figure 2.3, that includes obligational networks (informal, loosely linked groups of organizations having relationships of preferred exchanges), promotional networks (quasi-formal clusters of organizations sharing and pooling resources to accomplish concerted action), and systemic networks (formal interorganizational units jointly producing a product or service in pursuit of a supraorganizational goal). These three kinds of networks are distinguished by their increasing level of integration and interaction (Astley & Fombrun, 1983). Even systemic networks vary along this dimension, as do many business joint ventures (Killing, 1988), a topic that is analyzed in Chapter Four.

The differences among these three stages may be difficult to discern because they are hierarchical and they overlap. Together, they form a framework that describes a continuum of institutional forms, each with different purposes, structures, operations, and outcomes. This framework is not intended to be a rigid developmental sequence; it is theoretically possible, for example, for a network to originate as a production system, especially if mandated by law, as in juvenile justice systems. What Figure 2.3 does assert, however, is that the collective tasks necessary for one form are also necessary for each succeeding form in order for it to be successful.

	embryonic		developed
	obligational networks	promotional networks	systemic networks
Interorganizational Activities:	almost none ad hoc	peripherial segmented	essential enduring
Emergent Properties:	boundary spanners	pooling of resources	division of labor
Goals:	individual member needs	supra-ordinate member problems	supra-ordinate societal problems
Examples:	patterned resource exchanges	federations coalitions	service delivery systems
	groups supplier associations interlocking directorates	Sematech Chip United Way AFL-CIO	Japanese production systems Keiretsu

Figure 2.3 Model of Symbiotic Network Development

Exchange theory identifies the mutual dependence created when organizations in different sectors need goods and services from each other. This does not explain why purchasing or service networks would evolve toward promotional networks, however. Neither does it explain why systemic networks have emerged in the United States among public service organizations and not among for-profit firms and companies.

Traditionally Europe delivered welfare, health care, and education via centralized or poly-centralized ministries (Hage et al., 1989), which have been slow to decentralize, although this is now occurring quite rapidly. In the United States human services have, until only quite recently, been considered the responsibility of local voluntary organizations and charitable societies. Even in the 1930s, when the federal government began to play a major role, publicly funded services were delivered at the local level, with their control divided between state and federal bureaucracies (and between local organizations when there where significant amounts of local voluntary dollars involved). The interorganizational service field in U.S. communities is today a complex mix of voluntary fund-raising organizations (United Way plus more narrowly focused organizations), local offices of state agencies (departments of human services, public health, mental health, education, and so on) private nonprofit service organizations (family services, senior services, youth services, and so on), and for-profit agencies and clinics (home nursing, nursing homes, psychological and medical care, and so on).

Several factors push clusters of this mixed and complex field into interorganizational collaboration. First, service organizations have consistently been undercapitalized and underfunded, and organizations have been forced to join forces to seek government support and to solicit operating funds from the community. Because operating funds were seldom adequate to serve all individuals and families in need, those organizations making allocation decisions were able to dictate broad policy to the service organizations. One of the standard policies in most American communities is the "nonduplication of effort" rule, meaning that service organizations are forced into narrow niches. The only exceptions made are religious denominations, thus even medium-size communities have Jewish, Lutheran, and Catholic family service agencies. As a consequence, the interorganizational field of community service organizations today is highly differentiated, with many agencies providing narrowly focused service to a narrowly defined target population. When individuals and families have multiple problems and need multiple services or treatments, they must obtain them from multiple organizations. Thus, complex client referral systems and interagency collaboration are the only possible answer if clients are to be served effectively.

The resulting networks are the outcome of bartering interactions between administrators and workers across organizational boundaries (Granovetter, 1973; Mathiesen, 1971). As problems arise, information is exchanged, and the parties concert their action (Evan, 1966). If a problem is solved, then trust is built, and the basis for further collaboration is established (Gray, 1989a, 1989b; Johanson & Mattsson, 1987). This process happens every day in communities around the world, but has not, oddly enough, been well documented. What we know about interorganizational networks comes primarily from studying visible and formal structures that are, in actuality, only the tip of the iceberg (Lehman, 1975). The frequency of networks of preferred exchanges and obligational action is unknown, because they are embedded in the infinite number of market interactions that comprise the daily routine of organizations.

Earlier we observed that interorganizational collaboration allows large organizations to have it both ways—to maintain control over what they are doing without the necessity of building ever-larger bureaucratic structures. In the case of relatively smaller community service organizations, they do not need to create separate but jointly owned units; all they must do is decentralize their decision making so that their functional units have the necessary autonomy to develop interorganizational relationships with other needed organizations. In this way, even medium-size service organizations today have multiple departments—each belonging to and acting with a different network of agencies. Within these organizations the external relationships of departments may be so different that to study them requires treating each department as if it were a separate organizational unit. Each department may be involved in collective planning and program development with a very different set of actors. The next step, if joint product or service development is successful, is a symbiotic joint venture or multiorganizational network engaged in production.

The most distinguishing characteristic of production networks is that they occur in a large organizational field of highly specialized organizations. The more specialized the niche, the more likely there is a need for an elaborate pattern of purchases across a production chain or an extensive system of client referrals. When the organizational field is thus segmented into specialized organizational niches, then multi-organizational relationships can generalize themselves into more functionally complex relationships. Within these organizational communities, elaborate systems of collective production can develop. The factor that facilitates this elaboration is a climate of trust.

The need or desire to improve performance can cause network decision makers to develop collective production processes. In order to achieve joint operation among a multiple and diverse group of organizational units, adaptive efficiencies must be achieved. Thus, as networks develop toward a systemic form, they tend to become more differentiated; that is, members become more specialized in regard to their discrete function within the collective. When one department store agrees to both monitor suppliers in the Near East on behalf of a consortium of stores and make purchases for the group, functional differentiation exists in that system. Further, as functional specialization occurs, the number of communication and work flow channels tends to decrease, and with fewer channels, the collective is easier to comprehend and govern. These structural characteristics of systems—complexity, differentiation, and connectivity—have important influences on the ways in which administrators and workers must interact with one another.

One of the more important themes in institutional economics is the idea that changes in institutional rules create incentives for organizations to change their patterns of behavior (North, 1990). The federal government in the United States has altered a number of its rules and incentives, which in turn has encouraged the establishment of promotional and even production networks among welfare agencies in the United States. A number of examples of this are provided in the case histories given at the ends of Chapters Four, Five, and Six.

Two other structural properties of systemic networks—centrality and size—are also important. Systems can be centralized or decentralized, depending on whether the location of the decision-making authority is in a few or many parts of the system, and they can be lateral or hierarchical, depending on whether the source is within the system itself or at a higher level (Lehman, 1975). We believe, however, that networks are, in a normative sense, both non-hierarchical and self-regulating, and we hypothesize that poor performance results when structures are created that do not accommodate these inherent characteristics.

Likewise, systems are theoretically of any size, although in practice there are limits. The degree of centrality and the size of a system produce very important differences in structure and operating processes. All of these structural dimensions are discussed in Chapter Five.

Because production networks have a more definable structure, they are more easily identified than are exchange or promotional networks. They are more easily described because their boundaries are more visible, membership is often formal, and they have more permanency than the other forms. Systemic networks produce a common output by means of the operational processes of coordination and task integration, through differential structural characteristics and by developing specialized participation via function and role.

In summary, interorganizational networks constitute a distinct logical type and can be described in terms of their processes (Chapter Three), technologies (Chapter Four), structures

(Chapter Five), and performances (Chapter Six). There are, we assert, four normative characteristics common to all forms.

1. *Interorganizational networks are cognitive structures.* Antecedent to advanced network formation there must be a mutually shared conceptual framework held by the individuals who have common perceptions about their mutual technical competencies, and who have made similar judgments about strategies relative to their environments (Galaskiewicz, 1985; Gray, 1989a, 1989b; Vickers, 1968). As collective conceptualization is more widely shared, a domain is established based on mutually shared language, symbols, and beliefs about efficacy of methods (Benson, 1975). Although a common cognitive structure is a necessary antecedent of network development, the degree to which it is articulated or to which an explicit consensus exists can vary widely. Even exchange relationships assume a common perception of mutual dependence (Johanson & Mattsson, 1987); each party must have mutual knowledge of the other's capabilities, their own needs, and the match between the two. As one might expect, the Japanese have several terms for mutuality, one of which is *kyoei kyozon*, which means coprosperity and coexistence. Cognitive structures thus build commitment and trust.

One of the major problems in building networks is that while there may be a mutual objective in the cooperative relationship, it does not necessarily mean that there is agreement about the methods and strategies to be used. Conflict over means exists and is common. We will explore these problems in Chapters Six and Seven.

2. *Interorganizational networks are non-hierarchical.* Networks, as opposed to hierarchies, are constituted by lateral linkages but, like all organizational and interorganizational forms, are influenced, to a lesser or greater degree, by their environments and can vary in the degree of autonomy they possess. This is a critical point because transaction cost analysis (Coase, 1937; Williamson, 1975) has emphasized the choice of hierarchies versus markets, and later work (Williamson, 1985; Hollingsworth, 1991) views obligational and promotional networks as being midway between the two. We disagree and argue that the defining element in a systemic network is joint decision making and problem solving. This is a much more complex power structure

than a hierarchical one, and one more pervasive than the transaction cost perspective.

There are, of course, anecdotes about networks becoming dominated by one large organization. One reason why agricultural cooperatives are easy to create is that all units are small and no one dominates. But when a network is dominated by a single organization or several large ones, it is less likely to perform successfully. For example, the smaller companies in the Sematech Chip Consortia are leaving it, presumably for these reasons (Pollack, 1992b). The consequence of domination is less effectiveness, with ancillary costs of conflict, delays, and errors.

3. *Interorganizational networks have a division of labor.* Each firm or agency brings what Laage-Hellman (1989) called a technical competency to the interorganizational relationship. Failure to demonstrate this competency can lead to a termination of the relationship. But once demonstrated, it results in mutual dependency. This division of labor also militates against the development of a dominant actor who attempts to control the networks (Hage, 1965, 1980).

4. *Interorganizational production networks are self-regulating.* If networks are non-hierarchical, by extension their decision-making structures are horizontal. For a laterally linked cluster of autonomous organizations to act and work together, there must be a degree of solidarity achieved through democratic principles. The opposite side of the coin, of course, is that organizations must surrender sovereignty and operate under conditions of diffusion of power. In other words, order in networks is achieved through negotiated processes (Gray, 1989a, 1989b), which evolve through mutual adjustment of members (Thompson, 1967; Johanson & Mattsson, 1987). As Trist so eloquently put it, "Facing a future of increasing complexity means trying self-regulation within interdependency" (1983, p. 272).

We know that research consortia and production networks are more successful in Japan than they are in the United States, as measured by the number of new products and duration of participation. One reason for their success is that these Japanese networks have developed slowly over time, allowing for the development of interorganizational trust and a common cognitive structure that facilitates information exchange, creative problem solving, and collective action. We believe that many of the research consortia created in the United States will fail to develop into systemic production networks because they have been established without sufficient incubation time for exchange relationships to develop. Even among community service organizations, promotional networks will not evolve toward systemic production mandated by federal agencies unless the prior conditions that we specified in Figure 1.2 are met.

Even when the antecedent conditions are met; development time is abundant; and interorganizational relationships are a high priority for administrators, supervisors, and workers; systemic production networks will falter unless there is knowledge of the interorganizational technologies necessary for further development. Understanding these methods and processes is so important that we devote the next chapter to them.

THREE

What Is Coordination?

The prevalent image of organizations in the United States has been one of fierce competition and a struggle to survive and maximize profit. Even in the public sector, the dominant concept is of agencies battling over organizational domains. Despite these images of conflict there are, as we have seen, many instances of cooperation. These images are influenced by neoclassical models of human behavior and the power of the invisible hand.

But besides the invisible hand of competition, there is the visible hand of coordination and of cooperation. Chandler (1977) concentrated his analytical attention on the visible hand within an organization and on internal administrative coordination. External coordination across organizational boundaries is a much more difficult task because it requires much more cooperation. The normal mechanisms of rewards and punishments are not present.

COOPERATION AS COORDINATION

Cooperation has been described in the interorganizational literature. It is believed to be a predominant behavior of organizations in complex societies (Axelrod, 1984; Gray, 1985; Lincoln, 1985; Rogers & Whetten, 1982; Whetten, 1981). There are examples of successful interorganizational cooperation (Beder, 1984; Mathiesen, 1971; Mulford, 1984; Reid, 1964), as well as examples

81

of its limits (Frank, 1983; Gray & Hay, 1986; Hanf & Scharpf, 1978; Milner, 1980; Morrissey, Steadman, Kilburn, & Lindsey, 1984; Redekop, 1986), and considerable disagreement over the definition of cooperation and coordination. Some theorists consider these concepts to be analytically distinct: coordination involves deliberate adjustment and collective goals, whereas cooperation does not (Morrissey, Hall et al., 1982). We subsume coordination under cooperation as a specific form of cooperative activity (Benson, Kunce, Thompson, & Allen, 1973; Litwak, 1970), holding that few organizations would undertake joint activity without some deliberation and agreement on goals. The difference between the terms is one of degree rather than substance (Aiken, Dewar, DiTomaso, Hage, & Zeitz, 1975). Given this broad definition, there are two basic approaches in the literature for understanding coordination.

KINDS OF COORDINATION

Coordination as a Performance Objective:
A Program Goal

We often say, "That research project needs much better coordination," or "That patient's services are not well coordinated." What we mean in a general sense is that parts of the program or project are not congruent; rather than being compatible, they work together with friction and discord. If questioned, we find it difficult to describe what it is that would make the parts fit so that the program is a harmonious whole.

Since so many of the examples of collaboration between business firms have involved joint development of technologies or product innovation, we shall use this as the paradigmatic case for the private sector in our discussion of coordination/collaboration. In contrast, in the public sector the interorganizational literature is dominated by the discussion of service delivery. This, then, becomes the paradigmatic case for the public sector (see Table 3.2).

We are aware that federal program designers often use the term *coordination* as the intended result of system change efforts; thus, the goal of a program is "a coordinated system." The problem is that when one asks how to achieve a coordinated system, the answer is "by coordinating the activities of the system." This is a tautology, and such a program design cannot be evaluated. The answer is to conceptualize coordination as a network performance (Aiken et al., 1975; Dewitt, 1977). This is a useful way of thinking about coordination because it makes clear the *purposes* for which it is employed. Table 3.1 shows three performance criteria cross-classified with the four basic elements of service delivery that must be coordinated. These are only the most basic performances a network might wish to work toward; there undoubtedly are other important performances and many more intermediate objectives that are necessary for systems change.

Economists tend to emphasize the allocation of resources. Social workers tend to be client-focused and are concerned with how clients who are receiving services interface with the system. Our framework focuses on both of these perspectives. Just because a particular program or occupation is needed does not mean it is provided. Nor is this a function of our research's being in the public sector, where these problems are easier to see. Various joint ventures can fail because the wrong companies have come together (Laage-Hellman, 1989).

The first performance objective of coordination concerns whether all necessary resources and services are in fact present in the system and available to those who need them. Comprehensiveness, while seemingly a basic concept, is often omitted from discussions of coordination, implying that coordination applies only to those components or programs currently in the system. For this reason, critics such as Terreberry (1968) argue that a concept like coordination is inherently conservative and applicable only to stable, unchanging systems. We argue, however, that the most important objective of coordination must be to obtain the resources and expertise necessary to produce needed outcomes. As technology creates new interventions and products and identifies new problems, they must be included in considerations of comprehensiveness, especially if coordination is being defined in terms of its objectives. If sufficient resources are not present, then coordination efforts must focus on what can be done to generate additional resources. Using this definition, we might observe a high level of coordination among three components in a system, and yet judge the system to be poorly coordinated if consumer needs were not being met. In evaluating

Table 3.1 Objectives of Coordination by System Elements

System Elements	Comprehensiveness	Accessibility	Compatibility
Programs or Occupations	All kinds of expertise that are needed are available; continuum of care.	All needed expertise is accessible to those who need it; eligibility criteria are not barrier to intake entry.	All kinds of expertise are congruent; the parts complement, rather than contradict, one another.
Resources	Resources are adequate to support continuum of care or research project goals.	Resources allocated on basis of consumer need or project requirements rather than a priori resource categories.	Resource providers' goals and values are harmonious with needs and desires of consumer.
Supplies/ Consumers	Individual consumer's needs are meet; system is responsive to individual diversity.	Individual consumer has access; system provides sufficient outreach, information, and transportation.	Individual consumer is treated consistently by different parts of the system; multiple problem clients have one case plan.
Information	There is a central inventory of component parts (services), information and referral (resources), and central case files (clients) or research data bank, and continuous feedback on operation of the system at all three levels.		

SOURCE: Adapted from Aiken et al. (1975).

service delivery systems for a specific project or target population, we might find that only three of six necessary programs are available. There might be significant coordination among existing components, but such coordination would not produce desired outcomes if three program elements were missing.

The problem of comprehensiveness is not confined to the nonprofit sector. It pushes many of our largest corporations into consorting. For example, although IBM spends $1 billion on R&D each year, it is one of the most active corporations in research consortia. As knowledge becomes steadily more complex, it becomes increasingly difficult for even an IBM to maintain a comprehensive research program without coordinating with other companies in a number of research areas. Clearly, this is important for small high-tech organizations because they have a variety of needs for programs or occupational expertise. To invent a new product is not enough. The firm has to produce it, market it, distribute it, and so on; hence, the many joint ventures between small and large firms, such as in bio-tech (Powell & Brantley, in press).

Comprehensiveness is not enough, however. The availability of all necessary elements in a system does not of itself guarantee a desired output. A system is not coordinated unless the components are accessible to consumers and users. Access to program components may be conditional upon eligibility or access criteria that are incompatible or in conflict with the operational processes. For example, community organizations trying to serve the same client population, but doing so with funding from different sources, often have intake criteria that limit service access to only one group of clients. This is a problem decried by community planners for decades, and the movement toward "decategorization" is one solution currently being implemented in several states. The theory is that by eliminating categorical funding streams and allocating bloc grants equivalent to the sum of the categorical funds, communities will be able to overcome accessibility problems and thus be able to improve the coordination of their services.

Likewise, in promotional networks such as research consortia, goals are not always achieved because the individual business firms that are members guard their technological competencies and thus withhold either their best researchers or various kinds of technological information.

Finally, we know that a system is coordinated if the components work harmoniously together. By compatibility we mean appropriate linking and sequencing of elements. This is the most frequently used definition of coordination, but it is often equated only with the absence of conflict. We refer to the nature of the links between organizations, whether these links are for managing client flow or research development processes. In

Chapter One, we suggested that one of the distinguishing characteristics of interorganizational relationships is that they are conflict-ridden, so much so that we devote most of Chapter Six to this problem. It is conflict that explains why many of these interorganizational forms do not perform as well as they might. The Japanese succeed because they share profits. This is a lesson to be learned by many American businesspeople.

The same kinds of problems occur among firms engaged in joint activities, especially problems having do to with access to adequate, timely, and useful information. One of the most important skills and technologies of interorganizational project management is that which insures all actors have the information they need during the development process.

Coordination as Cooperation:
A Behavioral Attribute

Coordination is also described as the quality of the relationship between human actors in a working system and is often equated with cooperation. Cooperation includes both a behavior component (willingness to work together) and an attitude (absence of selfishness). In Figure 1.2 we have stressed the willingness to cooperate as a necessary but not sufficient condition for the creation of interorganizational forms because it is so central. Clearly, both the attitude and the behavior are important. Organizational theorists of the human relations school stress the importance of favorable attitudes in achieving coordinated action. Likert (1967), for instance, defined cooperation as favorable attitudes, confidence, and trust, and as a necessary condition within the organization. This would seem to apply even more to relationships between organizations. Others have suggested that agreement about organizational domains, what organizations have sanction to do, facilitates coordination (Levine & White, 1961). We can therefore define *cooperation* as the quality of the relationship between human actors in a system consisting of mutual understanding, shared goals and values, and an ability to work together on a common task.

Conflict is not necessarily the opposite of coordination, or the absence of coordination. Excessive conflict may prove to be inconsistent with coordinated action, but it may prove to be helpful in achieving coordination (Coser, 1956). Cooperation carried on despite some conflict has been referred to as "antagonistic cooperation" (Guetzkow, 1966) and might be helpful, for instance, in bringing to light all the various dimensions of clients' needs or of problems inherent in a development process. Thus, a fire inspector might initially oppose putting developmentally disabled clients in small residential homes because the buildings are difficult to bring up to institutional safety standards. A counselor, however, might find small homes vital because they provide the homelike atmosphere needed for personal growth. Much conflict may exist, but cooperation in our sense takes place if all can agree that rehabilitation, not just custodial care, is the goal of the treatment; if all can have some respect for others' points of view; and, most important, if all are willing to work together and make compromises necessary to settle differences. The controversy raised might mobilize public opinion and put pressure on the legislature to provide funds for outside fire escapes and other necessary equipment to bring small homes up to standards.

Given these considerations, we define *coordination* as the articulation of elements in a service delivery system so that comprehensiveness, accessibility, and compatibility among elements are maximized. We are suggesting that coordination is a necessary property of all social systems (Meyer, 1978), although the degree of integration and articulation, and hence the degree of coordination, may vary considerably. By comprehensiveness we mean the extensiveness and fullness of the components that should logically be a part of a delivery system, given a statement of its goals. Unless a sufficient number of elements needed to attain some desired state exist, coordination will be impossible to achieve. By accessibility we mean that eligibility criteria are not used as barriers to exclude clients or users who need resources or products from the system. By compatibility we mean the degree to which components are linked together in some coherent manner; that is, there is a fit between need and service, and services and technologies are provided to users in a meaningful and appropriate sequence. By cooperation we mean the degree to which collaboration exists among the elements in a system. In the context of interorganizational network systems, this refers to collaboration among units—agencies, professions, client groups, and resource controllers—so that social services are delivered to clients.

Coordination Across Hierarchical Levels and Different Functions: An Intervention Method

One way to understand the problems encountered by those who must coordinate in the public sector is to survey the narrow, special purpose, cross-hatched texture of government in the United States today. For example, at the foundation of U.S. federalism are 18,517 municipalities, 3,044 counties, 16,911 townships, 15,781 school districts, and 23,855 other special districts (Gawthrop, 1984). Layered on this base are 50 state governments with their substate regions, the 16 federal regions that administer federal programs, and the federal government itself.

Exacerbating the problem of multiple hierarchical jurisdictions is the explosive expansion of federal public policy programs during the decades of the 1960s and 1970s, a growth unequaled in the history of our nation and one that has continued. A brief review of *Congressional Quarterly* for the past 6 months finds federally funded programs targeted at school security, bridge replacement and rehabilitation, urban gardening, runaway assistance, pothole repair, rat control, noise control, education of gifted children, training for use of the metric system, alcohol abuse, tourist development, arson, repair services for the elderly, development of bikeways, solid waste disposal, aid to museums, rural fire protection, and displaced homemakers, to name only a few.

Because of constitutional prohibition of expansion of direct national control in the implementation of policy, these initiatives have taken the form of categorical or special purpose programs. It is this policy and funding structure—vertical, highly specialized, and inflexibly categorical—that makes coordination at the community level so difficult. Further, no programs have been created for the general support and management of these narrowly defined programs, and each has been "awarded" to a different local agency, some having first passed through regional and/or state agencies (Scott & Black,

1986). Further still, little attempt has been made to assist communities with their primary goals and necessary core processes, which have become increasingly more necessary as federal specialized programs proliferate. Communities are forced to finance an infrastructure that will support, coordinate, and integrate services neither conceived nor funded by themselves.

We agree with those who assert that federal and state initiatives that attempt to improve interorganizational coordination at the community level are simply an attempt by bureaucrats to modify the end of the delivery stream so they can avoid confronting the front-end inequities and inflexibilities (Morris & Lescohier, 1978; Wildavsky, 1979), and the burden caused by the failure of federal reform will be borne by communities into the foreseeable future. Attempts by federal and state governments to mandate improvements in coordination and integration will meet with limited success until federal and state governments are able to reform the most dysfunctional aspects of the categorical system.

A somewhat analogous situation exists in the private sector. Until recently, competing firms sharing the same niche seldom if ever interacted with one another; they guarded their own turf with care. Now, because consumers are more sophisticated and technology is more complex, firms must produce broader product lines. As a result, competition is industry-wide and there are fewer boundaries. The best example is the computer industry, where firms can no longer survive by using their own unique operating programs. With the convergence of computer and communication technologies, customers demand "complete solutions" and "complete interface" for their information-processing needs. Companies must, therefore, market and support a full line of compatible and expandable products. This means that to survive today, once fiercely independent companies are scrambling to enmesh themselves in alliances and coordinate their work with others in order to broaden their range of products and services.

When individuals must serve as linking pins—be they legislators, business executives, bureaucrats, researchers, project managers, or direct service workers—and must coordinate, they have similar objectives. They usually must coordinate across hierarchical levels and different functional units, and they frequently must use different institutional devices to achieve desired outcomes. This is why we believe it is important to specify that interorganizational coordination is *a method or a process*—not an outcome—that must occur at all hierarchical levels and that utilizes a wide range of methods. This idea is illustrated for the public sector in Table 3.2.

This simple cnart illustrates that coordination is a complex problem in the public sector, given our federal system of government with its separation of powers. There often must be exchange of information and meshing of tasks across functional areas as well as hierarchical levels. In the private for-profit sector, coordination is usually more easily accomplished than in the public sector. One reason that business firms use joint ventures is that, by doing so, they create a separate legal entity that combines in one hierarchy the policy-making, administration, and operational functions. Trade associations also represent the creation of a new entity with a specific focus that combines all three functions. In the private-sector not-for-profit organizations—such as the March of Dimes, Muscular Dystrophy, or the American Heart Association—policy might be controlled at the national level. These organizations might provide services at the local level, such as the Boy Scouts and Camp Fire Girls do, in which case they give up a considerable amount of the administrative and operational authority to the community. This makes coordination even more necessary.

The examples in Table 3.2 are all coordination methods and mechanisms, but there are important differences between them (March and Simon, 1958).

In our analysis of coordination throughout the balance of this book, we distinguish between the policy and administrative levels, or what we shall call administrative coordination, and the operational level, what we call task integration. Hage (1974), in a study that tested a theory of interorganizational coordination, and March and Simon (1958) found there are at minimum two levels that must be coordinated: administrative and operational. Much of interorganizational research has focused on the administrative and policy level of coordination, but has neglected the operational level.

Administrative coordination has been extensively studied in health and welfare organizations (Hage, 1974; Mintzberg, 1979) and in dyadic relationships between organizations (Aiken et al., 1975; Benson et al., 1973; Litwak, 1970; Mulford & Rogers, 1982),

Table 3.2 Public Sector Coordination Methods Used Across Different Governmental Functions

	Policy Making	Administration	Operations
Federal Level	Interagency Commissions Federations Alliances	Medical Waivers Integrated Grants Programs	
State Level	Delegation of Power to Local Authorities	Capitation Finance	
Community Level	Coalitions Welfare Councils Planning Authorities	Centralized Management Information Systems Joint Programs Collocation Referral Agreements	Case Management Interagency Teams

and is a critical dimension of interorganizational networks, given the frequent absence of a supraordinate body that imposes control. Much evidence exists to show that administrative coordination relies on formal methods of communication to achieve feedback of information, that is, regularly scheduled committees, written policies, and formal rules. As March and Simon (1958) suggested, standardization via the formalization of policy, rules, and regulations is one goal of administration, and one that can apply to both levels.

Coordination at the task level has been studied in few interorganizational settings. The organizational research of Van de Ven, Delbecq, and Koenig (1976) is important in this regard because they found that, although formal and impersonal methods were used, the operational level relied much more on informal methods of coordination. In interorganizational networks, we feel operational coordination is especially critical because that is where case management or mismanagement can occur. It is the core of the matter for effective service delivery. Surprisingly, there have been relatively few attempts to develop theories about the relationship between administrative and worker methods of coordination in network systems despite the large literature on conflict.

Even more glaring is the absence of research on network systems in the private sector. There are a number of reasons for this. Research consortia are a relatively recent phenomenon, and there has not been enough time to collect and to analyze data. Action systems—such as federations, joint ventures, and trade associations—all in various ways minimize problems of coordination. This is what makes systemic networks that much more interesting and important to study.

Methods of Administrative Coordination. March and Simon (1958) defined *coordination* as having two methods for meshing interdependent activities: coordination by plan and coordination by feedback. The primary difference between the two is the degree to which the activities are standardized; the key is the degree of division of labor and specialization. Although March and Simon referred primarily to *intraorganizational* processes, their discussion can be applied equally to *interorganizational* processes. Their essential question had to do with the number of program elements that can be combined into a workable set of interrelationships so that mutual goals can be achieved. Their answer was that it depends on the degree to which the work activity can be standardized: The more it is standardized, the greater the degree to which compatibility can be achieved through a plan or set of rules governing the program elements. The less the work activity is standardized, the greater the degree to which compatibility must be achieved via feedback that involves the transmission of new information (Hage, 1974). While one can cite a number of exceptions, we argue that human services, research projects, and high-tech endeavors require feedback, because it is difficult or even impossible to predict treatment or service outcomes and, therefore, interventions and processes cannot be standardized. This is especially the case when clients or products have multiple problems that require input from a large number of different organizations, each of which provides specialized professional services.

Building on the ideas of March and Simon, Thompson (1967) conceptualized coordination as methods that link parts so that performance objectives can be achieved. Like March and Simon, he emphasized the characteristics of the linkages and said that there are three types of interdependencies among organizations: pooled, sequential, and reciprocal. Coordination through standardization, or the use of routines and rules, is most appropriate for a network with pooled interdependence; coordination by plan is most appropriate with sequential interdependence; and coordination by mutual adjustment, in which there is a heavy emphasis on communication, is most appropriate for situations characterized by reciprocal interdependence. We shall use these ideas in Chapter Four when we build our theory of the kinds of collaboration that can occur within joint ventures and systemic networks.

Coordination means control (Georgopoulos & Mann, 1962; Hage, 1974); it refers to methods that regulate the work system within and between organizations or organizational units. When interorganizational coordination exists, many aspects of the work activity are so governed that the effort of each individual organization is directed toward common objectives and the supraorganizational goal. When coordination does not exist, organizations have few restrictions and are free to choose their own objectives and methods.

It is generally recognized that the nature of the work and the task determines the most effective methods of coordination. Following Thompson's discussion (1967) of work within organizations, we apply the same insights to work between organizations. Policymakers and administrators can use three methods for coordinating. At one extreme is interorganizational work, which has little uncertainty; the job can be specified, made concrete, and therefore programmed. At the other extreme is interorganizational work that has a great deal of uncertainty; there are so many alternatives at any given point in the network system that the tasks cannot be specified ahead of time. In the latter case, interorganizational work cannot be controlled with simple rules. It can only be shaped, improved, and adjusted by learning from experience—a process that returns information about the results of the interorganizational work back into the network system as participants engage in decision making. This process is termed *information feedback*. Several factors force systems into increasing the amount of information feedback. One factor is the complexity of the task (Hage, 1974). As complexity increases, feedback of information becomes more and more essential but difficult to achieve. Another factor that forces systems of organizations into larger and larger amounts of information feedback is concern over quality and customization of service.

As we discussed above, one objective that drives coordination is the need for compatibility of programs. From an administrative perspective, this means monitoring various problems that can occur when programs are in different organizations and workers have different perspectives about how clients should be treated. When systems move toward an increasing emphasis on individualized solutions and treatments, there is greater need for information feedback about how the process is progressing. The same is true for business organizations involved in subcontracting. As the product being jointly developed by two or more organizations becomes more complex, information sharing between organizations becomes critical, otherwise compatibility will be impossible.

Methods of administrative coordination can be thought of as varying with regard to the amount of information feedback required to implement them (Hage, 1974; March and Simon, 1958; Perrow, 1967). Three methods, which utilize increasing amounts of feedback, are defined in the following study:

1. Administrative Coordination by Impersonal Methods, including the utilization of plans, rules, regulations, agreements, contracts, or anything that removes discretion from individual workers and requires little information feedback.
2. Administrative Coordination by Personal Methods, including the use of person-to-person contact between workers, or the designation of an individual to act as coordinator in order to expedite planning and decision making across organizational boundaries.
3. Administrative Coordination by Group Methods, including feedback obtained through face-to-face communication by two or more individuals planning and making decisions by consensus.

Since there is little discretion left to workers when formal methods are employed, coordination by impersonal methods represents small amounts of administrative coordination. We say, therefore, that impersonal methods require little coordination, and group methods demand a large amount of coordination. Frequently, written rules are perceived as a way of achieving efficiency in coordination, but they have costs. Since these three methods are so critical to our theory, we include our questionnaire item used in Figure 3.1.

Methods of Task Integration or Operational Coordination. The second integrative mechanism is production flow, the paths by which materials or clients move from organization to organization in network systems. Thompson (1967) conceptualized production systems within organizations, but these same ideas can be applied to the interorganizational field. When they are applied to networks of organizations, a number of new insights can be gained about how networks are constructed. Rather than focus on flows at one time point, we begin to see the necessity of studying flows across time (Ashar & Shapiro, 1988; Hickson, Pugh, & Pheysey, 1969; Mohr, 1971; Van de Ven et al., 1976).

Since most interorganizational network systems about which we have data are in the public sector, we will illustrate the key ideas of Thompson (1967) with the flow of clients, but work flow can be measured by units of information or products. There are three patterns.

1. Task Integration by Sequential Client Flow, whereby the patient is treated by one agency, service is terminated, and the patient is referred to the next agency for service.
2. Task Integration by Reciprocal Client Flow, whereby the patient is treated simultaneously by more than one agency.
3. Task Integration by Collective Client Flow, whereby the patient is treated simultaneously by staff from several agencies who develop treatment plans together and systematically share tasks.

Client flow is a mechanism that utilizes time to integrate work. If the pattern is sequential, as on an assembly line, there is little integration of tasks across boundaries because patients or clients are treated by one organization at a time. At the other extreme is the collective pattern, which requires a division of labor and a high degree of task integration because the patient has to be "worked on" by an interagency team. Again, the concept of task integration is so central we have included the actual item in Figure 3.2.

If we apply these same ideas to the study of the private sector, we can find the same distinctions. Generally, the research on joint ventures has been concerned primarily with the kind of

Please indicate the extent to which each of the following methods are used to coordinate the work of the service delivery system in your county. Indicate the percent of time your system relies on each type of coordinating method to govern the work of the system (the percentages must add up to 100%).

Impersonal Methods:
Rules/procedures mandated by law or legally binding
(i.e., contracts)   _____ %
Written interagency agreements, protocols, or plans   _____ %
Unwritten (but firmly agreed to) interagency
agreements, protocols, plans   _____ %

Personal Methods:
Administrator or staff person acts as coordinator   _____ %
Informal communication between administrators
and staff   _____ %

Group Methods:
Standing interagency committees which meet
routinely to plan, coordinate   _____ %
Ad hoc interagency committee meetings held as needed _____ %

Percent of time your system uses impersonal,
personal, and group coordination   _____ 100 %

Figure 3.1 Questionnaire Item Measuring Administrative Coordination

administrative unit that is created. Almost all of the business studies cited in the previous chapter have been concerned with the kind of administrative coordination that occurs, rather than the issue of how it actually operates. For example, is there an informal arrangement or a formal contractual one (Hakansson, 1990; Killing, 1988; Moxon et al., 1988), or does a business firm choose a joint venture as opposed to establishing a subsidiary or buying its needed expertise (Hladik, 1988; Kogut & Singh, 1988)? Similarly, the strategic literature has emphasized the pros and cons of collaboration from an administrative perspective, rather than the issue of integration at the research project level (Contractor & Lorange, 1988; Jarillo, 1988; Nielsen, 1988).

There is some data, however, about the operational level in some studies. Our detailed example of how the Japanese supply network operates is based on a detailed description by Womack

We are interested in how your clients flow through the service delivery system in your community. There are three basic client flow methods. Please study these graphic descriptions:

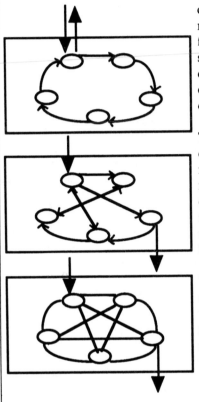

The Sequential Method—organizations make referrals to and accept referrals from other agencies in the system (clients flow from one organization to another but are served by only one at a time).

The Reciprocal Method—organizations make referrals to and accept referrals from more than one organization in the system (clients are served simultaneously by more than one agency).

The Collective Method—organizations share the work of serving or treating clients (clients are served by agencies whose treatment staff have developed one treatment plan together and who constitute one intervention team).

What percentage of your clients flows through your interagency service system in each of these ways? (Please make your answer add up to 100%)

by a Sequential Method	_____%
by a Reciprocal Method	_____%
by a Collective Method	_____%
Total clients	_100 %_

Figure 3.2 Questionnaire Item Measuring Task Integration

et al. (1990). The Hallen et al. (1987) study of the relationship between exchange of information and its impact on adaptiveness, while not consciously focusing on operational coordination, is laying the groundwork for the development of a theory of how successful collaboration can be achieved. Similarly, another Swedish study, that of Laage-Hellman (1989), has examples demonstrating how the lack of expertise can cause changes in partnerships and how they develop or become truncated by conflict.

Finally, we find Killing's (1988) discussion of the relationships between task and organizational complexity to be very much at this level of analysis. We shall return to these ideas in the next chapter. But in general the private sector research, as well as the public sector studies, have concentrated on the elites and the problem of administrative coordination and collaboration and have ignored the workers and the problem of operational integration. We feel that this is one of the distinctive advantages of our framework and of this research.

We need a number of case studies across time about the processes of interorganizational collaboration in both private and public systemic networks to build a process theory about its development. But in these theories, the operational level cannot be ignored.

Although there are no studies of problem solving in collective research involving multiple business firms and universities, we can imagine that problems in interorganizational R&D projects are passed back and forth between organizations in a way similar to client referrals. Here is an area of needed research.

The focus of the theory is interorganizational work activity, since this is the most important defining characteristic of these network systems. Specifically, the dependent variables are administrative coordination and task integration. A great deal has been written about governance mechanisms, but little research exists. Our contingency theory contains a set of hypotheses explaining two central problems of network systems: how organizations coordinate their decision making; and how organizations integrate their work flow when their staffs must work with the same clients. The former concerns policy and administrative coordination, while the latter involves operational coordination. We are thus not only establishing a theory about networks as governance mechanisms, but also indicating which form of coordination is used.

ILLUSTRATING THE CHOICE OF COORDINATION METHODS AT TWO LEVELS

In the following chapter we illustrate the problem of how to define the boundaries of systemic networks with our study of two counties located in two different states, although in the same metropolitan area. This same study provides a good example of how diverse and varied is the choice of coordination methods in service delivery systems, and how different are the types of administrative and operational methods used for different functions at different levels. Research methods that do not allow for this complexity miss a great deal. Much of network analysis in sociology has not considered the possibility that clients and products can be managed using different coordination methods.

The results of our exploratory study of systemic networks in Fulton and Farnam counties showed clearly that administrators and workers varied greatly in the degree to which they utilized feedback as a method for controlling and coordinating. Table 3.3 shows the mean scores for percent of time that each of the coordination methods were used by the service delivery systems in Fulton and Farnam counties.

Table 3.3 shows that administrators in these 15 systemic networks utilized formal methods of working together much more frequently (impersonal methods were used 44% of the time) than did workers (sequential methods were used only 28% of the time). The reverse was also true. Workers utilized collective methods of working together much more frequently (collective methods were used 27% of the time) than did administrators (group methods were used 17% of the time). It is interesting to note, however, that personal and reciprocal methods were utilized most equally at both administrative and operation levels.

Table 3.3 also shows there was a considerable amount of variation between the networks in regard to their choice of coordinating methods. The standard deviations and range of scores for impersonal coordination and sequential task integration showed

Table 3.3 Percent of Time Three Methods of Administrative Coordination and
Three Methods of Task Integration Were Used by Systemic Networks
in Fulton and Farnam Counties (N = 15)

	Mean	SD	Min	Max
Administrative Coordination				
Impersonal	.44	.16	.14	.82
Personal	.40	.10	.26	.57
Group	.17	.12	.04	.42
Task Integration				
Sequential	.28	.18	.04	.70
Reciprocal	.46	.12	.17	.66
Collective	.27	.17	.09	.60

the greatest amount of variation across the 15 systems. These
results are illustrated in Figure 3.3 and Figure 3.4.

Networks that manage special needs adoptions were found
to use primarily impersonal administrative coordination methods (70% of the time), whereas hospice systems relied most
heavily on group administrative coordination methods (more
than 42% of the time). Likewise, task integration in adoption
networks was achieved primarily via sequential methods (61%
of the time), while hospice systems used interagency teams
more than any other type of network in the study (53% of the
time). Once we observe this variation in the choice of methods,
we are led to questions about the causes of these choices and
whether there is enough coordination in these networks.

Predicting the Choice of Coordination Methods

One of the glaring omissions of the governance literature is
in regard to research on coordination. Much of the neoclassical
theory of markets assumes that markets coordinate. This may
be true in some sectors of the economy, but not everywhere. As
Hollingsworth, Hage, and Hanneman (1990) demonstrated, markets coordinate health care services poorly when compared to
state hierarchies. Similarly, network systems have emerged

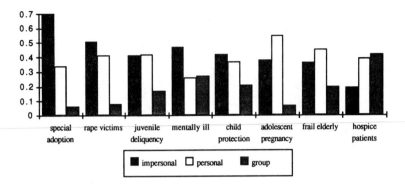

Figure 3.3 Percent of Time That Impersonal, Personal, and Group Methods of Administrative Coordination Were Used in Eight Different Types of Systemic Networks (*N* = 15)

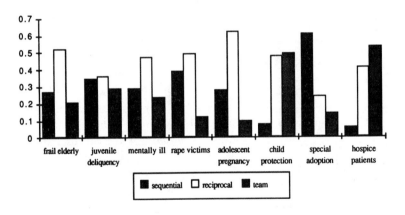

Figure 3.4 Percent of Time That Sequential, Reciprocal, and Team Methods of Task Integration Were Used in Eight Types of Systemic Networks (*N*=15)

because both markets and single organizations in the public sector have failed to provide comprehensive and compatible services to clients with complex needs; we must still reserve judgment as to whether they effectively coordinate.

We need a normative theory concerning alternative methods of coordination, and then we must test whether the movement away from the normative results in ineffectiveness. Just as neoclassical theories of the markets have gradually developed assumptions that must be met before markets are effective at coordination, we want to develop prescriptions about the problem of coordinating in network systems that serve multiproblem clients or solve multifaceted research problems.

Whether the type of coordination or integrative mechanisms used is due to choice or dictated by environmental conditions is, of course, a debatable question and is the basic question that distinguishes these theoretical perspectives. We believe that external forces and constraints, whatever their origin, do not account entirely for the internal processes of systemic networks. Rather, organizational members do have some capability to exercise discretion over the design and operation of their interorganizational relationships.

The key concepts and variables we consider when developing a theory to explain interorganizational choice are many and are shown in Figure 3.5. This conceptual framework is based on the work of Van de Ven et al. (1976), Van de Ven and Ferry (1980), Morrissey, Hall, et al. (1982), and Schermerhorn (1975) as well as our own—Aiken and Hage (1968), Hage (1974), Alter (1988a, 1988b, 1988c, 1990). Figure 3.5 organizes 19 variables into groups as a means of presenting a causal process of coordination. These are the concepts that have often been named as useful for understanding network processes; but because there is limited empirical research, we cannot at this time say with any certainty that there is a single best configuration or form. Consistent with the work of Aldrich and Mueller (1982), we argue a contingency approach to the problem of form. Different combinations of technology, network pattern, and coordination method are probably best.

Figure 3.5 is a heuristic that organizes this book, and it represents a complex causal model. The concepts are discussed at length in the coming chapters, and operational definitions and items are presented in Appendix A.

External controls (resource dependency, autonomy, and client status) and technologies (task scope, intensity, duration,

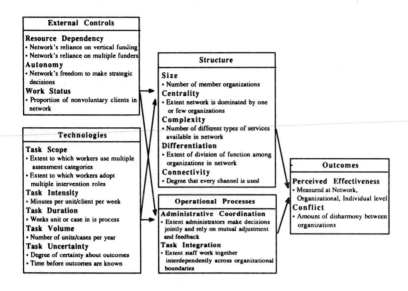

Figure 3.5 Conceptual Framework for Studying Systemic Interorganizational Networks

volume, and uncertainty) are our labels given to the clusters that represent environmental influence; they are discussed in Chapter Four. There is, of course, debate about the degree to which the environment determines the methods and strategies that administrators elect to use. For example, the amount of time an organizational member or individual worker within a network spends on a given project or client (task intensity) can be decided either by a hierarchical authority and mandated through contract or agreement, or it may be the choice of the agency, the worker, or the client. When a network operates under high resource dependency, low autonomy, and high proportions of mandated clients, then the chance that the network's technologies will be mandated by hierarchical authority, rather than freely chosen, will also be high. Resource dependency has been an important theme in the interorganizational literature

(Pfeffer & Salancik, 1978) and, therefore, it is important that it be included in our analysis.

Technology has not been emphasized in the interorganizational literature, and we believe this is one contribution of this book—the role of technology in shaping the form and processes of network systems. Generally, organizational theory lost interest in the debate about the relative merits of technology and size sometime in the mid-1970s. Yet, increasingly, there is evidence that technology is driving both private and public sector organizations. Whether the issue is American competitiveness, foster care, or health care, what we know and how we use this knowledge impacts decisively on the nature of organizational relationships and interorganizational network systems.

To develop this theme of technology, we build upon the work of Lefton and Rosengren (1966) and define a number of technological dimensions, including task scope, task intensity, task duration, task volume, and task uncertainty. Many of these dimensions have been significant for the organizational literature (Hage, 1980). Chapter Four is thus a dialectic between external control and technology, or between power and knowledge.

There is much more to be found in the interorganizational literature about the structure of networks—size, centrality, complexity, differentiation, and connectivity—than about their technologies or processes. There have been few attempts, however, to understand the causal link between external conditions, especially technology, and the patterns of associations that develop in networks. The five variables we discuss in Chapter Five are the most useful for understanding these relationships. Essentially, two questions are posed: How do external control and technology influence the network pattern described by these five dimensions, and does pattern have an independent effect on the choice of coordination method at each level?

Once we have considered how external control, technology, and structure affect the choice of coordination methods at both the administrative and operational levels, we present in Chapter Six a normative theory about the choice of methods and the amount of information feedback. This is then compared with actual practice, and the outcome is demonstrated to be less effective. In other words, we test our normative theory with measures of what we call performance gap and conflict.

In Chapter Seven, we attempt to account for the choices that administrators make when structuring and operating their systems. Synthesizing organizational theory, population-ecology theory, and institutional governance theory, we must answer this question: How can planners and managers, who must operate loosely linked interorganizational networks, coordinate their activities such that harmony reigns, performance objectives are met, and outcomes are effective?

Finally, in Chapter Eight we summarize our theory in a new model of interorganizational collaboration. This multidimensional model has specific implications for sociological theories and several specific applications.

Environmental Determinants of Network Systems: External Control and Technology

In the popular press there is a tendency to espouse the belief that there is one "best way" of accomplishing organizational objectives, such as Peters and Waterman's *In Search of Excellence* (1982), or that there are any number of models, such as Peters' second book, *Thriving on Chaos* (1987). Neither perspective appears sensible to us. We believe there are several alternative ways in which systematic networks can be coordinated: not just one or many, but a limited number.

Given that there are several different ways in which systemic networks can be coordinated, what influences the choice of means to coordinate and integrate systems? Our analysis of how planners should choose coordination methods within an inter-organizational network does not focus on exchanges or transactions, but instead the broader, more inclusive, properties of a production system. These more complicated kinds of systems have a number of properties that distinguish them. We consider here eight factors, either external to the network itself or intrinsic to the type of work being done. Most of these variables are general ones that apply to both public and private sectors. With them we construct a contingency theory about the choice of coordination methods in interorganizational network systems.

Essentially, our argument is that both external controls and task characteristics influence the method of administrative coordination and the kind of task integration that is employed. Our hypothesis owes a great deal to the work of James Thompson (1967) and March and Simon (1958), as well as the research of Van de Ven et al. (1976) and Hage (1974). Although all of these previous theoretical and empirical works examined the internal coordination of organizations, we believe they can be applied to the external coordination of organizations within network systems.

In this chapter we move considerably beyond prior conceptualizations of technology to include broader descriptions of task. There is a vast literature on the technology of producing products from raw materials and providing services within single organizations, but very little theoretical work on these issues in network systems that span organizational boundaries (for exceptions, see Alexander & Randolph, 1985; Provan, 1984b). To present the theoretical framework, therefore, it is necessary to conceptualized external controls and task technology.

THEORETICAL FRAMEWORK

Twelve kinds of interorganizational relations and forms of networks have been described in Chapter Two, but they do not include all of the institutional variety that exists. Each of these types can be further subdivided into subtypes that are similar, but different. The steel cartel in the United States and the steel cartel in Japan have operated very differently, in part because of governmental participation in the latter instance (O'Brien, in press). This leads to one of the major differences within each of the 12 kinds of interorganizational collaboration: the participation of the government as either a funding source or a regulator or both. Since we believe government involvement is becoming more important—not less, despite the dramatic changes occurring in Eastern Europe and the former Soviet Union—we have made it one of our basic dimensions.

The second dimension grows naturally out of the theory presented in Chapter One. Complexity of the task (along with a number of other variables) was used to explain the evolution of organizations toward interorganizational relationships, whether joint ventures, systemic networks, cartels, promotional networks, and the like. But this is a dimension that can be applied to all of the 12 forms described in Chapter Two. Consumer electronic production networks are simpler than automotive ones, which in turn are simpler than those for the development and construction of commercial aviation (compare Moxon et al., 1988, with Womack et al., 1990, and either of these with Sako, in press). Furthermore, one of the fundamental reasons why this dimension is so critical is that it helps explain why some networks have many more organizations in them, one of the basic categories used in the taxonomy of interorganizational collaboration described in Chapter Two.

Although it is not easy to demonstrate empirically, we believe that resource dependency of one kind or another involving the government and the complexity of the technology reflect two quite different ways of viewing both an organization and the nature of its relationships. The former derives from a political perspective (Pfeffer, 1981; Pfeffer & Salancik, 1978) on organizations, whereas the latter represents a contingency perspective (Hage, 1980; Lawrence & Lorsch, 1967; Perrow, 1967).

As we consider these dimensions we are able to make some important conceptual distinctions, such as the difference between network systems that are self-sufficient but not autonomous, and those that are both dependent and regulated. Similarly, networks vary in both scope and scale. In Chapter Six, after our analysis of these environmental determinants, we suggest one possible taxonomy of systemic network forms that combines eight technological variables with four structural patterns into a parsimonious and testable normative statement.

While there is no best way to categorize network systems, we have chosen to start building a contingency theory of coordination in network systems by selecting eight environmentally determined dimensions that appear to be the most basic. There are three external control or power variables: (1) resource dependency, (2) regulation, and (3) voluntary/nonvoluntary work. There are five technological variables: (4) task scope, (5) task uncertainty, (6) task intensity, (7) task duration, and (8) task volume. These eight variables have the advantage of combining a political-economy approach to interorganizational systems with a technological perspective, the combination thus reflecting two important intellectual traditions.

External Controls

There has been considerable attention paid to the issue of the external control of networks, especially in service delivery networks in the nonprofit sector where political influence is an important consideration. In the private sector, the intrusion of the government occurs either because it pays for the research, especially health, military or defense related, or because it sponsors the research consortia, which is increasingly important for our economy. It is possible to conceptualize interorganizational networks vis-à-vis their environment in somewhat the same terms as contingency theory conceptualizes single organizations vis-à-vis their environments. The question is, of course, to what degree does the organizational or interorganizational unit have the freedom to define its own future. To tackle this question we consider three different aspects of external control: resource dependency, regulation, and voluntary/involuntary work.

Degree of Resource Dependency. Our definition of resource dependency is:

> *Resource dependency* is the degree to which a network of organizations uses external resources from a single source for survival and goal achievement.

Probably the single most popular perspective on interorganizational relationships has been the resource dependency approach (Benson, 1975; Pfeffer & Salancik, 1978). It asserts that all interorganizational interactions—communication as well as joint activity—are ultimately and fully dependent on resource acquisition (Yuchtman & Seashore, 1967). Organizational decision makers' primary focus is on finding and defending an adequate supply of resources, and this orientation dominates the system and determines its superstructure. As Benson wrote, "Such an orientation becomes, for decision makers, an operational definition of the purposes of the organization and thus of their responsibilities as decision makers." (1975, p. 231). In sum, political economists argue that networks may be functional or dysfunctional, effective or ineffective, because of the political and economic forces affecting them, and the ability of members to change these dynamics and outcomes can be successful only within limits (Wildavsky, 1979). The amount of coordination and the choice of methods is, in this view, a direct result of the patterns of these external controls.

The degree of resource dependency has, therefore, been an important question because it is equated with degree of control. Do profit-making and nonprofit organizations, for example, differ in their degree of dependency? Are profit-making companies driven more by economic forces than nonprofits? The common wisdom has been that yes, organizations operating within free markets are more influenced by the needs and desires of their customers than nonprofits are shaped by their clients. What is overlooked, however, is that nonprofits vary greatly in the degree that their resource providers and consumers are the same. In some nonprofit service sectors the proportion of total resources derived from client fees is now substantial (Salamon, 1982; the estimate for the city of Baltimore is 42%), while elsewhere there are organizations where the total income is obtained from government or charitable sources. The degree to which human service networks are market-driven depends, therefore, on the definition of *market*. When the service is universally available, then the market is driven by user preferences; when the service is targeted solely on low-income clients, then the market is driven by public policy processes; and when the service is financed by client fees and by government sources, then controls are mixed, which is the usual case. In all three instances interorganizational networks are resource dependent, and preferences may change and change quickly. In our line of investigation the interesting question is how to explain and predict market stability in all types of sectors.

We believe there are not large differences today between resource dependency in the profit and nonprofit sectors. Both encompass organizations and interorganizational networks that are highly dependent on their markets, be it a consumer market or a governmental market, and both can have assets that reduce the degree of dependency. Two characteristics of resource dependency must be considered in this context: multiple versus single, and horizontal versus vertical sources of revenue.

Many for-profit organizations avoid reliance on single markets, such as contracts with a single branch of the military, and one of the motivations for developing multiple products, each with different markets and technologies, is to reduce dependency on any single customer group. Many nonprofit organizations likewise avoid reliance on a single branch of government for funds and strive to expand the number of different client populations they serve. The horizontal versus vertical dimension refers to the proportion of resources earned in local, national, or international markets. In nonprofit organizations, the distinction is between the percent of funds derived from the local community and from state and national government.

Further, it is not only the extent of dependency but the kind of dependency that affects system processes. A network of diverse organizations may be dependent on the same market, or because of their diversity, they may gain their resources through very different resource channels. Likewise, a network of organizations may be totally dependent on each other for needed resources, or they may be totally dependent on hierarchically ordered source(s) of resources. Interorganizational dependency seldom, of course, can be characterized exclusively by any one type of dependency, but rather by a mix of them. The effect of dependency cannot be assessed without knowing this mix of single versus multiple sources and local versus hierarchical sources.

Amount of Network Regulation. The definition of this variable is also straightforward:

> *Network regulation* is the degree to which a network is constrained in its ability to be self-governing, as opposed to being autonomous.

There has been much confusion about this aspect of interorganizational networks. Many IOR researchers have conceptualized resource dependency as strongly and positively related to constraint on decision making; or constraint has been considered as equivalent and thus treated as a proxy for resource dependency. Likewise, resource dependency and autonomy have been viewed as separate dimensions, but ones that are negatively related. Pfeffer and Salancik (1978), for example, asserted that reliance on external resources means greater external regulation and thus a constraint on autonomy, and that as autonomy decreases, interorganizational conflict increases and cooperation decreases.

Each of these conceptualizations may, in certain circumstances, be true. We believe, however, that at this stage of theory building, resource dependency and regulation should be thought of as separate variables. The reason is as follows. If dependency is conceptualized as the degree to which interorganizational networks must rely on external resources, then it is logical to conceptualize its absence as self-sufficiency, not autonomy. If autonomy is conceptualized as the freedom for stakeholders to make democratic decisions concerning the goals and operations of their network, then the absence of this freedom is regulation, not dependency. The important insight is that constraint does not necessarily derive exclusively from resource dependency or characteristics of the economy, but can emanate from laws and regulations or other political or altruistic decisions made by the state or other governance structure (North, 1990).

We are struck by the popular usage today of the term *community-based* in the nonprofit sector, a euphemism for network autonomy. Community-based programs are thought to be those where the locus of management and decision making rests at the community level. For a network to be community-based, of course, it must have the ability to adjust its objectives and methods to the specific needs of its community. And there are, indeed, community-based service systems to be found in American communities today that are "client driven" rather than being "bureaucratically driven." By our definition, however, it is probably impossible for a juvenile justice system to be truly "community-based" because of its total reliance on the state for funding and because its operations must adhere to state laws. The point is that all but a very few health and welfare organizations are equally dependent, but few are as regulated as juvenile justice systems.

In studying networks we are concerned with the ability of the network to secure financing and its ability to be self-regulating (to select its own outcomes and methods). It has often been assumed that vertical sources of funding are less desirable because they impose tighter restrictions on the use of resources than would horizontal resource providers. In other words, the closer to the action or production process the source of financing (even though the source provides a large percentage of the budget), the more latitude the network is thought to have to choose its own operating methods. Similarly, it is sometimes assumed that multiple sources are more desirable because it is less likely that the force of domination will be as intense as with single resource providers. These assumptions need to be tested empirically.

We believe, therefore, that it is useful to conceptualize resource dependency and regulation (not autonomy) as separate variables, and we doubt that there is always a strong negative correlation between them for two reasons. As suggested above, talented administrators can "play the market" and develop a mix of dependencies such that their autonomy is maximized. Indeed, networking is one such strategy (Sosin, 1985). Second, even though a network is highly self-sufficient and controls to a large extent the source of its needed resources, network operations may be highly regulated, depending on the service area in which it resides. This argument is made in Figure 4.1. Grandori and Soda (1991) have developed a related typology based on the importance of formal contracts, some of which are relevant in the public sector.

This typology makes the point that networks can be self-sufficient in terms of financing because of large endowments or stable markets and yet, as the exchange network for organ transplants demonstrates, be highly constrained by externally imposed laws or administrative procedures. Likewise, networks can be highly dependent on government agencies for financing or can exist within very unstable markets, and yet operate with little regulation, as illustrated by an R&D network. Having separated the concepts of dependency and regulation, we can consider separately their influence on interorganizational coordination.

Voluntary/Involuntary Work Status. Another way in which external forces influence network structure and process is by controlling the inputs of the system. Our definition of this determinant is:

Work status refers to the degree to which inputs of a network system are mandated rather than being voluntarily
agreed to by participants.

In the public sector one measure of mandated work in networks
is the proportion of clients who are involuntary, who are ordered
into the system by a legal authority. In the private sector one
measure of mandated work in networks is the proportion of the
funded products for which there are detailed input specifications.

This aspect of external control has been given little theoretical
attention in the IOR literature, despite its being a major issue in
social welfare literature. In service systems, many categories of
"raw materials" are involuntary: Felons, abusive parents, juvenile delinquents, and chronic mentally ill are only a few of the
clients who are under court jurisdiction or who are otherwise
effectively pressured into a service delivery system. In private
sector networks an analogous situation exists whenever external forces establish the materials and technologies to be used
by the network; subcontracting in automobiles in the United
States would be one illustration (Womack et al., 1990). The
clearest examples are in defense contracts.

*The Impact of External Controls on the Choice of Coordination and
Integration Methods.* The central theme and debate during the
past decade has been the necessity of reducing government
spending. Given this general political atmosphere and the perceived need to cut back funds for human services, there have
been many pressures to contain costs. Cost containment measures are, of course, one form of external control.

It is commonly accepted wisdom in the organizational literature that greater efficiency is achieved through the routinization of work, which is achieved, in turn, by bureaucratization
of structure (Thompson, 1967). These factors lead to the choice
of efficient processes—impersonal methods of administrative
coordination and sequential task integration. Further, if this is
the case, then we might expect that, in contrast, when interorganizational network systems are self-sufficient, there will be
a greater emphasis on the quality of work. Under these conditions
administrators will choose effective processes—group methods of
administrative coordination and team task integration. The hypothesis is:

	Low Resource Dependency (Self-Sufficiency)	High Resource Dependency (Dependency)
Low Regulation (Autonomy)	**Self-Sufficiency With Autonomy** e.g., an action network of well-endowed private foundations or organizations	**Dependency With Autonomy** e.g., a production network of firms or universities engaged in high-tech research
High Regulation (Constraint)	**Self-Sufficiency With Constraint** e.g., an exchange network of hospitals that allocate organs for transplantation	**Dependency With Constraint** e.g., a production network of public and private family service agencies charged with the protection of children

Figure 4.1 Typology of Resource Dependency and Network Regulation as Independent Concepts in Political Economy

Hypothesis 4.1: The greater the dependency on a single vertical source for needed resources, the more likely impersonal methods of coordination will be used and the work flow will be arranged in a sequential pattern; the less the dependency on vertical sources for needed resources, the more likely group methods of coordination will be used and the work flow will be arranged in a team pattern.

In spite of our insistence on the conceptual independence of resource dependency and regulation, it is illogical to generalize that the impact of regulation, if driven by an efficiency motive, would be any different for the two external controls. Therefore:

Hypothesis 4.2: The greater the regulation of networks, the more likely impersonal methods of coordination will be used and the work flow will be arranged in a sequential pattern; the less the regulation of networks, the more likely group methods of coordination will be used and the work flow will be arranged in a team pattern.

In networks where inputs or throughputs are involuntarily established, the major objective of the external force is, of course, control of the output. When human service systems must treat

involuntary clients—for example, these clients are resistant—
the therapeutic relationship is difficult to establish, and therapeutic objectives are much more difficult to achieve. When
R&D networks must undertake projects with firmly specified
objectives and methods, the nature of the throughput processes
will be affected. Military research is the prime example. This
variable, then, also has impact on the choice of coordinative and
integrative methods and, as we shall see in the next chapter, is
an important dimension affecting the shape and configuration
of the network itself. The hypothesis is:

Hypothesis 4.3: The less choice in the nature of the work (a large
proportion of involuntary clients, for example), the
more likely impersonal methods of coordination will
be used and the work flow will be sequential; the
more choice in the nature of the work (a small
proportion of involuntary clients, for example), the
more likely group methods of coordination will be
used and the work flow will be arranged in a team
pattern.

Technology: The Task Dimensions

It is not farfetched to assume that the nature of the technology
utilized within a network would be an important aspect in any
interorganizational analysis, yet this has not been the case.
During the 1960s the study of technology enjoyed a certain
vogue, but by the mid-1970s most researchers had lost interest
in the idea. Partially responsible was the proliferation of a large
number of variables (Scott, 1987), which frequently only tapped
a minor aspect rather than the whole production system (see
Collins, Hage, & Hull, 1988, for a critique and the need for a
new perspective). Another problem was the difficulty of finding dimensions that applied to both manufacturing and service
organizations. More recently, there has been a renewal of interest (see various issues of *Management Science* and the *Academy
of Management Review and Journal*), but it has been largely ignored in research on interorganizational relationships (exceptions are Gillespie and Mileti, 1979; Provan, 1984a). We believe
that network systems cannot be fully understood without tak-

ing into account the nature of the technology being used. There are five dimensions that are particularly important: task scope, uncertainty, intensity, duration, and volume.

Task Scope. This is a major variable and it refers to the complexity of the technology of the production or throughput process. The definition is:

Task scope is the degree to which tasks are variable and require a multidisciplinary or multidimensional approach.

The degree to which the problem to be solved must be examined from many different perspectives, or the degree to which human services must take in the whole biological space of patients and clients, is one measure of task scope (Lefton, 1970; Lefton & Rosengren, 1966; Rosengren, 1968).

As knowledge has grown, our perceptions of human behavior have become more complex, as we discussed in Chapter One. The knowledge base of the various professions has broadened, and today each is exhorted to engage in interdisciplinary research and practice to improve the quality of its work through a broadened perspective. This is an evolutionary process and can be captured by the variable we term *task scope* (Rosengren, 1968): It refers to the degree to which administrators and workers view their consumers in comprehensive ways. Network systems that have broad task scope are composed of organizations that use detailed theoretical frameworks for diagnosis or problem assessment, and have workers who assume numerous roles during the throughput process.

In a study by Killing (1988), which we did not discover until the last draft of this manuscript had been written, we found that he has an almost identical interpretation of the meaning and importance of task scope. His definition is the basis of their study—the number of business functions, the number of products, and the diversity of customers. He also includes the idea of duration, which we would keep separate for reasons that are delineated below. However, the key point is that there is a direct parallel between the private and the public sector, between joint ventures and systemic networks. They can be categorized on the basis of their task scope, and there are precise measures for this concept.

The most striking examples of networks with broad task scope, besides the many in the public sector that are provided in the following chapters, are what Hollingsworth (1991) calls promotional networks, especially the research consortia in Japan, the United States, and Western Europe. Airbus Industrie is perhaps the most complex arrangement because it involves four governments as well as a number of organizations (Moxon et al., 1988).

Lefton and Rosengren (1966) emphasized two dimensions of client characteristics that affect the kinds of services organizations provide. The first is scope of service: the degree to which clients are diagnosed as having multiple problems, and workers must perform many tasks. Because society's concepts of dysfunction and pathology are becoming more complex, the incidence of multiple problem clients is increasing; estimates range from 25% of total caseloads in family service agencies (Perlman, 1975) to almost 100% in prisons and child protection agencies (Cohn, 1979). An abusive or neglectful mother, for instance, is often thought of as requiring financial assistance, job training, day care, psychotherapy, and social support in order to change her behavior. These services are rarely available from one organization; most often they must be obtained from numerous autonomous organizations.

According to Lefton and Rosengren (1966), some professionals take in the whole biological space of their consumers. Hospice care systems, for example, are based on a well-defined and understood ideology having a set of clear values, beliefs, and unambiguous objectives. These are community networks of hospitals, home nursing agencies, volunteer organizations, and pastoral care programs dedicated to achieving the highest quality of life possible for the terminally ill. Hospice ideology is a complex one: It stipulates a holistic paradigm. Because the paradigm is so clearly conceptualized, however, workers can be more easily indoctrinated. Because they encounter few conflicting or competing attitudes, they can maintain the paradigm over time within their network and throughout their communities.

It is theoretically possible, of course, for workers and professionals in one community to use many assessment categories and take a comprehensive approach to their work, while the same type of workers in another community view problems in more narrow ways. In the first community, professionals will perceive the need for a much wider array of services than in the second community. A good case in point is juvenile justice systems, where network members may differ greatly in the breadth of their perceptions regarding assessment, goals, and objectives; they do not share a common cognitive structure.

Task Uncertainty. The concept of task uncertainty has been a factor in organizational theory for many years (Burns & Stalker, 1961; Thompson, 1967) but, like scope, is seldom used in the study of interorganizational networks. The definition is:

> *Task uncertainty* is the extent to which task processes or interventions have knowable outcomes.

Organizational theorists (Duncan, 1972; Lawrence & Lorsch, 1967; Tosi & Carroll, 1986) have shown that some kinds of work involve tasks that are difficult because the results or outcomes are unpredictable or unknown for a long period of time. The assumption is that as the amount of time needed for feedback increases, so does task uncertainty. Generally, organizations prefer to avoid uncertainty.

Killing (1988) has observed that, for business, uncertainty can occur about demand, customer preferences, competitors' actions, and supplier competence. He combines this idea with task scope as one dimension, which he then labels *task complexity*. In her discussion of the risks of being involved in joint R&D ventures across international boundaries, Hladik (1988) provides a similar list: the uncertainty of being able to develop a new product, or develop it fast enough, or develop it with enough quality; the problem of whether the new product will be acceptable to the consumer; and, perhaps most critically, the uncertainty of gaining a large enough market share to justify the expenditure of time and money and the other risks associated with collaboration.

Task Intensity. Tasks also vary in the amount of time devoted to them. This definition is:

> *Task intensity* is the amount of time spent on, or on behalf of, one client or work unit during a specific period of time.

Intensity is the degree to which workers have time to devote their energy, talent, and experience to a single case or unit of work. When intensity is low, the process is receiving a small portion of the workers' skill and effort. When intensity increases, the process comes closer to receiving all the workers have to offer. This concept is illustrated by the simple observation that it takes 1,120 times longer to produce a Waterford crystal goblet than to mass-produce a jelly jar (advertisement in *The New York Times*, 1988). As a variable, intensity is an indicator of effective and high-quality outcomes, and often covaries with task scope. Further, Dewar and Hage (1978) found that task intensity was strongly associated with the use of interdisciplinary staff and a wide variety of occupations in production processes.

In service delivery the intensity of services can vary greatly from community to community. Drug treatment programs for juveniles, for example, can range from those that require the adolescent to see a counselor for a half-hour once a week to residential treatment programs with very high staff ratios. The first service represents a very minimal investment, while the second indicates that a community has chosen to invest in high-quality treatment programs for their adolescents. Of course there are situations where low task intensity can be more effective than high, and intensity certainly does not guarantee effectiveness. But, in general, we believe that high intensity is associated with high quality.

Product and technological development tends to be highly intense work, as the book *The Soul of the New Machine* (Kidder, 1981) makes abundantly clear. The pressure to be first results in engineers working day and night, solving complex problems on the frontiers of knowledge.

Task Duration. There is another dimension of technology that uses time as a measure. The definition is:

Task duration is the total length of time it takes to produce or process one unit of output.

There are interorganizational projects that take years to complete (putting people on the moon), and there are those that take minutes. Duration differs from intensity in that it is concerned with how long it takes to completely process one unit from beginning to end. In the work of Lefton and Rosengren (1966), task duration was termed the *lateral dimension*. As with intensity, as duration increases, the resource investment also increases.

Typically, in the business literature, duration is used to refer to how long the relationship (Hakansson, 1990; Kogut et al., 1990) or contract (Laage-Hellman, 1989) is in effect, rather than the length of time it takes to accomplish an objective. Time frames for product and technological development tend to be highly variable, but they are still much shorter than the delivery of services to populations with developmental or chronic problems.

In human services, task duration is an indicator of the degree to which a service provides brief intervention or long-term care. It also can indicate the extent to which a system itself, composed of many organizations, provides service to a single client on a short- or long-term basis. For example, clients or patients may be "treated" or "reformed" by one organization, and at discharge be referred to another for ongoing aftercare. The offender released to a probation worker and the elderly man discharged from the hospital and linked to a home-care nurse have something in common; they experience duration and continuity of care because there is a network of organizations that takes an indeterminate rather than a truncated interest in them. In doing network research, however, a distinction should be made between how long a case is open and how long it should be open. In the Fulton and Farnam study, some clients were discharged because of lack of funds, rather than because they had successfully completed a treatment program.

Task Volume. This dimension is also related to the degree to which a worker can devote exclusive attention to a case or unit.

Task volume is the average number of units that must be processed simultaneously by a worker.

When systems have to produce large numbers of units or manage large client loads, the total amount of resources required grows geometrically (Lefton & Rosengren, 1966). This is especially true if the process is of long duration, such as in community support systems (CSS) for the chronic mentally ill. It can also be an important factor, however, even with brief processes if they are intensive, as in residential treatment facilities.

Task volume by itself, however, is not an adequate measure of the size of the operation and its cost. The total scale of a system is determined by combining intensity, duration, and volume. The Japanese automotive product network described in Chapter One, as well as some of the other production systems in manufacturing, would be examples of large volume and intense work. There are a number of models that have been developed for specific manufacturing sectors and industries, most for use in cost-benefit analysis, but in general they combine only two of these dimensions for an index of scale. In the Fulton and Farnam study we explored the effects of task intensity, duration, and volume separately, without creating a summative index, so that we could begin to identify alternative models of human service delivery.

All of these ideas about technology can be applied to collaborative efforts of private and public organizations, and to partnerships between the two. The basic idea is that the complexity of the problem and the scale with which it must be handled determine to a large degree the forms and processes of interorganizational networks, especially when they involve collaborative work. One reason that most of our examples of interorganizational relationships among business firms are of research efforts is because they are high in task scope—that is, they require inputs from different kinds of organizations—and they are large-scale—that is, intense effort of long duration requiring many tasks. And in business organizations the uncertainty of outcome is a well understood concept (see Duncan, 1972; Lawrence & Lorsch, 1967; and for criticisms of this idea, see Aldrich, 1979; Hage, 1980).

Just as we feel it is important to recognize that the concepts of resource dependency and regulation by rules are not necessarily the same, we also believe that task scope and uncertainty, and task intensity, duration, and volume require univariate analysis. In Figure 4.2 we suggest a fourfold typology that distinguishes between these various dimensions of task and provides some examples of the different combinations. Together the two axes have been useful in generating a typology of organizations (Hage, 1980) and in unifying organizational sociology and microeconomics.

The Impact of Technology on Choice of Coordination and Integration Methods. The importance of understanding task dimensions rests on the assumption that as technology increases or decreases, the pressure on organizations to interact covaries with it. Our central thesis is that as the complexity of technology increases there is increasing pressure toward coordination and integration. Three of our task variables influence interorganizational networks in this direction: task scope, uncertainty, and intensity. Conversely, while task volume and duration may also encourage entry into a network system, their pressure has the opposite impact on the choice of coordination mechanisms.

The accumulation of knowledge, and thus the process of complexification, has a variety of influences on the nature of work. It impacts not only on the choice of institutional arrangements, as we suggested in Chapter One, but also on the choice of coordination mechanisms, the argument made in the organizational literature. Greater knowledge about human or manufacturing problems leads to the recognition that they are multifaceted, thus requiring a variety of approaches and skills, thus leading to linkages to acquire complementary competencies and necessary resources. In turn, this growth in the number of linkages forces organizations to process the work in a collective pattern because decision making and tasks are too complicated to rely on dyadic communication (Hage, 1974).

If greater knowledge persuades us to see problems and tasks as multifaceted and thus broader in scope, then we are pushed to choose more complex kinds of coordination mechanisms, both administrative and at the case/task level. This was the central insight in both the work of Perrow (1967), who focused on the nonroutineness of technology, and Thompson (1967), who described the way in which production systems are organized. It was also an important thesis of Lawrence and Lorsch (1967) that increasing complexity leads to greater integration. The central idea is that as tasks become more complex, the work cannot be easily programmed but must be guided by constant communication and feedback (Hage, 1974), which is an interdependent process.

There are several reasons why workers do not get adequate feedback about their work. It may be that the client relationship is not sustained long enough for outcomes to become known, as in any emergency service or short-term product development with no customer follow-up. On the other hand, there are also long-term services that are provided under such difficult conditions that outcomes are very problematic.

Finally, complexity is also present when the performance objective of a network is quality. This is particularly true, of course, when the output is a concrete product, but it is equally true for human services. When the throughput process is perceived as requiring large investments of time in order to produce a quality output, then, given the interorganizational context of the activity, some of that time will be invested in interorganizational communication and integration. Put another way: The only way to assure quality of output when the throughput process requires participation from multiple organizations is to use cooperative administrative processes and team methods of case management. This is far more likely to happen when the time devoted to a single client or problem is large rather than small.

All of these examples, including the ones involving business organizations, involve discussions of the nature of internal work and not work that spans organizational boundaries, our focus here. Therefore, it should be recognized that we are extrapolating from one literature to another. Killing (1988) is the only researcher we know who explicitly described a variable similar to the one we have in mind, a variable that he labeled *organizational complexity*. He measured it in two ways: the routineness of the technology and the frequency of interaction. These are not the same as the administrative coordination, but they do bear a close resemblance to the ideas of task integration or operational coordination. Routine technology is the same as impersonal methods—indeed it is the way in which we measure this concept—and frequency of interaction at least taps the personal methods, even if it does not necessarily capture the idea of team coordination.

However, Killing (1988) starts with almost the exact opposite perspective from ours. He uses task and organizational complexity as dimensions to classify interorganizational alliances, but suggests that most managers believe that the simplest arrangement is the best. However, he suggests that the two are closely connected. Our intent is to test whether administrative

Task Scale (Volume and Duration)
Low   High

	Low	High
Narrow **Task Scope**	**Narrow Scope & Small Scale** i.e., care of dependent children (foster care and adoption services)	**Narrow Scope and Large Scale** i.e., management of juvenile delinquents (juvenile court services)
Broad	**Broad Scope & Small Scale** i.e., emergency services (trauma centers, domestic violence services)	**Broad Scope & Large Scale** i.e., treatment for multiple problem clients (programs for chronic mentally ill, child abuse treatment)

Figure 4.2 Typology of Task Scope and Task Scale as Independent Concepts

coordination and task integration are influenced by the nature of task scope and/or other technological variables.

How, then, does complexity of the work impact on the choice of administrative coordination and task integration methods? Three task dimensions are indicators of complexity and they push networks toward using collective methods of coordination and integration, and their absence tends to decrease the use of these methods.

Hypothesis 4.4: The narrower the task scope, the more likely impersonal methods of coordination and sequential work flow will be used; the broader the task scope, the more likely group methods of administrative coordination and team work flow will be used.

Hypothesis 4.5: The less the uncertainty of the task, the more likely impersonal methods of coordination and sequential work flow will be used; the greater the uncertainty of the task, the more likely group methods of administrative coordination and team work flow will be used.

Hypothesis 4.6: The less the intensity of the task, the more likely impersonal methods of coordination and sequential work flow will be used; the greater the intensity of the task, the more likely group methods of coordination and team methods of work flow will be used.

As we noted above, in addition to task intensity, there are two other ways that the scale of work can increase: the number of work units can be large and/or the total length of time required to process a unit can be very long. Task intensity, volume, or duration can each increase scale by themselves, but when two or even all three increase, then the scale of the operation grows geometrically.

We wish to speculate that as research accumulates about networks, the nature of task intensity will be shown to be fundamentally different from both task volume and duration, and that when very intense effort is devoted to a project or program, the motivation is to achieve very high-quality results. When, on the other hand, very large numbers of units must be produced/serviced, or when the duration of time they are in the system is very long, then the focus of the process will be efficiency. This is a simplistic analysis, of course, because different levels for each of the three variables will relate in different ways to both performance standards. Until we have studied a large number of different kinds of networks we cannot speculate about multivariate models of scale.

In the nonprofit sector the question of scale is really a public policy issue. Where services are perceived as a public utility, choices are made by politicians and administrators concerning levels of intensity, duration, and volume; and it has been only in the past few years that different models have been utilized for different client populations or for different clients with the same population. Research, for example, has shown that treatment services for a certain type of abusive parent are more effective if they are intensive and brief (Nelson, Landsman, & Deutelbaum, 1990). On the other hand, for populations for which there is no "cure," maintenance requires much less intensity but much longer duration.

If either task volume or task duration increases, then the total scale of service increases; if the volume of services increases simultaneously with duration and intensity, then total scale increases dramatically. In service delivery systems, as caseloads get larger, whether due to the influx of new cases or the failure to close old cases, there are strong pressures to rationalize the system in order to contain costs and maintain control. In this situation the system can become increasingly dependent on external sources for resources, which mandate cost control through written rules, formal procedures, and by avoiding the heavy resource investments required by case conferences, interagency teams, and case management.

The hypotheses are, therefore, straightforward:

Hypothesis 4.7: The longer the task duration, the more likely impersonal methods of coordination and sequential work flow will be used; the shorter the task duration, the more likely group methods of coordination and team methods of work flow will be used.

Hypothesis 4.8: The larger the task volume, the more likely impersonal methods of coordination and sequential work flow will be used; the smaller the task volume, the more likely group methods of coordination and team work flow will be used.

FULTON AND FARNAM COUNTIES: EMPIRICAL RESULTS CONCERNING ENVIRONMENTAL DETERMINANTS

There are a remarkable number of service systems in Fulton and Farnam counties. More remarkable, however, is how different they are. Qualitative data gave us knowledge of this diversity, especially the large differences among client populations and the services they require. An analogy from industry is that if networks producing Ford Tempos, limited edition prints, and cosmetics are different, then we can also expect differences between systems that deliver hospice care and community systems that provide indeterminant care for the mentally ill. One of our goals is to describe and account for this diversity.

Theoretically, resource dependency theory has been one of the means for explaining the nature of interorganizational networks. As discussed above, dependency for many years has been thought to be responsible for high levels of regulation. In Fulton and Farnam counties we found that this was indeed the case, as shown in Table 4.1.

Table 4.1 shows there was a strong association between vertical dependency and regulation ($r = .62$) in Fulton and Farnam counties. Likewise, the lack of choice in work inputs represented by the involuntary status of the client was even more strongly associated with regulation ($r = .80$). In fact, all three external control variables were positively associated, shedding some light on the issued discussed above. It may be that in a much broader sample of networks resource dependency and regulation will not always go hand in hand, but in this small sample they certainly did. In general the three external control variables shown in Table 4.1 (vertical dependency, regulation, and involuntary status) tended to covary and the correlations are high, but they did not appear to be related to any of the technology measures except intensity. The technology variables operated much more independently, as indicated by the relatively low correlations, none of which was significant.

The other finding on Table 4.1 is that while regulation and involuntary status had a strong positive relationship ($r = .80$), regulation and task intensity had a strong negative relationship ($r = -.71$). This suggests that there were conflicting demands upon those systems that had to manage involuntary clients: those networks required intense technologies but, because of the need for high levels of client control, they had to provide services within a highly regulated system.

External Control and Coordination

In Hypotheses 4.1 through 4.3 above, we speculated that there is a relationship between external controls and work processes. Cast in yet more theoretical language, we said that the control structure under which networks operate determines to some degree the choice of how they are internally coordinated and integrated. Since most interorganizational network systems are complex and, therefore, may potentially employ all three methods of administrative coordination and task integration, we asked the respondents to report the proportion of decisions handled by each method of coordination in their service delivery system and the proportion of clients treated by each mode of task integration in their service delivery system. Table 4.2 reports the zero-order correlations and regression coefficients for each of the external controls with each of the coordination and integration methods.

Table 4.1 Correlations Among Measures of External Control and Task Technology in Interorganizational Network Systems (N = 15)

	Vertical Dependency	Regulation	Involuntary Status	Task Scope	Task Uncertainty	Task Intensity	Task Duration	Task Volume
Vertical Dependency	—							
Regulation	.62**	—						
Involuntary Client Status	.60*	.80***	—					
Task Scope	.27	-.22	-.01	—				
Task Uncertainty	.27	.18	-.17	.26	—			
Task Intensity	.56*	-.71**	.53*	.36	-.27	—		
Task Duration	.17	-.19	-.16	-.01	-.13	.09	—	
Task Volume	.10	-.19	-.18	-.10	.00	.13	.48	—

$*p < .05$ $**p < .01$ $***p < .001$

In Hypotheses 4.1 through 4.3, we made the argument that external controls lead to a greater emphasis on impersonal coordination and sequential task integration. To our surprise we found that the Fulton and Farnam data did not support this reasoning. Only one of the nine correlation coefficients between external controls and administrative decision making was statistically significant; that is, the correlation was at least .50. Further, all of the nine coefficients were in the opposite direction to that which we predicted; that is, vertical funding was weakly but negatively associated with impersonal administrative methods ($r = -.31$) and involuntary client status had a strong positive relationship with group coordination methods. The correlation coefficients between the external controls and methods of task integration were somewhat stronger; that is, three of the nine were .50 or greater, but the direction of these correlations also contradicted the prediction. Specifically, vertical dependency led to a reduction in sequential task integration ($r = -.69$), but an increase in reciprocal ($r = .43$) and team methods ($r = .50$). The other two external controls followed the same pattern.

Why this reversal of the signs? We think there are two reasons, and they are qualifications and contingencies that should be added to any resource dependency or political-economy approach to network analysis. We now believe that to predict coordination, we must know who is controlling the resources and what their performance objectives are, for example, efficiency versus quality. In the case of Fulton and Farnam counties, the systems chosen for study were to a large extent dependent on federal funds, which for these programs meant more resources than would have been available locally, but also meant high expectations regarding quality. Where governance was by the participant organizations acting as a group, and where workers from different agencies had treatment plans made jointly and implemented jointly, it was, to some measurable extent, because federal funds made this possible. And therein lies an interesting finding.

We now believe resource dependency is not necessarily undesirable, as much of the resource dependency literature implies. Similarly, freedom at the local level from regulation does not necessarily lead to effective service networks. If we believe, given highly complex work technologies, that coordination and integration are necessary to produce high quality, then both adequate funding and the use of group governance and inter-agency teams for case management are necessary (the implementation of which may be mandated by vertical funding sources or adopted voluntarily by community participants). We have here in our findings the internal existential dilemma about the trade-offs between money and power, both of which may be used for either ineffective or effective ends. Organizations may go it alone or surrender autonomy in exchange for more resources, and in both cases the effectiveness of results will depend on the aims and values of those making the decisions.

Table 4.2 also shows the results of regression analysis combining the effects of the most useful variables on each of the coordination and integration methods. By using the external controls in the regression equations, we can determine which have the strongest effect on administrative coordination and task integration. However, because of our small sample size of 15, we were limited to only two independent variables per equation. The results do give us, nevertheless, some clues about the effects of external controls in Fulton and Farnam counties.

Overall, the six regression equations accounted for a significant amount of variance in coordination and integration. In particular, external controls affected the use of impersonal coordination (Adj. $R^2 = .20$, $F = 2.71$, $p < .10$), as well as the use of all of the task integration methods: sequential (Adj. $R^2 = .46$, $F = 6.97$, $p < .00$), reciprocal (Adj. $R^2 = .19$, $F = 2.60$, $p < .10$), and team (Adj. $R^2 = .19$, $F = 4.27$, $p < .05$). In Table 4.2 it is also clear that of the external control variables included in this study, vertical dependency was the most useful for predicting coordination and integration. Again, however, the signs were not as we hypothesized: The standardized coefficients for vertical dependency on impersonal coordination ($\beta = -.66$) and on sequential task integration ($\beta = -.88$) were negative, while they were positive for reciprocal task integration ($\beta = .69$) and team task integration ($\beta = .50$). These results, of course, are consistent with the correlations. It should be noted that involuntary client status also had a weak effect on sequential task integration ($\beta = .32$) and reciprocal task integration ($\beta = .44$). It is logical to generalize from this finding, if we can generalize at all from 15 cases, that court-ordered clients are for the most part referred in very structured and sequenced ways.

Table 4.2 Relationships Among Methods of Coordination and Task Integration and External Controls of Network Systems
(N = 15)

| | Methods of Administrative Coordination | | | | | | Methods of Task Integration | | | | | |
| | Impersonal | | Personal | | Group | | Sequential | | Reciprocal | | Team | |
	r	β	r	β	r	β	r	β	r	β	r	β
Vertical Dependency	-.31	-.66	.00	.00	.24		-.69**	-.88	.43	.69	.50	.50
Regulation	-.07		.28		.15		-.51*		.27		.41	
Involuntary Client Status	.49	.58	-.27		.51*		-.22	.32	-.02	-.44	.29	
Adj. R^2 =		.22		.00		.00		.46		.19		.19
F =		5.02		.00		.00		6.97		2.60		4.37
p <		.03		.00		.00		.00		.10		.05

Technology and Coordination

Although Table 4.1 shows that the correlation coefficients between the external control variables had a high and positive pattern, those between the task characteristics are consistently weak, suggesting that these dimensions vary independently (or are not well measured). Although task scope and task intensity were positively related ($r = .36$) and task volume and task duration were also positively related ($r = .48$), neither was statistically significant. These findings suggest that we should anticipate parallel impacts of task technology on the choice of coordination and integration methods.

This story is told in Table 4.3. Starting with the zero-order correlations, we note that only three task variables were strongly related to choice of administrative coordination methods. The index for task scope, a measure of the number of diagnostic categories and intervention roles, was negatively related to impersonal coordination ($r = -.50$) and strongly but positively related to group coordination ($r = .71$). The importance of this finding is the pattern of the signs: The associations shifted from negative to positive across the three coordination methods.

Based on this finding, we identify the following linear relationship as evidence for Hypothesis 4.4—decreases in the scope of service were generally associated with increases in the use of impersonal coordination methods, and increases in scope were associated with the use of group methods. The same pattern occurred with task uncertainty, evidence for Hypothesis 4.5, although overall the coefficients were not as strong. The reason why this finding is noteworthy is that task scope and uncertainty have been viewed as substitutes for each other in the management literature, while organizational theorists have been critical of the use of uncertainty (Aldrich, 1979; Hage, 1980). Here is empirical evidence that this is a variable for network analysis, and that it parallels scope in its influence on the choice of coordination methods.

The findings concerning task integration methods in Table 4.3 are even stronger. There are four statistically significant coefficients involving task integration, in contrast to only two involving administrative coordination. Further, the three task complexity variables show the same pattern of signs, with task scope being the clearest: Its association with sequential is negative

($r = -.69$), while its association with teaming is positive ($r = .83$). Task intensity also fits this pattern; negatively related to sequential integration ($r = -.60$) and positively related to teaming ($r = .50$). And although the signs for task uncertainty also fit the pattern, its coefficients are not statistically significant. This is consistent with the management literature that argues that uncertainty creates more problems for administrators than difficulty at the production level.

We were disappointed that the coefficients for task volume were not higher; we found no evidence for Hypothesis 4.7 in spite of the fact that many organizational theorists (Blau, 1970, 1972, 1973; Hage, 1980; Hall, 1990; Mintzberg, 1979; Scott, 1987) believe that this variable is one of the two most important factors shaping organizational structure. The coefficients for task duration were also insignificant, providing no evidence for Hypothesis 4.8. An examination of the raw score showed there was very little variation in the length of time clients spent in these systems in Fulton and Farnam. This was surprising, given the very different kinds of clients being served by these 15 network systems. We suspect that this was due to the fact that some of the systems we supposed would have a long duration of service—for example, child protective services and frail elderly services—in reality closed cases as quickly as possible (the average for the entire sample was only 7.7 months). With little variation in duration, there could be little impact on choice of coordination methods. We experimented with an index that combined volume and duration as a measure of scale, but this approach did not prove effective.

Table 4.3 also gives the results of regressing the five task characteristics on the methods of administrative coordination and task integration. As we already observed, these variables did a better job of accounting for variance than did the external control variables, ranging from team methods with the highest variance (Adj. $R^2 = .66$; $F = 28.55$; $p < .00$) to personal coordination having the lowest (Adj.. $R^2 = .23$; $F = 3.10$; $p < .08$). Given the correlation coefficients in Table 4.3, it was not unexpected that the first three technology variables (scope, uncertainty, and intensity) dominated the two extremes (impersonal and group; sequential and team), and the second two technology variables (duration and volume) dominated (either alone or together) the middle (personal and reciprocal). The regression

Table 4.3 Relationships Between Coordination and Integration Methods and the Characteristics of Tasks in Network Systems

| | Methods of Administrative Coordination | | | | | | Methods of Task Integration | | | | | |
| | Impersonal | | Personal | | Group | | Sequential | | Reciprocal | | Team | |
	r	β	r	β	r	β	r	β	r	β	r	β
Task Scope	-.50		-.27		.71**	.33	-.63	-.69**	.26	-.03		.83***
Task Uncertainty	-.53*	-.53	.17		.49		-.39	-.60	.28		.25	
Task Intensity	-.01		-.32		.10		-.60*	-.76	.05		.49	
Task Duration	-.01		-.25	-.54	-.19		.00		.59*	.59	-.01	
Task Volume	-.21		.34	.60	-.11		-.09				-.34	
Adj. R^2 =		.22		.23		.54		.64		.29		.66
F =		5.02		3.10		9.32		13.28		6.80		28.55
$p <$		.03		.08		.00		.00		.02		.00

*$p < .05$ **$p < .01$ ***$p < .001$

135

coefficients of task scope and task uncertainty on impersonal methods were negative (β = −.39 and β = −.43 respectively), but were positive on group methods (β = .63 and β = .33 respectively). Likewise, task uncertainty and intensity on impersonal methods were negative (β = −.60 and β = −.76 respectively) and scope was highly predictive of high levels of team task integration (β = .83). These findings suggest that task scope and uncertainty move networks toward greater knowledge about clients and products that is gained through feedback from team members, while task volume in various combinations of intensity and duration moves networks away from this outcome.

The regression coefficients for personal administrative coordination and reciprocal task integration were also consistent and, again, disconfirm our hypothesis. It was very apparent that when there were large volumes of clients, both administrators and workers tended to use personal and more direct methods of coordinating (β = .60) and integrating (β = .59). However, there is a special condition that seems to explain this pattern. A large volume of clients coupled with short duration leads to personal methods and, given this type of caseload, it may be that this is the most effective means of coordinating in this situation.

External Controls and Task Characteristics Together

Which, however, is the dominant set of determinants—external controls or task characteristics? We point out in passing that the line separating these two sets of variables is not as sharp as it appears. Task scope, intensity, volume, and duration are all political decisions, not just technological selections. Their values represent choices made by policymakers with their political and cultural environments.

The relative impact of the political-economy and the technological perspectives is reported in Table 4.4, where the two most significant variables for each method of administrative coordination and task integration are reported (again, we can have only two variables in each equation). The results shown in Table 4.4 are robust and, in fact, we experimented with three variables and found no improvement in the F statistic.

When we put the foregoing analysis together, a consistent story emerges. Table 4.4 shows that vertical dependency was the most useful external control variable because it enters four of the equations, and the signs are consistent with the idea that hierarchical resources make higher levels of coordination and integration possible. Among the technological dimensions, task scope was the most useful in its ability to predict high levels of coordination and task integration. High volume and short duration were both predictive of personal administrative methods.

The most successful equations were those for group coordination (Adj. $R^2 = -.54$; $F = 9.32$; $p < .00$), sequential task integration (Adj. $R^2 = .71$; $F = 18.10$; $p < .00$), and teaming (Adj. $R^2 = .73$; $F = 20.21$, $p < .00$). This result leads us to conclude that vertical dependency and task scope are the two most useful dimensions for understanding network systems, especially when the focus is on the opposite poles of the coordination and integration continuum. In other words, the combination of a political-economy perspective and a technological task perspective suggests the following principle governing the choice of administrative coordinative and task integrative methods: Given vertical source(s) of funding (or a single source that is concerned with quality and will pay for high levels of coordination/integration), there is a movement away from impersonal or bureaucratic methods of control. We believe the trend toward the utilization of group decision making among administrators and team integration is affected by the level of knowledge that administrators and workers have about the clients and products. This is an evolutionary process and is accelerated when federal, state, or local authorities value quality and effective outcomes, and decelerated when systems must manage high volume and large caseloads.

From these results we draw some very cautious generalizations about the effect of different kinds of client population on the choice of coordination/integration. For example, when involuntary clients are involved, it is clear that impersonal coordination is a necessity. When multiple problem clients are the target of service, then group methods of coordination are selected, even when there is vertical dependency. In contrast, if there is a large volume of clients receiving brief service, then personal coordination is the preferred mechanism. Large volumes of clients served for long periods of time did not occur in the sample.

The association between vertical dependency and quality is evident in the choice of task integration method. This variable is strongly associated with the avoidance of sequential methods and the adoption of either personal or team methods. Again, which method is chosen depends upon the nature of the client populations. High task scope seemed to require team integration, while large volume and presumedly short duration led to reciprocal methods of client referrals. There is, then, some evidence of a dialectic between scale and scope, but not exactly the one as envisaged in Figure 4.4.

SYSTEMIC NETWORKS SERVING HOSPICE PATIENTS AND CHRONIC MENTALLY ILL IN FULTON AND FARNAM

Of the 15 systemic networks in the Fulton and Farnam counties study, two were hospice care systems and one was a "community support system" for persons with chronic mental illness. We describe these three systems and the relationship between their external determinants and internal processes because they illustrate that variations in external factors can affect the type of coordination and integration to be found in interorganizational networks.

HOSPICE CARE AND ITS NETWORK SYSTEM

Background

Hospice was the name used during the medieval period for the network of way stations established for pilgrims traveling to the Holy Land. The term was adopted during the 1970s by the U.S. Hospice Movement to symbolize a new paradigm of care for terminally ill cancer patients. Hospice care values life while accepting its end, and strives for quality of life during its last phase by maintaining patients within their families and by recognizing the many physical, emotional, social, and spiritual needs of both patient and family. Like other service innovations

Table 4.4 Regression of Methods of Coordination and Integration in Network Systems on Measures of External Control and Technology ($N = 15$)

	Methods of Administrative Coordination			Methods of Task Integration		
	Impersonal β	*Personal* β	*Group* β	*Sequential* β	*Reciprocal* β	*Team* β
Vertical Dependency	-.66			-.54	.40	.30
Regulation						
Involuntary Client Status	.58					
Task Scope			.63			.75
Task Uncertainty			.33	-.55		
Task Intensity						
Task Duration		-.54				
Task Volume		.60	.54			.37
Adj. R^2 =	.22	.23	.54	.71	.40	.73
F =	5.02	3.10	9.32	18.10	5.57	20.21
$p <$	.03	.08	.00	.00	.01	.00

of the 1960s and 1970s, the development of hospice care was the result of changes not only in attitudes and demographics but also in knowledge.

Hospice patients are persons for whom curative treatment is no longer effective or desired by the patients and/or their family. Instead of attempting to prolong life by means of technology, the patients and/or family have opted to improve the quality of life that is remaining by means of hospice care, which owes its development to three technological advances. First, large gains have been made in our knowledge about the nature and control of pain. Findings from pain research have been applied by physicians to palliative care—heretofore an almost totally ignored field. As more was learned about pain control, it was recognized as an appropriate treatment goal in situations where curative medicine was no longer feasible.

The second discovery was described by Elizabeth Kübler-Ross, in *On Death and Dying* (1969), where she outlined the developmental process of dying and the psychosocial needs of the patient at each stage. She asserted that the needs of patients could not be separated from those of the family, and that the terminally ill could only be effectively served within their own social environments and then only with the participation of their significant social others. Furthermore, care was not complete until the cycle was complete, meaning that survivors must also be helped through their grief process.

Finally, these two events coincided with the movement in the United States toward holism—the integration of disparate parts of life in order to achieve harmony and fullness. This philosophy became the framework of the Hospice Movement. Not only did it dictate a treatment method—the interdisciplinary team including physician, nurse, social worker, spiritual adviser, family, volunteer—but it also became inseparable from the movement itself. It is not coincidence that the two life experiences that have changed most radically in the United States as a result of the sixties' notions about holism are our practices related to birth and death. With beginnings and endings, it is probably simpler to delineate the existential parts that compose the whole.

Contrary to popular perceptions, the patient populations of hospice programs are not exclusively the elderly. Where programs have pediatric care and encourage physicians to refer younger patients, about 35% of patient loads are under 55. Overall, however, hospice patients tend to be women, outnumbering men three to two, and they tend to be white, middle class, and married. In Fulton and Farnam counties there was an increasing acceptance of hospice, especially in situations where patients had family responsibilities—such as young mothers and elderly spouses. In such situations, the care plan included the needs of the entire family. For a patient to be accepted into these programs, four criteria had to be met: (1) The patient, family, and physician had to understand and accept the goals of hospice; (2) the patient and family had to understand and accept the diagnosis and prognosis; (3) the patient's life expectancy was a few months or less; and (4) the patient's primary physician agreed to continue providing care.

In the two hospice networks we studied, the programs grew quickly from their creation in the late 1970s. Staff and board members cited three principal reasons: (1) There was a growing public awareness that hospice care provides quality care to the terminally ill and a growing expectation that the dying deserve quality care; (2) there was a growing understanding of the financial, physical, emotional, social, and spiritual needs of families (families increasingly understood how the dying process saps their resources and they were not, therefore, constrained to ask for help); (3) there were a significant number of families who, due to geographic mobility, did not have extended family members for support and help. In addition, a fourth spur to growth was introduced in 1984 and will increase the growth of hospice care in the next decade: (4) Cost containment measures, such as hospital Diagnostic Related Groups (DRGs), will make institutional care of many terminally ill patients financially prohibitive. Because hospice care in the United States was conceived as an alternative to institutional care, its caseloads may increase dramatically as institutional care decreases.

The Hospice Network

Hospice services were delivered in both Fulton and Farnam counties by a small network of seven medical and service organizations:

1. Hospice Care, a free-standing private organization, did not provide direct medical or nursing care, but rather coordinated the care plan being delivered by an interagency team drawn from the member organizations.

2. Visiting Nurse Association, a public health organization that has a specialized hospice nursing unit, provided in-home health care. In some communities it is this organization that serves as the core hospice organization.

3. Family Social Services, a private agency, provided social casework services directed at the concrete and social needs of the family.

4. Voluntary Action Center, a public/private organization, sent volunteers to the home to provide respite for the family and friendly visiting for the patient.

5. The family's own church, or the hospital pastoral care unit, provided spiritual support and follow-up/bereavement counseling with the family for up to one year after the death.

6. The local chapter of the National Cancer Society provided essential medical equipment and supplies on a sliding fee scale.

7. A local hospital provided inpatient medical treatment, when needed, in a specialized hospice unit (approximately 20% of patient days were spent as inpatients).

The linkages between these seven agencies are depicted in Figure 4.3.

More than any other type of system we studied, the hospice networks appeared to be less dependent and regulated and were able to utilize highly coordinative and integrative methods, methods that best fit the requirements of the service technology they were using. There were several reasons for this conclusion.

The hospice care networks at the time of this study had been able to maintain a diversified resource base. The board of directors of Hospice Care was composed of representatives of the member organizations and prominent community lay people. They set policy, planned program direction, and worked hard at fund-raising to maintain the core hospice agency that provided the coordination and integration. Direct services in the system were financed through different funding channels (Medicaid, private insurance, allocations from public tax revenues, and private contributions) and, for the most part, flowed to the agency providing the service and not through the central hospice coordinating agency. These systems were not vertically dependent and were not subject to high levels of regulation, although the public health nurses complained loudly about some Medicare regulations. These systems appeared to be autonomous when compared to others, such as the child protection systems, and thus were free to fulfill the demands of the hospice paradigm.

Because of the combination of scale variables (intense multiple services of short duration), hospice patients were cared for by an interagency team composed of staff from the seven participating agencies. They met with the family every week. Figure 4.3 is a heuristic to illustrate the interdependency of parts of this network and to describe the fact that these agencies could not act alone because neither the service paradigm nor time permitted unilateral intervention. The ideology and crisis nature of hospice care demanded that the helping community come together and act together as one. Administrators of the seven organizations met regularly to assess and solve systemic problems, and workers perceived themselves to be a team. The point is a simple one: If local administrators and workers value interorganizational cooperation, then local autonomy will facilitate it.

The hospice systems in Fulton and Farnam demonstrated that a free-standing core coordinating agency can achieve interorganizational teaming when that behavior is part of culture of trust. These central coordinating organizations were highly successful because they were perceived by others as having no vested interest in specific client outcomes other than quality; they mediated, negotiated, and made case-related decisions based on the best interests of the patients. This seemed to stimulate trusting interorganizational relationships. There would have been no hospice service in either county if it were not for the ongoing working relationships between the Hospice Care agencies, the hospitals, and the home nursing agencies. The ultimate test of these hospice systems is to maintain these relationships, and they are their greatest weakness. At any time, acting out of self-interest rather than collective interest, any one of the member organizations can destroy its own creation.

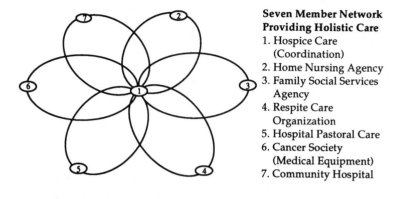

Seven Member Network
Providing Holistic Care
1. Hospice Care
   (Coordination)
2. Home Nursing Agency
3. Family Social Services
   Agency
4. Respite Care
   Organization
5. Hospital Pastoral Care
6. Cancer Society
   (Medical Equipment)
7. Community Hospital

Figure 4.3 Systemic Network of Home-Based Hospice Care

COMMUNITY SUPPORT SYSTEMS FOR THE CHRONIC MENTALLY ILL

Background

In the 1950s there were more than a half-million severely disabled psychiatric patients in hospitals throughout the 50 states. Today there are fewer than 150,000. The dramatic decrease is due to the closing of state mental hospitals and the return of the chronic mentally ill (CMI) to their communities. The total number of CMIs in communities, rather than in institutions, is estimated to be approximately 2 million.

The CMI population today is considerably larger than a decade ago because deinstitutionalization and the Baby Boom produced a new population of young adult chronic patients (National Institute of Mental Health, 1983). Today, the 64 million babies born between 1946 and 1961 are in their young adult years and constitute nearly one-third of the total U.S. population. The proportion of this cohort to develop schizophrenia has not been greater than for others, but in absolute numbers this group is very large: They become disabled at an earlier age, for some unknown reason, and the symptoms are very persistent (Bachrach, 1983). Nationwide, estimates of the young chronic population range from 400,000 to 750,000 (National Institute of Mental Health, 1983).

Young adult CMIs have been called a new patient population because they differ from older patients who have been deinstitutionalized. For young CMIs social failure is new, and they are still trying to be like their peers. They are rebellious and are resistant and difficult to treat; they act out, abuse drugs and alcohol, and often blame those who try to help them. They are the first generation of mental patients who have to cope, from the onset of illness and throughout their lives, with the tasks and stresses of community life.

Young CMIs have two predominant characteristics: severe deficits in social functioning and a tendency to utilize medical and mental health services inappropriately. As a rule, they are revolving-door patients; refusing to remain in therapeutic programs, they seek crisis help in emergency facilities and detoxification centers, or they land in detention or city jails. Few community psychiatric service systems today have either the structure or the programs to manage these young people.

This was the conclusion of a group of parents of young CMIs in Farnam County in early 1981. The Farnam County Mental Health Center had steadfastly refused to undertake residential care for them, but it was willing to assist in the development of "something," if the parents' group would take the lead. Over the next few years, a new agency was created—the Alliance for the Mentally Ill—that together with the Community Mental Health Center developed specialized linkages with other needed services in Farnam County.

The emergence of the CMI network was relatively swift and successful. Informants cite these major factors as contributing to its rapid development. The timing was right, they said. The state had just closed several of its institutions, putting severe strain on local resources. State and federal funds had become available for community support programs, and these funds were tied to the number of CMIs released from hospitals who had had community service plans developed for them.

Also, Farnam County had resources of its own. First and most important were the parents: a vocal, informed, and cohesive organizations of committed families. They had access to a good physical facility in which to develop a residential program, and encountered no neighborhood resistance when they did so; and a local option add-on to the property tax was passed and earmarked for mental health services. There was also a small but stable core of talented professionals dedicated to a shared vision of community care for the mentally ill, and they were willing to take risks to that end. They were skilled tacticians and they were able to mobilize and direct the resources at their disposal.

The CMI Network

Five organizations played major roles in this system:

1. A regional hospital provided periodic inpatient treatment for CMIs to reassess medication and to provide substance abuse treatment.
2. CMIs were discharged to the Community Mental Health Center, which was responsible for developing the client's service plan and for monitoring drug treatment.
3. CMIs were then referred to the Alliance for the Mentally Ill (AMI), where they were assigned to a worker who coordinated services for the client as long as he or she was in the community. These services were the concrete services of AMI (three levels of residential living, a sheltered jobs program and job finding in the community, and recreational programs), as well as two other services available in the community:
4. The State Vocational Rehabilitation Office that provided assessment and training, and
5. The State Public Aid Office that provided Social Security benefits.

Figure 4.4 is an illustration of the community-based systemic network that emerged.

The service paradigm of this network is quite different than that of the hospice network. Chronic mental illness is often incurable, and patients have episodes when intense treatment is needed. The goal of service is self-sufficiency—to enable clients to live independently in their community for periods of time that increase in duration over time. The client flow pattern is sequential and circular, with iterations of a single intense treatment service followed by multiple but non-intense services.

The operating processes we observed in this Farnam network were far more diverse than in the hospice system. Here, because of the vertical linkage with a state agency, there was more vertical dependency and more regulation. The state hospital controlled the pace of clients and financial reimbursement, and

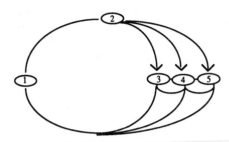

Community Support System
1. Regional State Hospital
2. Community Mental Health
   Center
3. Alliance for the Mentally Ill
   (3 levels of residential living)
4. State Vocational
   Rehabilitation

Figure 4.4 Systemic Network Serving Chronic Mentally Ill

state law governed other aspects of mental health treatment. This phase of the network was managed via impersonal methods of coordination. There was an interagency agreement between the hospital and the Mental Health Center that stipulated referral procedures, reimbursement rates, and payment schedules. In turn, there was a written agreement between the Mental Health Center and AMI that clarified roles and mutual expectations. During this phase of the cycle, from hospital to AMI, there was virtually no contact between workers other than perhaps a phone conversation at referral time.

In the community-based phase of the network, however, there was a need for more coordination. Because CMIs needed a fairly wide array of concrete services and because their situation had to be monitored closely, workers in the residential, training, and jobs programs frequently had to share information and make decisions together. But because the service objective was primarily maintenance for long duration, not intervention or treatment to produce change, teaming was far less frequent than in the hospice systems. Because time was not a critical issue, integration of task among workers was usually accomplished reciprocally through dyadic communication rather than collectively, but interagency staffing did occur in emergency situations when necessary.

When parents and administrators in this community support system were asked whether their system was resource-dependent, they answered, "Yes, and thank God it is." Without the combination of federal, state, and local tax dollars, they explained, their adult children would be among the drifters and homeless of our urban areas. The formality of the impersonal coordination methods and sequential flow pattern was viewed as a functional way of structuring a process by which their children could get intense help when needed, but be maintained on their own whenever possible. The community support system in Farnam County demonstrated to us the complexity of network systems. There was a wide range of services, utilized at different times, and needing different operational processes at different times. This confirmed for us that coordination and integration must be conceptualized as multiple category variables.

Structural Properties: Centrality, Size, Complexity, Differentiation, and Connectedness

Our usual conceptual image of a network is graph-like; that is, there are a number of points (or nodes) connected by a number of lines (or channels). These patterns are an abstract property, but one that has interested interorganizational researchers for quite some time (Burt, 1980). We refer to them as interorganizational network structures, to distinguish them from the coordination methods discussed in Chapter Three and the organizational structures that have been studied extensively in the past (Hage, 1980; Hall, 1990; Mintzberg, 1979; Scott, 1987). While there are analogs between concepts of organizational structure and network patterns, the idea of a network is quite different.

Graphs help us realize that networks have many critical properties; we used five variables in our conceptual framework (see Figure 3.3). Combining the five structural properties in different ways produces very different patterns of network structure, several of which are shown in Figure 5.1. First, there is centrality, the degree to which there is a central core to the network. Network analysis usually focuses on flows of information, clients, or resources, and in our use of the term it refers to the extent to which the heaviest volume of flow passes through a central location. The next four variables—size, complexity, differentiation,

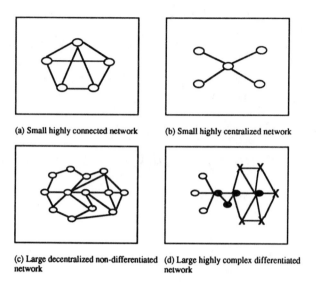

(a) Small highly connected network   (b) Small highly centralized network

(c) Large decentralized non-differentiated   (d) Large highly complex differentiated
network   network

Figure 5.1 Graphs Depicting Different Network Structures

and connectedness—are much less frequently mentioned in the literature on network analysis.

We include these other four dimensions of structure because they capture one of the important dilemmas of systemic networks; namely, as the network grows in size (the number of nodes in the graph), there is a tendency for connectiveness (the number of lines in the graph) to decline and differentiation and complexity to increase, which presents participants with many operational problems. This issue of size and how it impacts on the organizations in a network is less important in analyses of information or resource flows, but becomes critical when the network system is a production system. These last two properties, complexity (the number of different kinds of products or services produced by the member organizations) and differentiation (the degree of functional specialization represented by each member organization), can produce very different graphs and can be represented by symbols to reflect the different functions of organizations within a network or on flow charts (see Figure 5.1 d). Taken together these five properties—centrality, size, connectivity, complexity, and differentiation—help us describe the pattern of an interorganizational network system. Do these five properties vary randomly or are they themselves likely to covary? The examples provided in Figure 5.1 were not chosen at random but represent a few of the more common configurations. What shapes these configurations? Our objective in this chapter is to develop theory about various patterns of network structure. Organizational research has concentrated a great deal of attention on the theoretical problems of how technology impacts on complexity, structural differentiation, centralization of decision making, and formalization (Blau, 1970, 1973; Hage, 1980; Hage & Aiken, 1967; Hickson et al., 1969; Mintzberg, 1979; Perrow, 1967; Thompson, 1967), but little attention on communication rates and linkages (Hage, 1974). Although organizational and interorganizational concepts and their measures are not the same, the theoretical arguments are quite similar. External controls and technology should determine to a large extent the pattern of relationships between organizations in a network system, because the latter is a work system even if it spans a number of organizations. Therefore, resource dependency and technology should have an impact on work patterns and the configuration of the network.

In the first section below, we define and illustrate these properties and relate them to the external controls and task characteristics of the previous chapter. Finally, we compare all three sets of variables in their ability to influence the choice of coordination and integration methods.

THEORETICAL FRAMEWORK

In the previous chapter we dealt with a variety of task dimensions—scope, intensity, volume, autonomy, and a special one, the involuntary status of the clients—that impact on the choice of administrative coordination and task integration methods. In this chapter, we use these same dimensions to explain how networks are configured and shaped. Rather than present hypotheses about each of the environmental control and task variables with the five structural dimensions, our theory concentrates on developing ideas about which task characteristics are most likely to affect what pattern dimensions. Our approach is to view interorganizational network systems configured by a variety of environmental forces, which are then reflected in the definition of the task or supra-organizational goal of the network. These definitions then push and pull the network pattern into four alternative configurations, which in turn have distinctive methods of coordination and integration.

Centrality of Work Flow in Interorganizational Network Systems. Centrality of work flow is an important topic in the network literature, and there have been many definitions (Freeman, 1978, 1979). Hackman's definition (1985), used to study a large university, concerned the centrality of a unit's activities to the mission of the organization. On the other hand, Ashar and Shapiro (1988), using the conceptual definition by Hickson et al. (1969), conceived of centrality as the degree to which a unit's flow of work is centralized. We side with Hickson: "Centrality in interorganizational network systems is the degree to which the total volume of work flows through a single or few core organizations in the network." This conceptualization is one of dominance, because the organization that controls the flow of work is hypothesized to have influence over the production process of the collective (Ashar & Shapiro, 1988; Hackman, 1985; Mackenzie, 1978).

Our premise is that interorganizational networks develop dominant central cores when effectiveness is the performance objective of the system. There can be numerous criteria for effectiveness: Cost containment is an important one and predictability of outcomes is another. Effectiveness, whatever the criteria, is achieved in interorganizational network systems by coordination—either the coordination of decision making or the integration of treatment tasks. The need to use these methods of control springs from a number of imperatives, two of which are discussed below.

The first condition that leads to centrally patterned work flows in networks is growth in the volume of work. After an interorganizational network system is established, and as time passes, the number of clients perceived to need the service may increase— regardless of their status. Increased funding is then usually required, and community stakeholders often find it necessary to solicit state and federal funds. As increased state and federal support is obtained, service objectives and regulations are imposed by the funding authorities on the network system. Centrality, due to increasing vertical resource dependency, is for the purpose of controlling the behavior of organizations participating in the system. The federal government pays, and administers from afar. In a large-scale study of central government intervention in medical care, Hollingsworth et al. (1990) found that the usual pattern was for central governments to involve themselves in the collection of monies to fund the services or provide access—but inevitably, over time, to become more and more concerned with control, in part to ensure quality, but more critically to contain costs.

In the theoretical literature on organizations, this line of reasoning is consistent with the theory of resource dependency (Benson, 1975; Pfeffer & Salancik, 1978). The idea is that when resources come from a single source, then that source will want to control the decisions of the organization. Aiken and Hage (1968), however, made a further distinction. They found that in welfare agencies, the greater the proportion of the total budget that originated in a single organization, such as United Way, the fewer the innovations. In contrast, highly innovative welfare agencies had multiple sources of funding. These same ideas can be applied to the study of interorganizational network systems involving the production of goods or provision of service. Our concern here is not the degree of total dependency per se, but the extent of vertical dependency and the extent that vertical dependences are singular or multiple. The more that funding (and thus clients) is provided by a single hierarchically placed source, the greater the likelihood there will be a core organization controlling the flow of resources. Resource controllers want accountability and thus they usually demand that a single organization be held responsible.

The second condition that leads to centrally patterned networks is a concern for predictable outcomes. When clients are involuntary, for example, they have been ordered into the system by legal authorities, and communities view the treatment process as very important and inherently risky. When service delivery systems form as a formal extension of the state to treat abused children, for example, the system becomes centrally dominated in two ways. A core organization influences programmatic development through its control of purchase of service monies and in its interpretation of state law. Further, legal authority produces centrality of client flows, which gives the core agency power to affix organizational responsibility in cases of treatment failure. Centrality, due to the involuntary status of clients, is for the purpose of achieving sought for treatment outcomes.

Concern for quality occurs not only with involuntary clients, however. It is perfectly possible for a number of agencies, which desire to provide very high quality treatment to the same client population, to join together and create a centrally located structure to manage treatment planning and intervention. Many of the new case management projects currently being implemented are of this type and they are under the auspices of either a centralized program administered by the member organizations or a free-standing "governance structure" created by them for this purpose. Within this structure joint decision making by both administrators and workers can occur.

Although most of our task dimensions can be applied to network systems in the private and the public sector, as we have seen in Chapter Three, the involuntary status of clients does not have a direct counterpart in the private sector. The closest equivalent is perhaps when the federal government induces a group of firms to work on a military R&D project about which they are less than enthusiastic.

Quality and cost containment also lead to high centrality in the research consortia being established as National Science Foundation centers. There is most often a core university in these consortia, even when departments of other universities and business firms are involved, to insure the integration of the various research projects into a coherent intellectual attack.

Effectiveness, then, to control growth and contain costs during the operations of the network and/or to insure specified program outcomes, produces network structures that are centrally patterned. The hypotheses are:

Hypothesis 5.1: When network systems are dependent on a single vertical funding source, they will be high in centrality (and vice versa) in order to regulate work objectives and costs.

Hypothesis 5.2: When network systems must serve nonvoluntary work, they will be high in centrality to assure accountability.

These hypotheses suggest two alternative pathways to centralized work flows. One, resource dependency, is quite general and directly expresses a dominant theme in the literature (Pfeffer & Salancik, 1978). The second is the status of the work, be it voluntary or nonvoluntary. In human service delivery, any service network that is mandated by state or federal law is nonvoluntary. In the for-profit sector, it may be that there is no parallel concept, except that in cases such as military procurement, the relationship is so centralized and formalized that in many respects it resembles a mandated network.

The Size of the Interorganizational Network System. The term *size*, when applied to networks, represents the count of the member organizations in the network. This is not the same as the volume of clients or the amount of work, although we might expect there to be a relationship between size and the number of member organizations. Our definition is:

The *size* of an interorganizational network system is the number of organizations that participate in the work of the system.

Service delivery systems can vary widely in membership size, depending on the volume of work and the complexity of the work process. For example, adoption services are the smallest systems in this study because there need to be only three types of organizations in these systems—family service agencies, medical programs, and special education agencies. At the other extreme are systems that provide in-home services to frail elderly—large systems of organizations providing medical, social, environmental, nutritional, mental health, and recreational services. Large work volume by itself, however, does not guarantee large systems. One large bureaucracy, after all, could serve very large client populations if only one type of service is required (Aiken et al., 1975). It is the increase in the variety of kinds of inputs needed that pushes organizations to decouple units which can then participate in a network system.

An increasing volume of clients, especially if they have political influence, can, on the other hand, increase the variety of services and thus the number of participating organizations by lobbying state and federal governments for increased funding. The elderly are a good example. As the policy of deinstitutionalization has developed, and length of hospitalization of the elderly has decreased, the need for in-home care has increased. Core medical services, intended to prevent nursing home placements, have been augmented by a variety of other assistance, such as legal aid, chore services, shopping assistance, recreational opportunities—services not feasible as long as client volume was small. Economies of scale and the political power of the elderly have been the impetus toward greater numbers of organizations participating in these network systems.

Network size in the profit sector can also vary, from the two or three found in most joint ventures to the relatively large number typical of research consortia. If all of the research projects associated with a particular R&D area could be accomplished in one large bureaucracy, such as a Manhattan Project, then consortia would not develop. It is the complexity of the task, however, that requires the pooling of intellectual resources of a number of companies as well as those of universities. As in the treatment of clients with multiple problems, what is needed is the combination of a variety of backgrounds, perspectives, occupations, and experiences to be successful.

Our argument is the reverse of Blau's (1970) theory of structural differentiation. He suggested that as task volume for an organization increases, its internal structure becomes more differentiated into distinct job titles. Here we are suggesting that task volume, if it is coupled with a variety of services, will increase the size of the network system. This illustrates how distinct processes involving what seems like the same variables can impact differently at different analytical levels.

Another variable associated with large client volume is client status. Because involuntary clients must be tightly supervised, the service mix must be broad and include secure custody and/or residential treatment—24-hour care necessitates a large number of agencies. In our study, juvenile delinquents and abusive parents were provided a much broader range of services than, for example, either children in need of adoptive homes or hospice patients.

Two hypotheses are derived from this discussion:

Hypothesis 5.3: When network systems are vertically dependent, they tend to be large in order to provide the required mix of services.

Hypothesis 5.4: When task volume is high, the size of network systems is larger, especially if the market/need demands a variety of services or products.

Complexity of Interorganizational Network Systems. Complexity is one of the two or three most important structural properties of an organization, but frequently has been confused with structural differentiation. A careful reading of the original Lawrence and Lorsch (1967) work and Hage's (1965) axiomatic theory indicates that complexity and differentiation represent different properties. Lawrence and Lorsch (1967) started with the basic design of a manufacturing organization with departments for production, marketing, and research, and asked how different are the environmental demands to which each unit must respond. Hage started with Durkheim's (1964) concept of the division of labor and asked how many occupational specialties are needed. They both concluded that complexity should be measured by the number of occupational specialties (Hage, 1980; Hall et al., 1977).

At the network level, the analog for complexity is the number of different kinds of organizations involved in the network.

Complexity in interorganizational network systems is the number of different service/product sectors represented by the member organizations.

Theoretically a network can be very homogeneous and yet not be functionally differentiated, or a network can be heterogeneous and be highly differentiated. In practice, however, there is a positive relationship between the two variables because as the number of different kinds of organizations increases, there is a tendency for specialization by function to also occur in order for the network to overcome the attending chaos. In other words, as organizations increase the number of occupational specialties, they are grouped into departments. As networks increase the kinds of organizations involved, they are assigned limited roles (Paulson, 1985).

The same variables that affect size also explain complexity. As task volume increases and there is need for a broad array of services or perspectives, and if there is the political will to provide them, then the complexity of network systems will also increase. Our two hypotheses are:

Hypothesis 5.5: When network systems are vertically dependent, they tend to be complex in order to provide the required mix of services.

Hypothesis 5.6: When task volume is high, the complexity of the network systems is high if there is pressure for a variety of services or perspectives.

Complex tasks, especially when there is concern about quality, necessitate members of a system to work closely together and require the input of a wide variety of perspectives.

Differentiation of Interorganizational Network Systems. The concept of structural differentiation has not often been employed in the study of network systems, even though it is one of the important dimensions of organizational structure. In this study our definition is:

> *Structural differentiation* in interorganizational network systems is the degree to which there is functional and service specialization among the member organizations of the system.

In interorganizational systems, it is primarily the division of function and labor among organizations that is the best indicator of structural differentiation. When there is specialization, differentiation is high. Organizations within these systems each provide one or a limited number of services and fulfill one function. In these systems there is no modal technology. When specialization is low, there is little differentiation, and the agencies are generalists. Differentiation is: (a) the extent to which organizations fulfill specific functions (intake, assessment, or treatment) and (b) the extent to which agencies specialize by providing one service, as opposed to providing all the services available within the system.

Among the service systems in our study, a juvenile justice system had the highest differentiation score. This is a network system in which the police departments function as the intake points, court services do the assessment, a state agency provides detention and corrections, and psychosocial treatment is provided by family and youth service agencies. Because of this specialization, organizations in this system have different service paradigms. The police, for example, are responsible for applying the juvenile code routinely in each case—juveniles are treated as equally as possible. The staff of the mental health center, however, believes all clients are unique and treatment plans are therefore individualized as much as possible. When there is this wide divergence of service paradigm among organizations in a network, there is always the potential for conflict over service objectives and methods.

The system having the least amount of differentiation in our study was one that provided hospice services to terminally ill cancer patients. This system had little specialization, and there is a clear ideology and agreement among workers regarding the values, objectives, and methods of service delivery. There is a parallel in R&D networks. Typically, both university departments and research laboratories become dominated by a particular paradigm, theory, method, or way of thinking. There can be, however, a division of labor where companies are responsible for different phases of the development process or different kinds of research problems.

Network systems become highly differentiated when there is a perceived need for broadly based work that takes long periods of time. In service delivery, these systems stem from several environmental mandates, the most prevalent being the mandate that communities develop substitutes for state institutional care for chronic patients. The availability of comprehensive services is primarily a function of the scale of the service and an absence of the need for highly sophisticated services.

Task scope is sometimes thought to be the same aspect of service delivery as differentiation; in fact, they measure different dimensions of the same phenomena. Task scope represents the sophistication of technology; for example, the use of differential diagnosis and multiple treatment roles in service delivery. Differentiation, on the other hand, refers to how much functional specialization there is among organizations in the system.

It is theoretically possible, of course, for service systems to be high in both task scope and structural differentiation. This phenomenon occurs in network systems comprised of organizations that use very complex methods, but must respond to different mandates regarding the objectives of their service. The probability of conflict in these systems is very high, and the most visible examples at the community level are the child abuse systems.

In most systems, however, high task scope pushes networks toward nondifferentiation—and vice versa. It may seem counterintuitive that a complex approach to work is associated with less structural differentiation or organizational specialization. An explanation seems to be that it is easier to achieve and maintain both complexity and quality when there is a high degree of conformity to paradigm and program objectives and a high level of coherence in action. Highly differentiated network systems, on the other hand, develop when comprehensive, but long-term services must be provided. In these systems work must be routinized; this is achieved by division of labor within the network system.

Two hypotheses are derived from this analysis:

Hypothesis 5.7: In network systems where workers have a broad task scope, structural differentiation is low in order to achieve consensus about service paradigms and methods.

Hypothesis 5.8a: In network systems with high task volume, especially when duration is also high, structural differentiation is high in order to routinize and standardize service.

Hypothesis 5.8b: In network systems that have a large number of involuntary clients, structural differentiation is high because of the need for a high level of client control.

Connectiveness of Interorganizational Network Systems. Despite the large amount of research on networks, few studies of human service systems have looked at what has been called connectiveness. Our definition:

Connectiveness in interorganizational networks is the total number of linkages between organizations in the system.

In our study this is a measure of the density of client pathways. As we discussed in Chapter Two, exchange networks develop spontaneously and organically among clusters of organizations that have reciprocal needs and resources, and the channels through which resources flow can be few or very numerous. In the extreme, every possible linkage in the network is used, and this can produce highly successful exchange networks. Bavalas (1948), in his famous article on communication networks, distinguished between the configuration of a wheel, which is totally connected, and a yoke, which has little connectedness. In a production system, the structure of the wheel is useful for conceptualizing interorganizational teams, which, to operate effectively, must be highly connected.

A problem arises, however, because arithmetic increases in the number of member organizations produce exponential increases in the number of referral channels. If exchange networks are successful, and new organizations join the network, and they then want to move toward a chosen joint activity, they will find that unity of action is very difficult to achieve, given the large number of channels that must be used. Coordination and control among organizations in a large network tend to be highly problematic for the very reason that there are so many channels through which information and direction must travel (Litwak & Hylton, 1962; Pfeffer & Salancik, 1978). In other words, action networks and system networks form when organizational decision makers perceive a need to coordinate and control an activity or production process that they have undertaken jointly. To overcome the problematic of large densely linked networks, member organizations will concede some of their direct linkages to a centrally located organization and will be willing to interact with one another indirectly through the central core organization. By members being willing to surrender some autonomy over their own resource flows, the network is able to reduce the amount of effort required to maintain all channels.

By this analysis we hypothesize that the factors pushing networks toward large size, namely increasing vertical resource dependency and task volume, are the same that reduce connectivity. Our hypotheses are:

Hypothesis 5.9: When network systems are vertically dependent, network systems are low in connectivity in order to increase efficiency.

Hypothesis 5.10: In network systems with high task volume, the connectivity of the systems is low in order to control work flow.

These five structural dimensions of networks—centrality of work flow, membership size, complexity, functional differentiation, and connectedness—are shaped by environmental forces and work technologies. To test these 10 hypothesis, we return to the findings from our network study in Fulton and Farnam counties.

FULTON AND FARNAM COUNTIES: EMPIRICAL RESULTS CONCERNING NETWORK PATTERNS

The 15 network systems we studied in Fulton and Farnam counties were structurally very different. Qualitative data collected in the interviews with administrators and workers led us to this conclusion, and the empirical results confirmed it. In fact, the structural dimensions do not vary randomly but form identifiable patterns. The first evidence of this assertion was found in the correlations between the five dimensions as shown in Table 5.1.

Among the 15 systems in this study, centrality was moderately associated with size ($r = .54$), but had almost no relationship to structural complexity ($r = .37$) or differentiation ($r = .06$) and, as we suspected, was strongly but negatively related to connectedness ($r = -.65$). Highly centralized work flows resulted in a reduction of connectivity. Centrality appeared, therefore, to be a basic axis for describing network patterns—a finding that was hardly surprising, given its prominence in the literature.

A different axis of network patterns was the combination of size, structural complexity, and differentiation. As may be seen in Table 5.1, all three of these dimensions vary together: size and complexity ($r = .87$), size and differentiation ($r = .68$), and complexity and differentiation ($r = -.70$). The point to note is that because centrality was not strongly related to size, and not related at all to either complexity or differentiation, we believe

Table 5.1 Correlations Among Structural Dimensions of Interorganizational Network Systems (*N* = 15)

	Centrality	Size	Complexity	Differentiation	Connectivity
Centrality	—				
Size	.54 *	—			
Complexity	.37	.87 ***	—		
Differentiation	.06	.68 **	.70 **	—	
Connectivity	-.65 **	-.70 **	-.72 ***	-.30	—

*p < .05 **p < .01 ***p < .001

that size, complexity, and differentiation are best treated as one axis. Given the large organizational literature on size (Blau, 1970, 1972; Hage, 1980), there is some advantage to selecting this variable as a basic descriptor. Furthermore, much of the network literature has examined very large networks isolating various clusters and, given this tradition, size recommends itself.

Connectedness is clearly the third and quite different dimension of network structure since it was negatively related to all the other structural dimensions. Presumably we can infer from this study that connectedness occurs only when the network is small and there is little centrality of work flow. Thus, a large network, high in centrality and connectiveness, is ruled out on logical grounds; and a large, noncentral but connected network is probably equally as unlikely.

We surmise from these results that there is a continuum of patterns represented by the 15 systems in our study, a continuum that runs from networks that are small, highly connected with low complexity and differentiation to those that are large, loosely connected, and highly complex and differentiated. One way to examine this possibility is to recall that in the developmental theory described in Chapter Two, it was suggested that the structural patterning of networks does indeed change, and it changes over time as networks develop and mature. We cannot test this proposition properly with time series data, but we can categorize our cross-sectional data by age of network, dating the network's "birth" from the month in which the first interorganizational agreement was concluded that established some method of coordination. This procedure allows the comparison of mean scores for each structural dimension for the immature systems ($N = 8$) and the mature systems ($N = 7$). The results are shown in Table 5.2.

Table 5.2 shows that when these 15 systems were compared, using length of time they had been in existence, there are significant differences between younger and older systems. Consistent with the developmental theory proposed above, as systems aged they become larger, more complex and differentiated, and less connected. Unlike these four dimensions, however, the mean scores for centrality were not statistically different. We believe this finding provides some evidence that not only can network patterns differ significantly, but network structures can change over time. Furthermore, it suggests that

Table 5.2 Analysis of Mean Scores for Five Structural Dimensions of Interorganizational Networks Categorized by Age of Network ($N = 15$)

	Centrality		Size		Complexity		Differentiation		Connectivity	
	Actual	z-score	Actual	z-score	Actual	z-score	Actual	z-score	Actual	z-score
Immature Systems * (N = 8)	.46	-.27	8.38	-.54	3.63	-.74	.31	-.45	.50	.73
Mature (N = 7)	.58	.32	12.14	.61	6.86	.85	.44	.53	.29	-.83
F =	3.34		7.12		27.07		4.65		23.40	
p <	—		.02		.00		.05		.00	

*Immature networks are defined as those that had been in existence 9 years or less; mature networks were 10 years or older.

external controls influence centrality while the nature of the task is impacting on the other structural characteristics.

Determinants of Structural Patterns

To test the 10 hypotheses of this chapter, the five structural variables were each regressed on the external control and technology variables. As noted in Chapter Four, our small sample size means that we can include only one or, at most, two variables in the regression equations. We shall, therefore, examine the zero-order correlations with more attention than would otherwise be the case. These coefficients appear in Table 5.3.

On the whole, our environmental variables are quite useful in explaining and predicting the patterns of network structures. For example, centrality of work flow was associated with three of the task variables and had a coefficient of .40 or higher. Task scope was the highest ($r = .51$), but task volume ($r = .49$) and intensity ($r = .41$) also had a weak association with centrality, which was not unexpected. We assumed that systems with high demand would need to contain costs via centralized referral pathways. More important, the correlations between the three external control variables and centrality were higher, suggesting that environmental demands were also a determinant of these network structures. As we suggested in Hypotheses 5.1 and 5.2, both vertical dependency ($r = .47$) and involuntary status ($r = .52$) pushed systems towards centralized client referrals so as to maintain control. Perhaps the most interesting relationship is that between autonomy and centrality. Not unexpectedly, autonomous networks were not highly central. Given a choice, the members preferred to share equally in the work and control over its flow.

The thrust of our argument about why interorganizational network systems are controlled was twofold: concerns about system effectiveness and concerns about client control. In the stepwise multiple regression (F to enter = 4.0; POUT = 3.99) of centrality on the eight variables (see second column in Table 5.3), vertical dependency and scope enter the equation (Adj. R^2 = .54; F = 9.27). Indeed, the βs are little different from the

Table 5.3 Relationship Between Patterns of Network Systems and Measures of External Control and Task Characteristics

	Centrality		Size		Complexity		Differentiation		Connectivity	
	r	β	r	β	r	β	r	β	r	β
Vertical Resource										
Dependency	.47	.48	.69	.66	.57		.47		.56	
Autonomy	-.61		-.73		-.80	-.73	-.61		.73	.74
Involuntary										
Client Status	.52	.38	.52		.62		.52	.62	-.59	
Task Scope	.51		.13		.08		-.49		-.37	
Task Uncertainty	-.20		-.16		-.31		-.20		.20	
Task Intensity	.41		.49	.38	.60		.41		-.60	
Task Volume	.49		.44		.41		.49	.59	-.07	
Task Duration	.35		.40		.48	.35	.35		-.12	
Adj. R^2 =	.54		.55		.70		.54		.51	
F =	9.27		9.70		17.51		9.27		15.42	
p <	.02		.00		.00		.00		.00	

zero-order correlations, indicating that they are both separate pathways toward centralized work flows.

Networks grow for a variety of reasons, as can also be seen in Table 5.3. Task volume was the most obvious reason ($r = .44$), but intensity ($r = .49$) and duration ($r = .40$) had a similar impact. As clients were treated more intensely and for longer time periods, it meant a greater demand for a variety of organizational resources, thus increasing the size of the interorganizational system. In this instance we found that duration and volume had a similar impact. Like centrality, however, the external control correlations were higher. As hypothesized, vertical resource dependency was the most strongly related ($r = .69$). Federal funding was most necessary when large client populations had to be served; thus volume and vertical funding impact most strongly on the size of the network (Adj. $R^2 = .55$; $F = 9.70$; $p < .00$).

Given the strong associations between membership size and structural complexity and differentiation, we did not expect the correlations to be very different for the latter two. As noted on Table 5.3, the zero-order correlations between the environmental and technological variables and structural differentiation and complexity were quite similar to size. The only major difference was that scope had a negative, but relatively weak, association with differentiation ($r = -.49$). The regression equations, however, are not similar.

Each of the three network variables was explained by a different combination of variables, with autonomy being associated with an absence of complexity, differentiation, and size. Only small, noncomplex, and undifferentiated networks were autonomous and vice-versa. Low autonomy and long duration were associated with a complex network, while involuntary status and high client volume produced a differentiated network. Given the association between complexity and differentiation, this was an interesting finding. Large volume of many services pushed these systems toward rationalization and thus differentiation, while the necessary mix of services for clients of long duration created pressures for complexity.

A word about autonomy. We asserted in Chapter Four that vertical dependency and autonomy were not necessarily negatively related, because there are vertically placed funding sources that allow a good measure of autonomy to community decision makers. Based on the data from these 15 systems, it appears that we were wrong; the correlation of autonomy with centrality, size, complexity, and differentiation are all negative and very strong. We are not willing at this time, however, based on this exploratory study, to concede that we are indulging in wishful thinking. Finally, we can examine connectedness, which is our third basic dimension. The interesting observation about connectedness is that it was negatively associated with all of the environmental and technological variables but two. Task volume and duration had little impact, suggesting that it is not the number of clients that is critical, but the variety of agencies or client needs that requires parsimonious channels. The most interesting result, however, was that the only variable to enter the regression equation was autonomy, more evidence that our developmental theory makes sense. Highly connected systems are highly autonomous—the small and simple exchange networks that we believe to be the young and unorganized early network form.

In summary, these many discrete findings can be reduced to three basic observations about the ways in which interorganizational network systems are shaped:

1. Centrality and size of networks increase together when there is a heavy reliance on vertical sources of funding and either the process is high-tech or there is a heavy volume of work.
2. Complexity and differentiation also covary, but they are influenced by different factors. It appears that complexity does not develop as a result of concerted action by members (diverse organizations are not invited to join networks unless there is an hierarchically produced incentive or mandate). Differentiation, on the other hand, develops when the system must serve involuntary clients and work flows are heavy.
3. Connectivity exists only when there is little or no hierarchical involvement and, therefore, member organizations are free to refer clients in their own ways.

Fundamentally, the major conclusion is that interorganizational network systems are shaped by a variety of factors. Just as in the organizational literature, technology has an important impact on the shape and configuration of networks, but unlike this literature, two political variables—vertical resource dependency and involuntary status of clients—are equally important. For once, "politics" matters a great deal, but it is the external decisions about who should control and who will be controlled that dominate the system.

We conclude from these results that the structural patterns of our 15 systems can be arranged on a continuum, at one extreme being the small, unorganized but highly connected networks, and at the other extreme those that that are large, highly organized, and unconnected. In fact, this is exactly what we will propose in Chapter Seven. Before presenting this typology, however, we must return to the original theme.

Determinants of Coordination and Integration

In this and the preceding chapter we have been laying a foundation so that we can answer this question: What determines coordination? Why do some networks rely on very informal methods of working together, and why do some routinely work together in groups? Is the answer related to factors in the external environment of networks, or does it lie in the type of work being done, or are coordination methods those that will fit best with the structural pattern of the collective? On the basis of a large literature on organizations (Hage, 1974; March & Simon, 1958; Perrow, 1967) we might assume that specific dimensions of network structure might determine the choice of administrative coordination and even task integration, although the argument has been that technology is more likely to be decisive (Thompson, 1967; Van de Ven et al., 1976).

When we regressed all 13 of the variables on the three methods of coordination and integration, using a stepwise procedure, we found that 6 variables entered the equations at least once. The most successful were the technology variables, as shown in Table 5.4. This table presents our six methods of administrative coordination and task coordination regressed on the three sets of determinants, using the stepwise process. Allowing no more than 2 variables to enter each equation, the unused variables have been deleted from the table. As can be seen, the technological variables are by far the most useful, with an external control and structural determinant each entering only one equation. The results shown in Table 5.4 are summarized as follows:

Administrative Coordination:

- Written rules and contract were used when outcomes were predictable.
- Personal coordination and communication were used when work volume was heavy and work processes were brief.
- Group decision making by administrators occurred when task scope was broad.

Task Integration:

- Clients were served sequentially when both vertical dependency and technology were low.
- Clients were served simultaneously when caseloads were large.
- Clients were served by teams when the operational processes were high-tech and, interestingly, there was at least a moderate level of centrality in the system.

SYSTEMIC NETWORKS SERVING FRAIL ELDERLY IN FULTON AND FARNAM COUNTIES

The earliest interorganizational networks to help frail and homebound elderly were established in the United States by the Older Americans Act (OAA) during the mid-1970s. The act mandated planning regions administered by Area Agencies on Aging (AAA) as a prerequisite for OAA funding. The AAAs were charged with the planning, coordination, and pooling of resources for the development and maintenance of community-based service delivery systems. The AAAs patched together interorganizational systems by utilizing funds available from various titles of OAA, as well as the Social Security amendments, HUD, UMTA, CETA, and state and local governments. These early systems tended to be large, sprawling exchange networks with many linkages that used a mix of impersonal and personal methods of coordination targeted primarily at the well elderly population (Benjamin, Lindeman, Budetti, & Newacheck, 1984).

Table 5.4 Regression of Methods of Coordination and Task Integration on External Controls, Task Characteristics, and Structural Dimensions (N = 15)

| | Methods of Administrative Coordination | | | Methods of Task Integration | | |
	Impersonal β	Personal β	Group β	Sequential β	Reciprocal β	Team β
Vertical				-.54		
Resource Dependency				-.55		
Task Scope			.71		.59	.61
Task Volume		.60				
Task Duration		-.54				
Task Uncertainty						
Centrality	-.53					.43
Adj. R^2 =	.22	.23	.47	.71	.30	.80
F =	5.02	3.10	13.49	18.10	6.80	28.52
p <	.04	.05	.00	.00	.02	.00

Policy changes have pushed these community-based elderly service systems toward a second generation of network systems. The first important shift was the 1978 OAA Amendments that mandated AAAs to establish coordinated relationships with health planning agencies. As a result, elderly service systems became increasingly focused on elderly clients with medical problems (Benjamin et al., 1984). The next shift was the substitution of in-home for inpatient medical care (Evashwick, 1985). Between 1981 and 1985 the Reagan administration succeeded in making fairly substantial cuts in Medicare and Medicaid funding (Storey, 1986), putting pressure on hospitals to discharge early, and causing states to tighten nursing home eligibility standards (Nocks, Learner, Blackman, & Brown, 1986). These events stimulated the use of in-home services, one result being that many in-home health agencies have chosen to serve the chronically ill needing long-term care, rather than recently discharged patients needing acute care (Birnbaum, Burke, Swearingen, & Dunlop, 1984).

A second factor was the federal government's adoption of a decentralization policy. This shift meant bloc grants, rather than rigid categorical programs, and gave states the flexibility to develop Medicaid Waiver programs that allowed integration of Medicaid-funded in-home health care services into existing well elderly service systems (Benjamin et al., 1984).

This second generation of elderly service systems can now be observed in Medicaid Waiver states: OAA systems have developed into stable bureaucratic forms with structures that are more centralized, complex, and differentiated than their predecessors, but capable of delivering a much greater volume of service. These new systems have been termed Alternative Delivery Systems (Freund, 1986). A comparison of first- and second-generation elderly systems illustrates how the structures of interorganizational networks are affected by factors external to the systems themselves.

Fulton and Farnam counties were a nice laboratory for observing change in network structures because Farnam was in a Medicaid Waiver state and Fulton was not. As a result, the elderly service system in Fulton County had changed little since its establishment in the mid-1970s, whereas the Farnam County system had undergone considerable development since the introduction of the Medicaid Waiver program in 1981. We present data supporting this statement in two forms.

First, standardized scores for the structural variables are shown in Table 5.5. Taken together these z-scores paint a profile of each county's interorganizational system, and when compared, they produce deviation scores that describe how much the Farnam County system had been affected by the Medicaid program. As can be seen, the two systems differed widely, with Farnam being more dependent on vertical sources of funding (Medicaid) and considerably broader in scope. Further, all of its structural dimensions were intensified except connectivity.

The First Generation: OAA Elderly Service System in Fulton County. A second method of presenting empirical evidence of structural change is to utilize matrices and diagraphs. A matrix of all asymmetrical referral channels was constructed, and from this a diagraph was drawn, as shown in Figure 5.2.

This diagraph was constructed from information about the functions, type of services, and duration of service supplied by each of the participating organizations. The matrices show the volume of referrals made and received by each member organization. These two sources of information provide us with detailed descriptions of these two systems. The Fulton County system, as shown in Figure 5.2, was similar to many early elderly service delivery systems created by the Older Americans Act. It was large and sprawling, the epitome of a community service network that confounds clients seeking help and frustrates decision makers trying to rationally plan and allocate resources. There were 14 organizations identified as participants in this system, as listed in Table 5.6.

These 14 organizations offered a diverse set of 16 discrete services: 2 social services (adult protection and social casework), 4 health care services (hospital care, medical screening, ambulatory medical clinic services, and home nursing care), 9 environmental support services (financial, legal, housing, meals, transportation, shopping, weatherization, homemakers, and day care), and 1 mental health treatment service. The member organizations are listed in Table 5.6 with their type of organization, services provided, the function they performed for the system, and a centrality score representing the degree to which they were central to the client referral flow of the network. This is

Table 5.5 Standardized Scores for External Factors, Pattern Dimensions, and Methods of Coordination and Integration in Fulton and Farnam Counties ($N = 15$)

	Fulton County	Standardized z-Scores Deviation Farnam County	Scores
Environmental and Technological Factors			
Vertical Resource Dependency	.52	.99	+.47
Task Scope	-.61	.63	+1.24
Pattern Dimension			
Centrality	-.63	.24	+.87
Size	1.29	1.01	-.28
Complexity	.43	1.41	+1.23
Differentiation	.30	.89	+.59
Connectivity	.77	-.39	-.38
Methods of Administration Coordination			
Impersonal Coordination	.28	.43	+.15
Personal Coordination	.55	.34	-.21
Group Coordination	.16	.24	+.08
Methods of Task Integration			
Sequential Client Flow	.30	.24	-.06
Reciprocal Client Flow	.60	.41	-.19
Team Client Flow	.10	.35	+.15

175

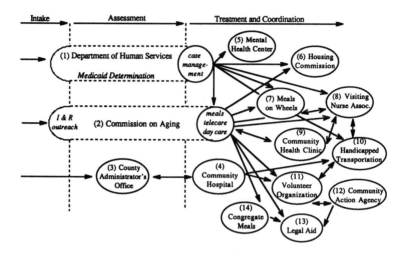

Figure 5.2 Diagraph of Fulton County Elderly Service System

the system created by the Older Americans Act: not as tightly coordinated as it might be, but certainly as comprehensive as intended.

The diagraph in Figure 5.2 makes clear that the Fulton County system was not highly centralized. No single core organization existed through which all or a large proportion of clients flowed. Rather, the system had many intake points and flow-through paths. It was nondifferentiated—there were four intake points and 14 direct service agencies. Organizations in this system are not highly specialized because there is overlapping of the intake, assessment, and treatment functions.

The scale of the Fulton County system was relatively large, but provided considerably less volume of service than the Farnam County system. A comparison of the total number of referrals shown on the matrices confirms this observation: Fulton County completed 4,060 referrals per year, compared to 6,276 in Farnam County. This is interesting, given that the Fulton system had a larger number of participating agencies. One explanation is that scale of service is related to the degree that services are state-financed and not to the number of participating agencies.

Table 5.6 Fourteen Organizational Members of the Fulton County Elderly Services System

Name of Organization	Type of Organization	Services Provided	Service Function	Centrality Score
1. Department of Human Services	Government	Medicaid Determination Adult Protection Case Management	I, A, S, C	.053
2. Commission on Aging	Social Services	Outreach and I & R Volunteer Visiting Telecare Adult Day Care Center	I, S, C	.179
3. County Administrator's Office	Government	Public Guardianship	I, A	.000
4. Community Hospital	Medical Care	Inpatient Acute Care	S	.072
5. Mental Health Center	Mental Health	Outpatient Therapy	S	.001
6. Housing Commission	Government	Subsidized Housing	S	.001
7. Meals on Wheels	Support Services	Home-Delivered Meals	S	.006
8. Visiting Nurse Association	Medical Care	In-Home Nursing	S	.066
9. Community Health Clinic	Medical Care	Outpatient Treatment	S	.007
10. Handicapped Transportation	Support Services	Specialized Transportation	S	.020
11. Volunteer Organization	Support Services	Specialized Transportation	S	.003

continued

Table 5.6 Continued

Name of Organization	Type of Organization	Services Provided	Service Function	Centrality Score
12. Community Action Agency	Support Services	Subsidized Drugs Utility Assistance Home Weatherization	S	.009
13. Legal Aid	Support Services	Legal Aid	S	.000
14. Congregate Meals	Support Services	Nutrition and Education	S	.020
Overall Indices		16 Different Services		.399

I = Intake   A = Assessment   S = Service   C = Centralized Case Management

Fulton County did not receive the level of state financial support that was available to Farnam County.

Limited state funding meant that the amount of autonomy in the Fulton County system (autonomy $z = -.15$) was high, compared to Farnam County (z-vertical $= -.73$). OAA service delivery systems in this state had had a relatively high degree of autonomy in the design and delivery of elderly services to their communities. Furthermore, without the formal controls that accompany state financing, the Fulton County system relied on personal forms of coordination and did not have to rely on impersonal and written controls. Decisions were made by administrators making contacts horizontally across organizational boundaries, the bases of which were friendship, trust, and a history of successful interaction.

These structural features—low centrality, differentiation, and scale—combined with a fair amount of local autonomy and personal coordination methods, made this system appear to be unorganized, lacking the hierarchical control mechanisms that produce organizational efficiency and accountability in bureaucracies. For example, the Fulton County delivery system had few systemic mechanisms to control the flow of clients, mandate the intensity or quality of services, and impose monitoring of evaluation procedures. The use of personal coordinating methods, rather than hierarchically imposed impersonal rules and regulations, indicated there was some measure of decision making left to the participating organizations. The strengths and weaknesses associated with this type of structure are discussed below.

The Second Generation: Combining OAA and Medicaid Services in Farnam County. The diagraph in Figure 5.3 shows that the structural characteristics of the Farnam County and Fulton County systems are quite different, most probably as the result of combining an OAA-funded system with the Medicaid Waiver program. In the Farnam network there are 12 participating organizations and 14 discrete services (missing are mental health treatment, social casework, and shopping services).

The Farnam County system had a core organization, Alternativies for Seniors, as can be seen in Figure 5.3. It was created by the state to provide screening and assessment, and to establish client eligibility for all state-financed elderly services in the county. In addition, Alternatives provided ongoing case management and monitoring of patient care. The centralizing effect of this core organization can be clearly seen on the diagraph in Figure 5.3. When client referral pathways are centralized through one agency, such as Alternatives, it puts the state, through its agent, in control of the system.

Also obvious in the diagraph and Table 5.7 is the fact that there is a high degree of differentiation in the Farnam system. In Farnam County there was a high degree of specialization and division of labor: Only the AAA and Alternatives did intake and assessment. As shown in Table 5.7, no agency in this system was a generalist, and there was very little overlapping of functions and client pathways, so the system appears to be rational and efficient.

As expected, there was a larger scale of service in Farnam County—more referrals, a larger unduplicated count of clients, and a longer duration of service. All three of these variables contribute to larger scale.

Last, examination of the standardized scores in Table 5.7 indicated a large difference in the integrative mechanisms used by these two elderly systems. The Farnam County system relied to a greater extent on impersonal coordination than on any other coordination method, but utilized group administrative decision making to a slightly greater extent than did the Fulton County system. The most interesting observation, however, was that in Farnam workers provides service and treatment as a team with more frequency than in Fulton. The development toward formalized controlling mechanisms appeared to have encouraged the use of higher levels of task integration. These structural characteristics—high centrality, differentiation, scale of service, and vertical control—made it possible in Farnam for large numbers of clients to be channeled in preplanned paths by a centralized organization having a large amount of decision-making power. This model, too, has its strengths and problems.

Effects of Increasing Vertical Dependency

Prior to the integration of the Medicaid programs with the OAA system in Farnam County, its elderly system was very

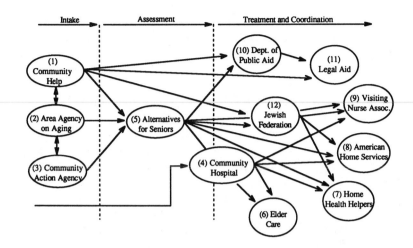

Figure 5.3 Diagraph of Farnam County Elderly Service System

similar to the Fulton County system. After the inclusion of the Medicaid program, the structural configuration of the system had changed.

The Farnam County elderly service delivery system was not the only one in the parent study to experience these changes. In fact, this developmental pattern is apparent in all the systems studied to date in this research project. Specifically, these effects of increasing state control can be observed in Farnam County:

1. Increasing vertical dependency in the Farnam County system resulted in an intensification of all its structural characteristics, except for connectivity.
2. Increasing vertical dependency in Farnam County reduced the amount of administrative coordination, but increased the amount of task integration.

The changes occurring in community-based elderly service delivery systems seem a paradox. Services for elderly clients

Table 5.7 Twelve Organizational Members of the Farnam County Elderly Services System

Name of Organization	Type of Organization	Services Provided	Service Function	Centrality Score
1. Community Help	Social Services	Information & Referral	S	.022
2. Area Agency on Aging	Social Services	Adult Protection System Administration	I, A, C	.011
3. Community Action Agency	Social Services	Outreach/I&R Specialized Transportation Telecare, Volunteer Visiting	S	.107
4. Community Hospital	Medical Care	Inpatient Acute Treatment	S	.023
5. Alternatives for Seniors	Social Services	Assessment Case Management	A, C	.172
6. Elder Care	Social Services	Adult Day Care	S	.000
7. Home Health Helpers	For-Profit Corp.	In-Home Health Aides	S	.015
8. American Home Services	For-Profit Corp	Homemakers	S	.017
9. Visiting Nurse Association	Medical Care	In-Home Nursing	S	.008
10. Dept. of Public Aid	Government	SSI-Income Assistance	S	.031
11. Legal Aid	Social Services	Legal Services	S	.002

| 12. Jewish Federation | Social Services | Congregate Meals
Home Delivered Meals
Specialized Transportation | S | .002 |

14 Different Direct Services

Overall Indices   .399

I = Intake   A = Assessment   S = Service   C = Centralized Case Management and patients in Farnam County were improved. Badly needed in-home health care is now available to the most needy to prevent unnecessary institutionalization. After the implementation of these service improvements, however, community administrators and workers felt their system was less effective. Furthermore, there was a large degree of conflict and low morale in this inter-organizational system. Based on the data collected for this study, it appeared that these current problems were to some extent a result of the structural changes that had occurred in the Farnam County elderly service delivery system.

The paradox is partially explained by the history recounted by residents of Fulton and Farnam counties. The elderly services systems in both counties were first created by local initiative. Churches and volunteer groups started the programs and then created agencies to institutionalize their efforts. A community delivery system did not exist: There were simply a number of unconnected services that were beginning to experience increasing demands for service as the community's expectations were raised by the public debate concerning the plight of the elderly. When the Older Americans Act was passed, the Fulton County and Farnam County agencies had to become somewhat coordinated and more centralized and had to accept some measure of control from the newly created Area Agency on Aging to receive badly needed OAA funding. The Fulton County system remains at this stage today, the first generation of service delivery systems.

The Farnam County system, however, entered another stage of development. Service improvements in this county have been accomplished by the utilization of Medicaid dollars, which has been accompanied by more state control. As this vertical financial support increased, local autonomy over programs and service delivery has been eroded still further. As Farnam County became a second-generation system, the loss of initiative was keenly felt by community participants.

The unorganized form of the Fulton County system has its advantages. The Fulton system is decentralized and, as such, has a capability for innovation, flexibility, and the tailoring of services to specific subpopulations of clients. The Fulton system is able to incorporate volunteers into the service delivery system, people who bring warmth and commitment to elderly clients. The involvement of volunteers maintains community involvement and support, a necessary ingredient of successful service delivery. The weakness of this organic structure is that it is not well organized, it cannot provide a large volume of service, nor does it have a high level of accountability among participating organizations. The latter, of course, are the strengths of the bureaucratic structure.

The paradox of service delivery is epitomized by the Farnam County system. It has the capability of allocating resources rationally, of processing clients more efficiently, and of providing health care for increasing numbers of elderly patients. This is an improved service delivery system. There are problems associated with this tightly linked structure, however, and they seriously affect community service delivery. Primary effects are the loss of local autonomy and the professionalization of the system, which excludes volunteers and community support.

Based on the limited data of this study, it is concluded that state and federal planners should be aware that there are negative effects to the consolidation of power and the centralization of community-based service delivery systems. It is clear that the need for coordination and task integration increases as systems become more complex (Hage, 1974, 1980). It is also predictable that the amount of coordination will not keep pace with the need as state control increases. State planners should sort out the decisions that must be made at the state level from those that should be made by participating community agencies, and then allow community systems to operate with as much flexibility and autonomy as possible.

Stated another way: Service delivery managers at all levels must understand different intra- and interorganizational structures and be able to manage those that are simultaneously loose-linked and tightly linked (Peters & Waterman, 1982). Effectiveness of the Farnam County system will be improved when there is firm vertical control coexisting with horizontal autonomy, and coordination that encourages flexibility and innovation.

Currently there is much turbulence among Farnam County agencies and very low morale among their staffs. Some of the negative effects of system changes could have been avoided if more autonomy and coordination were allowed in Farnam County. This will not entirely solve the developmental dilemma of control versus flexibility, but it may reduce its negative effects.

SIX

Conflict and Interorganizational Effectiveness

In this chapter we examine network failure. Specifically, we explore the factors associated with conflict and perceptions of performance gap among organizational members of interorganizational networks. One of the central issues in governance theory is what institutional arrangements are most effective and efficient, given specific situations. Although our data do not allow us to contrast the relative efficacy of network systems versus single organizations versus markets, we can at least examine the relative causes of ineffective networks. The performance of interorganizational networks is just now beginning to be of interest to chief executive officers and managers of for-profit and nonprofit organizations. As U.S. firms make strategic alliances with foreign corporations, characteristics of these interorganizational working relationships will become important indicators of success and failure (Harrigan, 1988).

The theme of interorganizational conflict has been a popular one in both the organizational and interorganizational literature (Benson, 1975; Boje & Whetten, 1981; Corwin, 1969; Hage, 1980; Hall et al., 1977; Lawrence & Lorsch, 1967; Walton & Dutton, 1969). Both organizations and interorganizational networks are likely to experience more conflict when people with different perspectives must work together. Community-based networks with little autonomy are particularly vulnerable to dysfunctional conflict because there is no central authority to settle arguments and negotiate settlements. It is now emerging as a critical topic in the business literature as well. The sources of conflict are different—sharing profits (Laage-Hellman, 1989; Moxon et al., 1988) or the difficulty of getting the right competencies (Laage-Hellman, 1989). Harrigan (1988) has used duration of relationship as a criterion of success. Short duration might be conceived of as relationships in which conflict has not been managed well.

Perhaps one of the most interesting case studies is that of Airbus Industrie (Moxon et al., 1988). While Britain, France, and Germany had a clear common enemy, namely the dominance of Boeing in the commercial aircraft industry, each government had differing political and economic agendas. Britain left the consortium at one point and then reentered. The negotiations have been quite complex because each government was interested in helping its local industry and giving the country a competitive technological edge. The French appeared to have won in these conflicts.

We suggested in Chapter Two that there are currently strong pressures forcing organizations to decouple their units and departments so that they can become involved in interorganizational relationships. These decoupled units gradually develop reciprocal referrals, preferential contracts, and other patterned resource exchanges. Slowly over time, first an obligational network, then a promotional network, and then a systemic network emerges by trial and error. As we observed in the first chapter, most of the research on interorganizational relationship in the late 1960s and 1970s judged networks to be ineffective and conflicted because they were being viewed at early stages in their development (Aiken et al., 1975).

Networks develop incrementally and their different parts may not develop at the same pace. Exchange networks do not just develop overnight into promotional networks, and promotional networks do not evolve into full-fledged systemic networks without a good deal of muddling and conflict, an inherent characteristic of developing systems. Systemic networks have a division of labor, a pattern of decision making, and other structural characteristics, and these processes do not necessarily change simultaneously in all parts of the system. Even when the parts do develop in tandem, they do not necessarily employ optimal arrangements or choices of coordinating mechanisms evenly throughout the system. In short, the development process is anything but coherent and rational.

The same is true on the joint venture side, even when it involves symbiotic relationships (by definition and experience, the competitive joint ventures are filled with even more conflict, as the Airbus Industrie case illustrates). A variety of studies stressed the number of different managerial functions that can be undertaken collaboratively (Contractor & Lorange, 1988; Killing, 1988; Powell & Brantley, in press). Successful product development does not necessarily mean successful production and marketing, or even the choice of the same partner for further product development. Laage-Hellman reports the experience of a Swedish pharmaceutical company deciding not to continue with Genetech, even though they had a successful product development, because Genetech wanted to maximize its profits.

Just as we explored the relationship between environmental conditions and the choice of coordination methods, here we explore the relationship between the performance of networks, the external controls and technological variables discussed in Chapter Four, and the structural dimensions discussed in Chapter Five. We want to determine the conditions under which conflict and negative perceptions dominate a network. It is possible that the same forces which propel organizations into complex collective arrangements can also establish constraints and make effectiveness difficult to achieve. If this is the case, then we must ask whether coordination is able to reduce or ameliorate these network failures. As we shall observe, the relationships between these variables can be quite complex.

THEORETICAL FRAMEWORK

The analysis of conflict and ineffectiveness in systemic networks reflects a fundamental issue in population ecology, namely, which form is effective and why. Forms are defined as the combination of technology, structure, and control mechanisms (Aldrich & Mueller, 1982). By exploring the associations between technology, structure, conflict, and ineffectiveness, we may be able to decide which forms are likely to be selected across time. In this chapter we consider conflict and perceived effectiveness as dependent variables that are affected by a range of environmental and structural conditions. This analysis is continued in Chapter Seven, where the issue of failed evolution is considered.

Conflict in Interorganizational Networks

Conflict and cooperation have often been thought of as extremes of a single interorganizational dimension, different ends of a single continuum descriptive of relationships within and between organizations (Gillespie & Mileti, 1979; Hage, 1980). In fact, a major concern of the management literature has been to find methods to increase control via cooperation and coordination in order to reduce conflict (DeWitt, 1977). Although this may be an effective strategy, conceptualizing conflict and coordination in this manner is not necessarily the most helpful because it views them as opposites, with conflict being inimical to effective working relationships. Actually, these terms describe two separate and differentiable dynamics that are not mutually exclusive, but that occur simultaneously within interorganizational networks (DiStefano, 1984; Killing, 1988; Litwak & Hylton, 1962). Similarly, ever since the concept of coordination was first advanced (Georgopoulos & Mann, 1962; Lawrence & Lorsch, 1967; March & Simon, 1958), it has been assumed that coordination and effectiveness were synonymous. But as Lawrence and Lorsch (1967) demonstrated, in a seldom-replicated study, the kind of coordination method used makes a difference. Some coordination mechanisms can be ineffective.

Until recently conflict was thought to be the dominant behavior of interorganizational relationships (Zeitz, 1985). The development of conflict as a conceptually discrete organizational property, however, has not progressed significantly since Simmel wrote *The Conflict in Modern Culture* (1968), and there still is not consensus about the nature of conflict within the interorganizational context. Some treat conflict as a cause of poor outcomes (Assael, 1969); others use it as an outcome itself (Schmit & Kochan, 1972). Some models describe it as covarying with cooperation (Gillespie & Mileti, 1979), while others treat it as an independent variable (Litwak & Hylton, 1962). Conventional wisdom has held that conflict within and between organizations is frequent and dysfunctional. Marxists believe that conflict is inevitable in organizational life: The resolution of old conflicts sets the stage for new conflicts in a dialectic process that is a vital component of creativity and innovation (Hage, 1980; Zeitz, 1985).

Theorists have categorized organizational conflict in a number of ways. Molnar and Rogers (1979) describe types of structural conflict resulting from rules, policies, or procedures. Pondy (1969) and Frazier (1983) believe that conflict can best be described as "frictional" (relatively minor disagreements) or as "systemic" or "manifest" (clashes over fundamental issues), and it can occur in interorganizational systems at the individual level and/or at the collective level (Galtung, 1967). Individuals can direct angry or frustrated feelings at other individuals, they can verbally disagree with others, or they can act with the intent of neutralizing, excluding, or injuring others. By the same token, organizations can undertake communication or action meant to neutralize, exclude, or harm other organizations. Corwin (1969), in one of the most extensive studies of organizational conflict, found that there was a significant difference between the causes of interpersonal disputes and those responsible for intergroup conflict.

This study conceptualizes conflict as an organizational behavior that occurs and recurs at different times during the life cycle of a network system. Conflict can occur between individuals and organizations as they strive to maximize their control over their dependency on the collective (Leach, 1980), or as an oppositional process in which one individual or organization attempts to change, block, or impede the activities of another (Morrissey et al., 1982). The resolution of interorganizational conflict produces outcomes that range from withdrawal to adjustment to strengthened ties. Development occurs when the resolution enhances common perceptions, improves role clarity, and lessens task ambiguity (Frazier, 1983). This conceptualization, then, regards conflict as a property of work processes, one that is legitimate and necessary (Zeitz, 1985) and has long-term benefits (Guetzkow, 1966; Warren, 1973). In summary, we define interorganizational conflict as:

Interorganizational conflict is disagreement, disharmony, and strife about objectives, methods, and policies between individuals and organizations in an interorganizational network.

Conflict, because it can occur at the individual level as well as the organizational level, is as difficult to measure as is coordination. There have been two basic approaches—both are perceptual and both have inherent problems. The first uses a 6-point semantic scale to measure the frequency of disagreements or disputes between individuals and units within an organization (Van de Ven & Ferry, 1980). This approach does not make explicit the difference between individual behavior and organizational behavior as they may affect interorganizational relationships. The second approach (Figure 6.1), designed by Alter and Hage for research on service delivery systems, does acknowledge this difference.

The problem with any attempt to measure conflict, however, is that administrators and workers may be reluctant to divulge the extent of conflict in their networks because it is a subject laden with political connotation and possible negative consequences if confidentiality is breached. But since this limitation operates uniformly, we might expect either of these measures to underreport the intensity of conflict but not its distribution across systems.

In retrospect, it would have been better to measure disagreements about specific aspects of the systemic network, such as its goals, methods, and policies. An issue that produces conflict in juvenile services, for example, is, what works best—treatment or punishment? The framing of questions about conflict in this manner might eliminate some of the interpersonal conflict that exists in any complex institution or organization.

*Factors Associated With High Levels
of Conflict in Network Systems*

In the preceding chapters we considered a wide range of factors that characterize network systems. Here we consider each cluster of concepts and hypothesize about the role it plays in either inhibiting or stimulating conflict in these networks. Rather than provide multiple hypotheses as we did earlier, here we use only the variables we found to be the most predictive.

On an average, how many times per month do the following incidents occur
while you are working with administrators or staff from other participating
organizations in your SEDS service system?

Number of Times

you and a person from another organization have:
angry feelings toward each other   _____
verbal disputes between each other   _____

you act overtly or covertly toward a person from
another organization to:
negate or neutralize him or her   _____
exclude him or her   _____
injure him or her   _____

your organization acts overtly or covertly toward
another organization to:
negate or neutralize   _____
exclude   _____
injure   _____

Figure 6.1 Questionnaire Item Measuring Conflict at the Individual and the
Interorganizational Levels

First, of course, is the degree to which the working relationship is controlled and regulated by forces outside the network.
Environmental controls, if they inhibit the work process and
rob local personnel of initiative and autonomy, may well engender conflict between organizations that are working together, especially when these organizations belong to different
vertical networks. If organization A in a local network is highly
dependent on vertical funding sources and is also highly regulated, then there is a strong likelihood that other organizations in
the network might not understand the restrictions that organization A must place on its participation, and their frustration will
manifest itself as conflict on several levels. In the business sector,
joint ventures vary in the degree of external influence or interfer-
ence, even though this is what they are designed to avoid.

Hypothesis 6.1: The higher the level of external control and the less
autonomy of network systems, especially if there are
differential levels of external control among members,

the greater the amount of conflict among individuals and organizational members within a network.

A common theme in the literature on role conflict (Biddle, 1986; Merton, 1957) is the different expectations of various actors. This same principle applies to boundary spanners in systemic networks (Aldrich, 1979). One cause of differential expectations is the differing demands of different funding sources.

With the technological variables it is a different story. There is no theoretical reason we can think of that explains why the use of one type of technology over another, absent other factors, should increase the amount of conflict between organizations. This may surprise those readers who remember the introduction of new technologies such as milieu therapy or deinstitutionalization in the public sector, or the introduction of automation and computers in the business world (Mann & Williams, 1960; Walker, 1950, 1957). These, however, were single technologies within an organizational context, designed to replace an existing technology. In network systems, the technologies of individual organizations are being pooled together (which is what task scope measures), rather than one technology replacing another.

Hypothesis 6.2: There is no relationship between the technology of work in network systems and the amount of conflict between individuals and organizational members.

There are good reasons, however, why structural characteristics should engender disagreement and disharmony in networks. Technology per se may not be a contributor, but when different actors use different technologies and when they play different roles in the production or action process, then the opportunity for conflict caused by lack of information or understanding, and disagreement over methods, is very possible and even likely. In general, our theoretical framework specifies that all of the structural variables except connectivity are associated with increasing levels of conflict. An exception is made for this last variable because when units are tightly connected, communication is increased, which works to militate against misunderstanding and disagreement, as the original studies of intraorganizational communication argued (Georgopolous & Mann, 1962; Hage, 1974).

Hypothesis 6.3: The higher the centrality, size, complexity, and differentiation in network systems, the higher the levels of conflict among individuals and organizational members.

Hypothesis 6.4: The higher the connectivity in network systems, the lower the level of conflict among individuals and organizational members.

The fundamental causal assumption that undergirds Hypothesis 6.3 is that, in various ways, bureaucratic structures generate conflict. Centrality, for example, means that only a few people or organizations are making key decisions, and this situation is associated with conflict, as the literature on organizational conflict demonstrates (Corwin, 1969; Hage, 1980). Large size (more organizational members) inevitably increases the probability of misunderstanding and differences of opinion and expectation. Complexity and differentiation, associated with the problems of pooling different technologies, means that the range of differently trained workers, different perspectives, and unrealistic expectations will be high, which in turn increases opportunities for conflict and combat.

Last is the popular belief that coordination decreases conflict. We suggested above that conflict and cooperation are separate processes occurring simultaneously in fully operating systems. Using this conceptualization, then, there are three possible relationships between the two: Conflict and cooperation are (a) completely independent, (b) positively related, or (c) negatively related. The third possibility is the view commonly found in the management literature, where it is often asserted that more cooperation in any form will reduce the level of conflict.

Hypothesis 6.5: The more coordination of administrative decision making and task integration, the lower the levels of conflict that will be found in network systems.

The meaning of this hypothesis must be fully understood. Typically the literature has discussed coordination as a dichotomous variable, either being present or not (March & Simon, 1958; Mintzberg, 1979). Lawrence and Lorsch (1967) introduced the notion that integration exists as a continuous variable. Thus, when we say "more coordination" and "more integration," we call attention to the fact, not widely appreciated, that when we go from impersonal to personal to group methods, we are achieving much higher levels of coordination because of the greater amount of feedback (Thompson, 1967). In fact, the weights we assign to the three coordination and integration scores to derive the summative coordination and integration indexes are based on an assumption that group methods achieve three times more coordination than do impersonal methods, and team methods achieve three times more task integration than do sequential methods (see Appendix B). Hypothesis 6.5 suggests, therefore, that a system moving from impersonal to personal to group methods of administrative coordination and the parallel methods of task integration should experience a decline in conflict.

Interorganizational Effectiveness and Performance Gap

Most of the work to date on interorganizational relationships has been done for the purpose of understanding networks and explaining their antecedents, processes, and structures. Understandably, there has been little attention paid to their effectiveness. We say understandably, because there is still a general lack of agreement about the best approach to effectiveness in organizations (Cameron, 1981; Goodman & Pennings, 1977), although progress has been made in the past decade (Van de Ven & Ferry, 1980; Zey-Ferrel, 1979). If this is a problematic concept in organizations, it is doubly so in networks.

One problem associated with conceptualizing effectiveness of complex systems is establishing the focus of investigation (Wooldridge, 1981). There are several unique approaches to studying organizational effectiveness; they can be categorized as distinct models and applied to interorganizational structures, as shown in Table 6.1. This diversity of perspectives has led some to argue that the concept should be abandoned (Goodman & Pennings, 1977). While it is true that effectiveness is an exceedingly broad concept, its use in practice is so well established as to be impervious to assaults by theorists. We believe that a framework such as the one shown in Table 6.1 helps with the problem of focus.

Table 6.1 Four Models of Assessing Interorganizational Networks

Theoretical Model	A Network System Is Effective to the Extent That	When Useful
Goal Model	it accomplishes its consensual goal(s)	Goals are clear and measurable
System-Resource Model	it acquires needed resources	Inputs can be specified and measured
Internal Process Model	it has an absence of internal strain; exhibits smooth internal functioning	Clear causal connection between internal processes and desired output
Strategic Constituencies Model	all strategic constituencies are at least minimally satisfied	Constituencies have powerful influence

SOURCE: Adapted from Cameron (1981, p. 5).

Much of the existing government and foundation sponsored research on interorganizational systems has adopted the third approach in Table 6.1, the internal process model. This choice has been based on the assumption that the outcomes of the system, the product or the service, will be of higher quality if the system functions smoothly and with a minimum of conflict. There are currently several attempts to evaluate service delivery systems using the goal model.

In the organizational literature a variation of the first model in Table 6.1 has been suggested by Goodman and Pennings (1977). They argue that effectiveness should be conceptualized as an outcome, but measured relative to the constraints that exist in the system. For example, if the entire economy is in recession, then business executives are usually not fired when their companies experience lower profits. The expectation of what is a reasonable outcome, given the context and the barriers to goal achievement, is usually the best measure of effectiveness. In fact, one way of using the other models in Table 6.1 is to view each as a potential constraint. Under these circumstances, effectiveness is achieved when goals are met within the context of technological and resource constraints, given certain levels of internal conflict and pressure from external constituencies. This logic can be applied to systemic networks, but it is apparent, as we discuss below, that this global perspective encounters methodological problems.

There are additional reasons why it is difficult to conceptualize effectiveness of network systems. First, as we tried to show in Chapter Two, interorganizational networks go through phases, each phase having a set of developmental tasks that must be accomplished before the next phase can be successfully entered. Evaluation of networks must be phase-specific, or expectations will be inappropriately high. In our opinion, this was the case with much of the IO evaluative research of the early 1970s.

A third area of concern when assessing interorganizational effectiveness is the level of analysis. In network systems, even if it is possible to specify system level goals and objectives, one is faced with deciding the level at which data will be collected. This is difficult because the production process is a hierarchy of cause and effect in a cybernetic process, with change occurring at different levels, and the outcomes at each level acting as determinants for the next set of outcomes. This process is pictured in Figure 6.2.

Network systems are the result of changes at the state and federal level that have outcomes at the systems, organizational, and client/product levels, which in turn are fed back to the system's larger environment. Indicators of success in program, service, or product development or delivery can, of course, be identified at any of these levels. There have been few studies to date that have used organizational or client/product outcome measures to assess the effectiveness of network systems. One exception is the current mental health studies that are attempting to predict patient outcomes from system variables (see future results of Robert Wood Johnson funded research).

We have outlined above some of the possibilities available to researchers to make the point that there is no one best way to measure effectiveness in networks. For the purpose of the study reported in this book, we conceptualized interorganizational effectiveness at the systems level.

Effectiveness in interorganizational systems is a perception among administrators and workers that their collective effort is achieving what it was intended to achieve, that it works smoothly, and that it is reasonably productive.

The item we used to measure this conceptualization of effectiveness was perceptual, and it collected data at the individual level. Because we needed an item that could be administered to workers and administrators within a wide variety of systems, it was not possible to use a fixed performance scale. We designed, therefore, an item to yield a gap score—the difference between the current situation ("what is") and an idealized standard ("what could be," given realistic restraints on best practice) (Figure 6.3). This approach is useful when baseline data is unavailable. The index derived from this item we term *performance gap*.

We believe this measure of effectiveness (or performance gap, as it is conceptualized) is akin to the solution proposed by Goodman and Pennings in their conference on the problems of organizational effectiveness: Performance is always relative to resources. They suggested that effectiveness is always defined relative to prevailing conditions, and managers, for example, are not fired when their businesses are doing poorly if all businesses are doing poorly (the exception, of course, is professional sport teams). Nonprofit organizations are usually underfunded, and there are states today where child welfare workers carry caseloads of 200 or more. Under these conditions, it is very difficult to be effective. An item trying to measure effectiveness must, therefore, be sensitive to differences in available resources if the item is to be used across different market sectors.

Factors Associated With High Levels
of Performance Gap

Here we consider each cluster of interorganizational variables and speculate about what role it plays in influencing how participants judge their system's performance. First is the cluster of environmental controls. The effect of vertical dependency, regulation, and involuntary status on performance gap is similar to their impact on conflict. It is strong and positive. Whereas we see the driving force behind conflict as primarily the differential expectations about the process and outcomes of working together, the

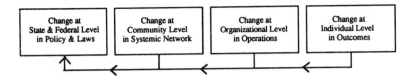

Figure 6.2 Model of Hierarchical Levels of Change

major sources of negative gaps in performance are the barriers that prevent systemic networks from reaching their potential.

Hypothesis 6.6: The higher the level of external control and the less autonomy within network systems, the larger the gap perceived between actual practice and best possible practice.

Our hypothesis incorporates a basic idea from resource dependency theory, namely, that lack of control over resources implies lack of control over essential decisions. Hypothesis 6.6 makes explicit that ineffectiveness is often caused by the inability to make the "right" decision.

Whereas we hypothesized little association between the technological variables and conflict, we believe that scope, uncertainty, and intensity do play important roles in perceptions concerning effectiveness. When technologies are sophisticated and the production process requires diverse and highly skilled workers, then the likelihood of dissatisfaction with outcomes is much greater. The better workers are trained, the higher the standards and, paradoxically, the more fault-finding there is. This means that the use of perceptual measures of effectiveness adds a useful dimension to the subject, especially in the public sector, where resource scarcity is endemic and where professionals' expectations regarding outcomes are rarely realized.

Hypothesis 6.7: The higher the levels of scope, uncertainty, and intensity associated with the task, the larger the gap perceived between actual practice and best possible practice.

The reason for this hypothesized relationship between the technological variables of scope, uncertainty, and intensity, and

This question has to do with the effectiveness of your network system. Seldom are systems as effective as they can be, because of the capabilities of the people that work in them. On the other hand, there are usually forces beyond the control of workers that prevent systems from being as effective as they can be (for example, resource scarcity, inhibiting rules, and the like). This question is constructed to determine the gap between how effective your system is in actual practice, and how effective it could be (the best practice that is potentially possible), given the existence of these restraints.

Please indicate (on the 11-point scale) the extent to which each of the following statements applies to your network system:

	in actual practice	highest level that is potentially possible given existing restraints
System goals are achieved	0 1 2 3 4 5 6 7 8 9 10	0 1 2 3 4 5 6 7 8 9 10
System generates adequate resources	0 1 2 3 4 5 6 7 8 9 10	0 1 2 3 4 5 6 7 8 9 10
System works smoothly	0 1 2 3 4 5 6 7 8 9 10	0 1 2 3 4 5 6 7 8 9 10
System is productive	0 1 2 3 4 5 6 7 8 9 10	0 1 2 3 4 5 6 7 8 9 10
System is effective	0 1 2 3 4 5 6 7 8 9 10	0 1 2 3 4 5 6 7 8 9 10
Overall, I am satisfied with the performance of this system.	0 1 2 3 4 5 6 7 8 9 10	0 1 2 3 4 5 6 7 8 9 10

Figure 6.3 Questionnaire Item Measuring Performance Gap in Interorganizational Networks

performance gap is not necessarily the same. Scope most often measures sophisticated technology and the use of highly trained professionals. Intensity, and to a lesser extent uncertainty, is often associated with the involuntary status of some clients, their attitudes, and the necessary use of intense and controlling strategies rather than therapeutic ones. In general, however, high levels of technology mean that tasks are difficult and expectations are higher, and thus goals are less likely to be achievable.

Third is the cluster of structural variables. Again, we speculate that as a system moves toward a bureaucratic structure—becomes larger, more centralized, differentiated, and complex—the greater the chance that workers will perceive the outcomes of their work in negative terms. This is a very old and classic theme in the organizational literature (Blau & Scott, 1962); namely, professional versus bureaucratic control. Again, we are taking this old idea and applying it to new arenas of research and indicating new implications. The large size of networks and our inexperience of managing large size are also important variables. Their complexity is a quantum leap beyond a single organization. These two factors alone make expectations at times unreasonably high. But as we speculated above, connectivity can play a mitigating role. If communication channels are dense and the volume of communication is high, then the barriers that impede effectiveness may be bridged.

Hypothesis 6.8: The higher centrality, size, complexity, and differentiation are in network systems, the larger the gap perceived between actual practice and best possible practice.

Hypothesis 6.9: The higher connectivity is in network systems, the smaller the gap perceived between actual practice and best possible practice.

Last are the methods of coordination—administrative decision making and task integration. Here, as with conflict, we believe there is a negative relationship. Especially if effectiveness is operationalized as smooth operations, then it is logical to assume that the methods and amount of coordination employed will have a major impact on increasing or decreasing that perception. This is a major assumption of the IO and management literature: Not only will coordination reduce conflict but it will also improve effectiveness.

Hypothesis 6.10: The more coordination of administrative decision making and task integration, the smaller the gap between actual practice and best possible practice.

FULTON AND FARNAM COUNTIES: EMPIRICAL RESULTS CONCERNING CONFLICT AND PERFORMANCE GAP

As with other aspects of networks that we studied in Fulton and Farnam counties, we were surprised at the variation in levels of conflict and performance gap that we found. We interviewed workers in one network and found almost a team spirit, people who were focused on clients and on how they could collectively improve client outcomes. We interviewed in another network where workers accused one another of poor practice and where police officers were having social workers arrested for dereliction of duty. We had, of course, expected to encounter conflict and poor perceptions of performance because the resource dependency perspective holds that resource scarcity will engender discord and contest, and this data collection was done in 1985, after cutbacks in social programs were well under way. We had not expected to find as much variation in conflict and performance gap as we did, however, and it allowed us to test our theoretical statements.

Conflict

The raw scores for size and amount of conflict in each network are shown in Table 6.2. As can be seen, the amount of conflict varies significantly in these 15 systems. On this 10-point scale, the least conflicted system we studied was the special needs adoption network in Fulton County and the most conflicted were the chronic mentally ill system in Farnam County and both of the child protection systems. We include the size of these networks only to refresh readers' memories.

Table 6.3 shows the zero-order correlations between conflict and the 15 factors we discussed in earlier chapters. Overall, it can been seen from the zero-order correlations that conflict is most closely associated with loss of autonomy and the structural characteristics and, contrary to popular wisdom, has surprisingly little to do with either administrative coordination or task integration.

Hypothesis 6.1 predicted positive relationships between conflict and external controls. Table 6.3 shows that this was indeed the case. The correlation coefficients for both autonomy ($r = -.55$; $p < .05$) and involuntary status ($r = .57$; $p < .05$) are statistically significant, and vertical dependency is close. As we have suggested at other points in our analysis, these three environmental variables are highly intercorrelated. When networks are highly

Table 6.2 Raw Scores for Amount of Conflict in 15 Interorganizational
Networks

System Network and Location	Size of Network	Conflict (Scale of 1 to 10)
1. Special Needs Adoption (Fulton)	5	2
2. Special Needs Adoption (Farnam)	6	4
3. Hospice Care (Farnam)	6	7
4. Hospice Care (Fulton)	7	3
5. Maternal Health Care (Farnam)	9	4
6. Rape/Domestic Violence (Fulton)	9	8
7. Rape/Domestic Violence (Farnam)	9	5
8. Chronic Mentally Ill Support (Farnam)	10	10
9. Maternal Health Care (Fulton)	11	6
10. Juvenile Justice (Fulton)	11	8
11. Frail Elderly In-Home Care (Farnam)	12	9
12. Juvenile Justice (Farnam)	13	6
13. Frail Elderly In-Home Care (Fulton)	14	6
14. Child Protection Services (Farnam)	15	10
15. Child Protection Services (Fulton)	15	10

dependent for resources on vertical units, clients are often involuntary and networks therefore have little autonomy.

There was no significant association found between the technological variables and conflict, as predicted in Hypothesis 6.2. Task intensity came close ($r = .49$), but in general these findings suggest that technology per se does not breed contentious relationships. Structural variables, however, are a different story.

Hypothesis 6.3 predicted that the first four structural factors are related positively to conflict. The results confirmed this and showed that the most conflicted systems were those that were highly differentiated ($r = .75; p < .01$), complex ($r = .59; p < .05$), and large ($r = .49; p < .06$). Centrality, however, did not appear to be statistically related to conflict, as we had predicted. We expected that there would be a fair amount of conflict in systems where client flow was tightly controlled by a core agency, but our results show there was little conflict in these centralized systems ($r = .13$). Clearly this finding suggests that conflict is generated much more by large unwieldy systems, which, via the process of structural differentiation, exacerbated the problem of different expectations. Further, and contrary to Hypothesis

Table 6.3 Relationship Between Conflict and 15 Antecedent Factors ($N = 15$)

Variables	Coefficient
Environmental Controls	
Vertical Dependency	.46
Autonomy	−.55 *
Involuntary Status	.57 *
Technological Characteristics	
Task Scope	−.11
Task Uncertainty	.08
Task Intensity	.49
Task Duration	.27
Task Volume	.27
Structural Characteristics	
Centrality	.13
Size	.49
Complexity	.59 *
Differentiation	.75 **
Connectivity	−.25
Administrative Decision Making	−.06
Impersonal Methods	−.15
Personal Methods	−.19
Group Methods	.13
Task Integration	.10
Sequential Pattern	−.30
Reciprocal Pattern	.29
Team Pattern	−10

*$p < .05$ **$p < .01$

6.4, we were surprised to find no relationship between the level of conflict and connectivity. This finding suggested that the number of communication channels, as a structural variable, did not improve or suppress the level of mutual understanding and agreement among organizations.

Hypothesis 6.5 speculated that coordination and task integration both have the effect of reducing conflict. We were surprised, again, to find that for the most part we were wrong. The summative index for the amount of administrative coordination did not correlate with conflict ($r = -.06$), nor did the summative score for task integration ($r = .10$). Contrary to popular opinion, the level of conflict in these networks did not appear to be affected by the amount of coordination or task integration. What, then, were the most influential determinants of conflict? To answer this question we selected the statistically significant and near-significant variables from Table 6.3 and regressed all possible pairs on conflict. The resulting 21 models are shown in Table 6.4. From this table it is clear that the two factors that accounted most strongly for conflict are autonomy and differentiation. Model 11, combining (loss of) autonomy and differentiation, accounted for almost two-thirds of the available variance (Adj. $R^2 = .64; F = 13.28; p < .00$). We interpret this result in this way: When administrators and workers feel their work is not under their control and others make the decisions that count, especially when they work in systems with high divisions of labor, then conflict, disagreement, and disharmony will reign. This is a significant finding, in spite of its exploratory nature and the probability that the value of the R^2 is inflated because of the small sample size.

There are a number of interesting insights that emerge from the analysis in Table 6.3. Vertical dependency, as we suggested above, does not necessarily mean loss of autonomy. When it does, then and only then is conflict generated within the network. It is not large size in systemic networks that generates conflict but rather how networks are structured. If structural differentiation is necessary, then these functional barriers prevent disagreements from being satisfactorily resolved. Further, the combination of external control and functional differentiation produces the most conflict. In other words, while conflict is existential, it is the presence of problem-solving constraints that prevent it from being resolved.

If this is the case and further research confirms that these are the two characteristics that produce the most difficult interorganizational environments, then what can managers do? One response, of course, is to increase the amount of coordination as a way of reducing the level of conflict. Certainly this is what the organizational literature would suggest (Lawrence & Lorsch, 1967; Walton & Dutton, 1969). Looking back at Table

Table 6.4 Standardized βs for Environmental, Technological, and Structural Variables Regressed on Conflict ($N = 15$)

Model	1	2	3	4	5	6	7	8	9	10	11	12	13	14	15	16	17	18	19	20	21
Vertical																					
Dependency	-.01	.19	.27	.26	.25	.15															
Autonomy	-.77																					
Involuntary							-.84	-.83	-.90	-.95	-.50										
Status							-.11					.43	.45	.40	.26	.34	.28	.23	.09	-.04	
Intensity		.46						-.10				.26				.30					
Size			.34						-.20				.22				.35				
Complexity				.29						-.24				.27					.44		.00
Differentiation					.38	.66					.43				.60			.64		.76	.72
$R^2 =$	.50	.24	.17	.13	.19	.48	.51	.51	.52	.53	.64	.27	.26	.26	.52	.20	.20	.51	.15	.46	.46
$F =$	8.06	3.18	2.46	2.07	2.67	7.39	8.19	8.21	8.67	8.77	13.28	3.58	3.43	3.48	8.43	2.69	2.79	8.15	2.21	6.89	6.86
$p <$	.01	.08	.12	.16	.11	.01	.01	.01	.00	.00	.00	.06	.07	.06	.01	.11	.11	.01	.15	.01	.01

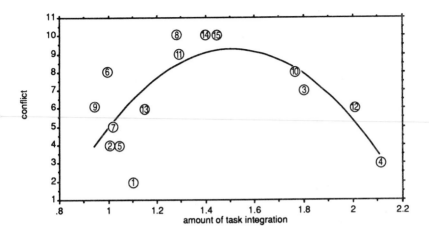

Figure 6.4 Scattergram of Conflict Regressed on Task Integration. The regression equation was computed with the polynomial term Y *(conflict)* $= -28.73 + 50.187x$ *(task intergration)* $- 16.544x^2$. The date points on the scattergram represent the numbers given to the interorganizational service delivery system in Table 6.2.

6.3, however, shows us that coordination and integration did not affect the level of conflict. Because this was an unexpected result, we examined the data to determine the appropriateness of the linear model. Using a curvilinear equation showed that administrative coordination still had little effect on conflict, but the variance for task integration on conflict was improved significantly. This regression equation produced an Adj. $R^2 =$ .55 with $F = 7.32$ and $p < .008$. The plot using this equation is shown in Figure 6.4.

Figure 6.4 shows this nonlinear convex relationship between conflict and task integration. There appeared to be little conflict when the levels of task integration were either low or high, but much conflict with moderate task integration, suggesting the following analysis. It can be argued that there were two groups of networks among the 15 in this study. The first group was made up of the 11 systems shown in the left-hand column below Figure 6.4—Special Needs Adoption (1. and 2.), Maternal Health (7. and

9.), Rape/Domestic Violence (5. and 6.), Chronic Mentally Ill (8.), Frail Elderly (11. and 13.), and Child Protection (14. and 15.). For them it can be said that conflict and task integration were positively related: As the level of conflict increases across these 11 systems, the amount of task integration also increases.

The second group was made up of the 4 systems shown in the right-hand column below Figure 6.4—the Hospice systems (3. and 4.) and the Juvenile Justice systems (10. and 12.). These 4 had very high task integration scores but low to moderate conflict scores. For these systems, task integration and conflict were negatively related. In fact, it appeared that the large amount of coordination occurring among workers in these systems did indeed serve to suppress the level of conflict. In the Juvenile Justice systems, for example, the court in Fulton County required that there be interagency case staffings whenever a youth was released from detention or residential treatment, and mandated that periodic reviews be held between probation workers and private agency staffs until such time as the child was no longer under Court jurisdiction. In the Hospice systems each patient had an interagency treatment team that met weekly for consultation and case planning. Both of these types of systems—one a state system with involuntary clients and the other a community-based system with private patients—were the most highly centralized systems in the study. All juvenile offenders were "taken in" through the Court, and all terminally ill patients were first referred from, and then often returned to, the hospital.

There were four systems where there appeared to be a great deal of conflict accompanying a moderate amount of task integration. Two of these systems, Chronic Mentally Ill (8.) and Frail Elderly (11.) were young, newly forming systems that did not as yet have a dominant core agency to play the coordinative role. It can be argued, however, that the other two, Child Protection systems (14. and 15.), *should have been* in the second group. These systems were high in centrality and their services were very broad in scope, which should have meant that they had an adequate amount of task integration. Qualitative data collected during the study, however, revealed that the Child Protection systems did not have the resources available for adequate coordination and task integration—they had extremely large caseloads and inadequate state funding. Here is evidence that adequate funding for coordination in these systems could have had significant benefits for the systems as well as their clients

It is possible that conflict is highest at the moderate level of task integration because the systemic network has moved from sequential, where conflict has less chance of surfacing, to reciprocal, where there is more personal contact between workers and therefore more opportunity for differences in expectations to become visible. A little bit of communication can be worse than none at all. The presence of conflict in the newer systems suggests this possibility because there has not been enough time to construct the appropriate coordination and integration mechanisms.

The generalization that can be drawn from this analysis is as follows. Conflict is a characteristic of all interorganizational service delivery systems and should be thought of as a collective variable. There tend to be high levels of conflict in systems that are very dependent with little local autonomy, and are highly differentiated in terms of function. Conflict exists simultaneously with coordination and task integration and is generally related positively to them, especially in newly developing systems. There is a threshold, however, beyond which a negative relationship exists, where higher levels of task coordination among professional staff will reduce the level of conflict.

There is a sense, then, in which the managerial wisdom about conflict is correct. In very complex systems, one needs intense coordination mechanisms, namely team integration. Inadequate resources or experience can prevent this from occurring. In their studies of differentiation, Lawrence and Lorsch (1967) did not analyze why it is that, as their structural differentiation increases, organizations fail to increase their level of integration. In our data there are some possible answers.

Applying this analysis to the management of networks requires us to ask how easy is it for managers to change either the lack of autonomy or the structural differentiation in their networks. Through collective action, administrators of the organizations within a network can attempt to influence those officials who set the policy and rules that govern the network, in order to gain greater local autonomy and reduce the level of differentiation. In cases where there must be functional differentiation, then administrators should seek enough resources to provide very high levels of coordination and integration through frequent cross-organizational in-service training, interorganizational planning groups, and teams.

Interorganizational Effectiveness and Performance Gap

The raw scores for performance gap in each network are shown in Table 6.5. Here, too, there is a fair amount of variation but not as much as with the scores for conflict.

The network with workers who perceived their system as having the smallest performance gap was the Special Needs Adoption network in Fulton County. Those with the highest performance gap scores were the Chronic Mentally Ill system, the Juvenile Justice systems, and the Child Protection systems. The correlation coefficients for the antecedent variables with performance gap are shown in Table 6.6.

Consistent with Hypothesis 6.6, the environmental variables were all significantly related to perceptions of performance gap. Most remarkable were the correlations for performance gap with vertical dependency ($r = .75$; $p < .01$) and autonomy ($r = -.62$; $p < .01$), which provide more support for resource dependency theory. When local networks were controlled to a large extent by hierarchical forces, there was likely to be a high level of dissatisfaction with performance among workers and administrators. These coefficients as shown in Table 6.6 were higher than the coefficients for conflict.

Hypothesis 6.7 speculated that scope, uncertainty, and intensity would all be positively related to performance gap. Intensity ($r = .76$; $p < .01$) was the only significant association we found. There are a number of explanations for this finding. It may be that whenever workers devote large amounts of time and effort to single clients or production units, they are more invested in the outcomes and their expectations concerning quality will be higher. When their expectations are not realized they blame "the system." Another possible interpretation is that clients or production units that require large amounts of time are those where the technologies are not necessarily ade-

Table 6.5 Raw Scores for Amount of Performance Gap in 15 Interorganizational Networks

System Network and Location	Size of Network	Performance Gap (Scale of 1 to 10)
1. Special Needs Adoption (Fulton)	5	2.75
2. Special Needs Adoption (Farnam)	6	5.63
3. Hospice Care (Farnam)	6	6.40
4. Hospice Care (Fulton)	7	5.47
5. Maternal Health Care (Fulton)	9	4.49
6. Rape/Domestic Violence (Fulton)	9	4.38
7. Rape/Domestic Violence (Farnam)	9	4.10
8. Chronic Mentally Ill Support (Farnam)	10	7.19
9. Maternal Health Care (Fulton)	11	5.91
10. Juvenile Justice (Fulton)	11	8.76
11. Frail Elderly In-Home Care (Farnam)	12	5.78
12. Juvenile Justice (Farnam)	13	5.95
13. Frail Elderly In-Home Care (Fulton)	14	5.50
14. Child Protection Services (Farnam)	15	7.29
15. Child Protection Services (Fulton)	15	5.29

quate to the task. The systems in our study that scored highest on performance gap—Juvenile Justice, Child Protection Services, and Chronic Mentally Ill—serve populations that are very resistant to treatment, have caseloads that are very high, and must work with methods that have outcomes that are usually not known for a long time. We were surprised at the relatively high scores for the Hospice Care and Frail Elderly systems. These, too, may be high because the services are relatively new and have yet to develop workable technologies.

The relationships between performance gap and the structural characteristics were very similar to those for conflict, but stronger. An increase in perceptions of performance gap appeared to be related to an increase in all of the structural variables but one: centrality ($r = 59$; $p < .05$), size ($r = .48$; $p < .06$), complexity ($r = .57$; $p < .05$), differentiation ($r = .44$; $p < .06$), with connectivity ($r = -.64$; $p < .01$) as the major exception. These findings confirmed both Hypotheses 6.8 and 6.9. Connectivity—the number of communication channels—was negatively and strongly related to performance gap, providing some evidence that when communication channels are few and workers do not have

Table 6.6 Relationship Between Performance Gap and 15 Antecedent
Factors

Variables	Coefficient
Environmental Controls	
Vertical Dependency	.75 **
Autonomy	−.62 *
Involuntary Status	.55 *
Technological Characteristics	
Task Scope	.23
Task Uncertainty	.04
Task Intensity	.76 **
Task Duration	.20
Task Volume	.01
Structural Characteristics	
Centrality	.59 *
Size	.48
Complexity	.57 *
Differentiation	.44
Connectivity	−.64 **
Administrative Decision Making	.11
Impersonal Methods	.00
Personal Methods	−.37
Group Methods	.25
Task Integration	.54*
Sequential Pattern	−.69 **
Reciprocal Pattern	.36
Team Pattern	.54 *

$*p < .05$ $**p < .01$

access to adequate interagency dialogue and information, they
will have negative assessments of the performance of the system. Large and complex systems are difficult to make effective.

Last, the summative score for administrative coordination did
not correlate with conflict ($r = .11$), contrary to what we predicted
in Hypothesis 6.10. Task integration, however, did appear to be
weakly related to performance gap ($r = .54$; $p < .05$). Of the
coordination methods measured separately, only sequential task

integration($r = -.69; p < .01$) and teaming ($r = .54; p < .05$) were significant.

Table 6.7 regressed all possible pairs of the independent variables (with sufficiently high correlation coefficients) on performance gap. Across all 21 models, the variables that were most predictive of performance gap were vertical dependency and intensity. Vertical dependency combined with intensity to account for more than two-thirds of available variance (Adj. R^2 = .67; F = 16.28; $p < .000$), and when combined with autonomy it accounted for almost as much variance (Adj. R^2 = .61; F = 11.71; $p < .00$).

Although performance gap and conflict are related ($r = .51; p < .05$), comparison of Table 6.7 with Table 6.4 shows that there are some subtle differences. Whereas conflict was generated more by a lack of autonomy, it appeared that vertical dependency was more responsible for perceptions of performance gap. It was, however, not only the lack of autonomy that reduced effectiveness, but also the need to rely on external funding sources. This is suggested by the first column in Table 6.7, where both vertical dependency and autonomy have bs that are statistically significant. Another obvious difference is that structural differentiation had a strong influence on conflict but none on performance gap. Rather, it appeared that task intensity had a more significant influence on performance than did differentiation.

Even though no linear relationship existed between performance gap and coordination and task integration, we wanted to determine if there wasn't a curvilinear association. The results are shown in Figure 6.5. There was indeed a relationship when a polynomial was inserted into the regression equation and the variance accounted for was high (Adj. R^2 = .59; F = 8.67; $p < .01$).

The plot in Figure 6.5 is very similar to the plot for conflict in Figure 6.4, leading us to the conclusion that, although the causative factors may be somewhat different, performance gap and conflict are both measures of network ineffectiveness and, in their extreme, of network failure. The generalization that can be drawn from these data is that there is a gap between actual performance and best possible performance in all systems, but it may be larger than the norm when environmental controls are tight, the network's structure is bureaucratic (centralized,

Table 6.7 Standardized βs for Environmental, Technological, and Structural Variables Regressed on Performance Gap ($N = 15$)

Model	1	2	3	4	5	6	7	8	9	10	11	12	13	14	15	16	17	18	19	20	21
Vertical																					
Dependency	.50	.66	.47	.62	.63	.57															
Autonomy	-.41																				
Involuntary							-.76	-.35	-.57	-.72	-.54										
Status	.16						-.06					.20	.40	.32	.27	.63	.66	.59			
Intensity			.50					.52				.66							.43	.30	
Centrality				.23					.36				.45	.37		.27	.17		.41		
Complexity					.21					-.00											.22
Connectivity						-.32					-.24				-.48	.58	.53	-.28	.40	-.44	-.47
R² =	.61	.51	.67	.53	.52	.57	.43	.53	.56	.43	.46	.55	.40	.28	.36	.58	.53	.57	.40	.36	.33
F =	11.72	8.16	16.28	8.81	8.61	10.24	6.26	10.70	9.87	6.22	6.93	9.42	5.63	3.76	4.97	10.46	8.98	10.78	5.63	5.01	4.51
p<	.00	.01	.00	.00	.00	.00	.01	.00	.00	.01	.01	.00	.02	.05	.03	.00	.00	.00	.02	.03	.03

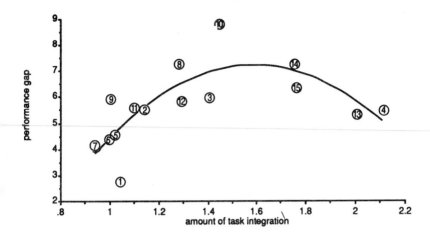

Figure 6.5 Scattergram of Performance Gap Regressed on Task Integration. The regression equation was computed wth the polynomial term Y *(performance gap)* $= -13.167 + 25.647x$ *(task intergration)* $- 8.058x^2$. The data points on the scattergram represent the numbers given to the interorganizational service delivery systems in Table 6.5.

large, complex, and differentiated), and it utilizes task-intensive technologies. If, however, the network is highly connected by communication channels among a large proportion of the organizations, and if there is a sufficient amount of coordination and integration used throughout the system, then it appears from our data that those working within the system may perceive the level of performance gap to be relatively small.

Constructing explanatory or predictive models of interorganizational behavior using data from cross-sectional exploratory studies is difficult in any case, and especially so when the unit of analysis is the system, and the sample size is small. The results of this study should be considered exploratory because it has not been possible to use normal regression techniques to test its multivariate model. Nevertheless, there are ideas here that are worth future attention and study. If the results of this study turn out to be valid, then there are a number of important conclusions here for community planners and decision makers in various service and manufacturing sectors.

Conflict and poor perceptions of performance undoubtedly are unavoidable processes in all interorganizational service delivery systems. They are a necessary component of the developmental process, whereby information is shared between organizations, roles and functions are clarified, and disagreement over objectives and methods is mediated. We found, however, systems that were experiencing extraordinarily high levels of these negative factors because of the way they were structured and operated.

If this is the case, then administrators and planners should be aware of these possibilities and be prepared to prevent systemic dysfunction. This is the case in many child protection and juvenile justice systems today. The results of this study showed that prevention of excessive conflict is possible by using integrative mechanisms, but the most lasting remedies would be the granting of more autonomy to networks and the reduction of structural differentiation. These would reduce the barriers to conflict resolution, allowing for coordinative methods to have more of an impact.

In his qualitative study of prison/probation systems during the 1970s, Mathiesen (1971) showed that networks in which administrators and workers must coordinate their tasks are very different, and that it is between workers that interorganizational relationships have the most profound consequences for system operation and for service outcomes. This is not to say that coordination across organizational boundaries between policymakers and managers is unimportant, but it does say that integration at the client level is at least equally important, an insight that has not often been used in interorganizational research. Neither is it a concept that is acted upon by federal and state agencies responsible for categorical programs delivered at the community level. Their approach most often is that formalized contracts and protocols, agreed to by the organizations in a system, will serve to establish and maintain working relationships. Seldom are there incentives and/or resources available to workers to develop task coordination. This study showed that interagency diagnostic teams, case conferences, joint intervention and monitoring units were methods that were effective in preventing dysfunctional conflict.

In addition to making sure that workers have ample opportunity for integrating their work, system managers should understand that the amount of coordination must match the structural requirements of the system. The more differentiated and complex a system becomes, the more there is a need for cooperative working arrangements. Another means of controlling conflict, then, is to prevent the system from becoming unnecessarily differentiated and complex. This is a conundrum, of course, for systems that must serve clients with multiple problems, and for development/manufacturing systems that require high-tech and differentiated processes. To whatever extent possible, however, operating rules should not replace personal contact between administrators and workers.

The inclusion of many different kinds of units within a system should be recognized as a complexification process for which conflict is the price (Hage & Powers, 1992). This is not to say that functional specialization and complexity are bad; there are systems, such as child protection, where the delivery of effective services requires these structural properties. It does suggest, however, that the principle of simultaneous tight and loose linkages also applies to interorganizational systems (Peters & Waterman, 1982). Those who control state and federally funded service delivery should analyze policy and operational decisions that affect community level systems, and separate what has to be decided vertically from what should be within the domain of local administrators and workers.

The problem of performance gap is somewhat more complex. It is not just an issue of constraints on autonomy, but also the fact that multiple external sources of funding appear to reduce network effectiveness. Here is an area where more research is needed. Resource dependency theory has been concerned primarily with the power of organizations. We have suggested a wider range of issues in our study and have indicated how they can prevent systemic networks from becoming effective. The relationship between task intensity and performance also needs much more detailed research.

CHILD PROTECTIVE SYSTEMS
IN FULTON AND FARNAM COUNTIES

For most of U.S. history, children were legally the possession of their parents to do with as they wished. Child public dependency could occur only if a child was orphaned. In 1968, however, Drs. R. Helfer and C. Kemp wrote *The Battered Child*, and in its aftermath a national consensus developed that extended dependency to other classes of children, namely, the physically abused and neglected and the sexually abused. Fifty states passed child abuse and neglect laws in the early 1970s that codified the states' responsibility for children of parents unable to provide appropriate care and nurturing.

State Child Abuse and Neglect Laws

Laws that were passed in the 50 states had to conform to model legislation developed by Congress in the early 1970s if the states were to be eligible for Child Abuse and Neglect (CAN) program funds. When the state codes were implemented, they created interorganizational systems to protect children in every U.S. community. At the entrance to the system were "mandatory reporters"—child care workers, teachers, physicians, social workers, nurses—who were required to report to the state's family services agency if they suspected a child was being abused or neglected. The state Department of Human Services was then required to investigate within a specified time period (immediately if imminent danger, or within a day if not) and file an assessment with the juvenile court, stating whether the allegations contained in the report were founded or unfounded. If founded, the case would then come under the jurisdiction of the court, and courts had wide latitude regarding disposition. Those cases that were kept in the system because of various actions of the juvenile court were referred to community agencies for concrete and treatment services, sometimes under court order and at other times through voluntary cooperation of the family. The creation of these community-based child protection systems, through the passage of state laws, brought many changes to local child welfare programs, one of the most important of which was that many community organizations were forced to work together for the first time.

The major effect of the laws on social service delivery was that the child became the focus of service rather than the family, and the identified population of children entitled to services increased exponentially. In 1972, the year Fulton County's abuse law was enacted, the Department of Human Services (DHS) received 39 referrals of children in need of protection; 9 years later referrals were running 2,000 per year, and foster care placements were 250 per year.

This is a very young client population. In general, about 50% of referrals are under age 5, about 25% are 5 to 10, and 25% are 10 to 18. Boys and girls are about equally represented, but boys predominate at the younger ages and girls at older ages. About 40% of these children in Fulton and Farnam counties are minorities, even though minorities are only 10% of the general population. And although data are not available, workers say that virtually all these children are from low-income homes. Because these children are viewed by the public as being highly vulnerable and because the law spells out in great detail a mandated model of how the system must operate, child protective systems have had much public scrutiny since their inception. Errors in these systems become public knowledge through florid newspaper accounts, whereas effective outcomes are hidden from public view because of client confidentiality.

Functional Differentiation and Service Complexity

Prior to the passage of the child protective laws, there were child welfare and family services in most counties across the United States. Dating from New Deal Legislation and funded by county and voluntary dollars, public social service agencies provided income assistance and family services to those who, for a wide variety of reasons, were not self-sufficient. The staff in these agencies were usually generalists, caseworkers who provided whatever services the agency had available and who worked with all members of the family.

At the time that the child protective laws were passed, there were decisions being made in the political arena that would limit the size of the public sector in the future. In order to implement the law and yet manage with the restraints placed on growth of their staff size, the state agencies had to bring private nonprofit agencies into the service delivery system through contracting mechanisms, such as purchase of service agreements. This process greatly increased the level of functional differentiation and service complexity within the system. The development of foster care services in Fulton County illustrates this process. The first major change occurred when DHS reorganized to include a specialized foster care unit. This change led to others:

- As reports increased, the need for foster homes increased. Because the state agency's (DHS) staff size was being frozen, they could not provide enough foster care directly as they always had done. DHS began to purchase foster care from private agencies. Contracts were developed with three private family service agencies to recruit and license foster homes and provide casework services to children in foster care.

- A year after the contracts were in place, it became evident that the need for foster homes was outstripping the three agencies' recruitment capacity. In order to mount a effective recruitment campaign, DHS and the private agencies together implemented a joint publicity campaign. As potential foster parents responded to this very visible publicity, they were assigned to one of the private agencies on a rotating basis for investigation and licensing.

- After this rotating system had been operating for a year or two, it became evident that the process of placing children in these homes could be improved. As a result of a study of the system, every home recruited and licensed by a private agency was put into a "common pool" administered by DHS. This procedure had two major advantages over the former one. First, the number of multiple placements experienced by children was greatly reduced because they were not moved from home to home as the payee changed. Second, the number of successful placements increased because matching improved—all children had access to all foster homes under the new system.

Another change that simultaneously increased differentiation and coordination occurred in 1978. To improve the outcomes of foster care and prevent long-term placements, the state offered counties grant funds to finance innovative in-home counseling services. Fulton County applied and was awarded a large demonstration grant. After several months of internal discussion, the following plan to utilize these funds was adopted:

- DHS would specialize in the three functions mandated by the law and needed by the system: intake, assessment, and monitoring. Because DHS recognized that it could not provide the volume of treatment service needed, it chose to specialize in these functions and tasks at the front end of the system.
- The treatment function would then be delegated to private community agencies. Four "alternatives" to foster care contracts were developed; three for in-home counseling and one for homemaker services. One year later a contract for specialized day care was added.

Informants now say that things were "tough" at DHS during this period. The decision to go outside the department for foster care and treatment services was hard for many of the department's social workers to accept. To give up their clients to other workers and to share their domain with other agencies was not a welcome prospect. Department workers feared they would end up doing "second-class" work and that, in fact, the number of department jobs would decline. Informants attribute the final acceptance of the plan to one major factor, namely, the success of the foster care program. Department workers could see that their intake role was important to the success of the foster care program, and that in-home treatment was badly needed—an expansion without which the immediate successes of the foster care program would be lost.

Vertical Dependency and Scarce Resources

These community-based child protective systems were mandated by federal and state legislation. By definition, they are vertically constructed and dependent systems. By definition, their ability to respond to local conditions, to be effective, and to provide quality service for children is determined by hierarchical forces.

During the 1970s, after the publication of *The Battered Child* (Helfer & Kemp, 1968), public interest in the problem of child maltreatment continued to increase. The print media, but also television news and feature programs such as *60 Minutes*, devoted considerable attention to appalling stories of children mutilated, abducted, and killed. There developed among the public-at-large a "child saving" attitude that demanded immediate help for children who were at risk. There did not develop, however, the political will to demand and pay for public child protection services. But because of this public attention, there has been a continuous increase in reports, without a concomitant growth in staff and services needed for children and families once they are in the system. By the mid-1980s Fulton County DHS was responding to 2,500 reports annually, of which approximately 800 were remaining in the system because the allegations were substantiated. Several services that were added to the system in the late 1970s and funded from many different vertical sources were cut during the 1980s, services such as the Parent Help Line, educational groups for parents, Volunteer Parent Aides, and Support for New Parents. Furthermore, specialized treatment services were funded at totally inadequate levels. One example is sexual abuse treatment, added to the system under a demonstration federal grant in 1978. This treatment program did survive the cut-off of federal funds in the 1980s and was funded with state resources, but the current contract purchases services for 35 Fulton families and only 10 Farnam families per year. Since the showing of "Something About Amelia" on CBS in the summer of 1984, the story of a sexually abused girl, both counties have been confirming 10 cases of sexual abuse per month.

Because of the public attention to this social problem, there is also much scrutiny of the public bureaucracy's management of the front end of the system, but virtually none of the treatment end of the system. Furthermore, because the structure and operating procedure of the system are mandated by law, DHS is unable to respond in a flexible way to children in need. Combining these elements—vertical dependency, total lack of autonomy, inadequate level of funding, and inability to meet the public's expectations—means that these are very fragile systems. It should be no surprise that they are very difficult to work in, that staff turnover often approaches 50% per year, and that these workers are the most dissatisfied we encountered.

Today's Child Protective System
in Fulton and Farnam Counties

As stated above, the systems in the two counties are remarkably alike. While a few details differ, Figure 6.6 summarizes their structural and functional features. The core organization is the local office of the State Department of Human Services (DHS), which is required to investigate all reports of child abuse or neglect. As can be summarized from this graphic, specialization is high within DHS and among the many organizational members of this system.

The intake units of DHS receive reports 24 hours a day from the many mandatory reporters named in the law—doctors, police, schools, and other social and educational organizations. The DHS intake unit receives these reports and responds to "priority one" reports within one hour and others within one day, and has 10 days to collect enough information to make the initial decision. About 35% of all reports are founded and referred to the judicial system; immediate custody and placement in shelters or foster care occurs in about 10% of all reports.

When the DHS intake unit substantiates a report and refers the case to court, it then flows to the DHS assessment unit, which opens a case and provides brief service. Cases that must remain open longer than 45 days (between 5% and 12% of total reports) are transferred to the ongoing family counseling and case management units. At this point referrals are made to the network of private treatment programs shown in Figure 6.6. Cases that reach the case management unit are open from 6 months to one year, and "revolving door" families are not uncommon.

These systems are characterized by the very large number of DHS linkages that were formalized by purchase of service agreements, interagency agreements and protocols, and, of course, the laws that specify how the intake and assessment functions shall operate. We were not surprised when workers indicated that impersonal coordination and sequential task integration methods predominated throughout the system, although reciprocal contacts between caseworkers were also very important.

We found in these systems extraordinary examples of interagency linkages forged between organizations in order to create

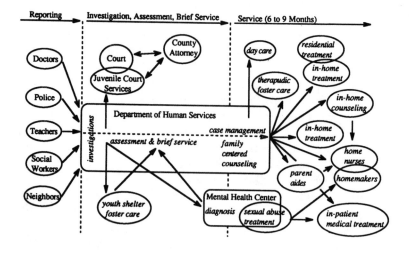

Figure 6.6 Child Protection System in Fulton and Farham Counties

needed services or to improve existing care. The integrated foster care program described above was one. In Farnam there were three outstanding conjoint programs: a day treatment program that was a joint effort of the public special education district and a private family service organization; a job program that was staffed by the state employment security agency and housed in the DHS offices; and a private community-based coordination council that provided multidisciplinary diagnosis and case management to any organization that requested it. All of these programs were locally initiated attempts to close service gaps and/or improve accessibility by co-location and by pooling resources.

We found the structure of the systems in Fulton and Farnam to be almost identical. We had thought they would be highly centralized, but were surprised to find they were not. Because of their large size and because of the large volume of activity that occurs among the peripheral organizations in these large systems, they were considerably less centralized than were other systems in our study.

The service paradigms in the child protective systems were also remarkably alike: The scores on task uncertainty were the highest in the study, and the only task scope indexes that were higher were in the hospice systems. And finally, as discussed above, conflict was higher in these two systems than in any other system and the perceptions of performance among their workers were among the worst.

If these systemic networks are staffed by people who operate within a comprehensive framework, who obviously care about their clients, and who have built and maintained relatively well-coordinated working relationships, why is there so much conflict and performance gap? This is a complex question and, as we demonstrated with the empirical data above, not one we can answer definitively at this time. We are convinced by our qualitative experience, however, that the answer lies in the facts of vertical dependency with little autonomy, combined with large amount of public scrutiny and the potentially serious outcomes resulting from errors in judgment.

Last and most important, however, the cause of conflict and performance gap lies with the differences between the individuals and organizations that must work together in these systems. We found the beliefs, values, and methods of the police, social workers, and psychiatrists to be extremely diverse. On every measure that we took from individuals (92 respondents in these two systems), when we grouped the scores by type of organization or by function, the group means were statistically different and the between variance was greater than the within variance. On the technological variables in particular, the average scores for workers in mental health and social service agencies were all significantly higher than those for workers in medical, educational, and law enforcement organizations. This did not mean that one set of professionals was better trained than the other. It meant, specifically, that the psychologists and social workers perceived clients differently, more broadly, than did the nurses, teachers, and police we interviewed.

The verbal battles in these systems were often fought between organizations at opposite ends of the system. Mandatory reporters, such as teachers and doctors, had unrealistic expectations of the system's capacity to rescue children, and they quarreled often with workers at DHS and the service organizations about methods and outcomes. Mandatory reporters expected the system to intervene immediately and to take children out of their homes at a far greater rate than workers at DHS were either willing or able to. Arguments and bitter relationships developed between workers in service organizations who had to work together with the same families, and families often exploited and fueled these conflicts. If public expectations had been lower, if caseloads had been smaller and operating rules more flexible, if administrators and workers had had more time to work out differences, then we believe that the conflict in these systems would have been lower and their performance much better.

SEVEN

The Failure of Evolution

We have tried to establish that there are different types of inter-organizational collaboration; we described 12 kinds in Chapter Two. Our objective in this chapter is to summarize the empirical results of the past three chapters, which give details of these differences, into a parsimonious typology of systemic networks. And while our typology is based on an analysis of delivery systems in the public sector, we believe it has application to the private sector as well.

The hypotheses of our theory are normative statements about how different types of systemic networks should be organized. For example, we have hypothesized that products and services which must utilize sophisticated technology in the production process should use group coordination and team task integration as coordination mechanisms. But what if high-tech networks do not use adequate amounts of coordination (like a number of the systems that we studied)? Should the theory be changed, or does this represent the wrong choice that administrators have made during the evolutionary development of the network? How do we decide whether we are looking at bad theory or failed evolution? We believe that by using conflict and performance gap as criteria, we can make this distinction. Where conflict and performance gap are unusually high, then we argue that the theory is correct and the choice of coordination and/or integration methods has been wrong.

The thrust of this analysis is critical because researchers in the social sciences seldom confront their ideas in this way. As a consequence, it is often difficult to draw practical implications from research. Many are afraid of delineating normative theory, which is understandable; however, as a result, sociological theory becomes reduced to describing what is, rather than what should be. If the exceptions to our theory are associated with some undesirable outcome, in this instance conflict and/or ineffectiveness, then these exceptions prove the general rule, and we know that the deviations must carry considerable cost.

Throughout our discussion of systemic networks in Chapter One, we suggested there are strong evolutionary pressures forcing organizations to decouple their departments so that individual units can participate in interorganizational relationships. The source of these pressures is the complex problems facing many organizational leaders today. It may be they have to launch a new product in a different market or culture (solution: joint venture), or design a product for multiple markets with economies of scale (solution: three- or four-way matrix structures), or undertake fundamental research for an entire industry (solution: a promotional network such as the Sematech Chip), or design a service for a target population that has multiple needs (solution: systemic network as a delivery system for both public and private services). Gradually, the departments that have been decoupled begin to engage in patterned referrals or preferential contracts, as we described in Chapter Two. Slowly over time, first as exchange, then as action or promotional networks, and finally as joint ventures and systemic networks, clusters of organizations build working relationships that become more complex and sophisticated. This is an evolutionary process, one that accelerates and decelerates and does not proceed at a steady pace.

In addition to understanding the reason for departures from the normative theory and deciding when the theory can provide practical guidelines for administrators and managers, our analysis in this chapter also speaks to a seldom explored topic in population-ecology, namely, the issue of dead ends in an evolutionary process. Population-ecology theory postulates that efficient forms are selected and other forms disappear. In this chapter we have an opportunity to ask whether certain forms result in extinction over a period of time. In the previous chapter we demonstrated that performance gap was associated with certain types of technology and interorganizational structure. Here we ask whether specific combinations of technology, structural patterns, and coordination methods represent failed evolution—forms that cannot survive because they are ineffective and too filled with conflict. Unfortunately, our data do not allow us to explore whether some ineffectiveness reflects an evolutionary pace that is too rapid. Likewise, it is likely that networks may be trying to solve a problem for which there exists no effective solution at the present time. These caveats must be taken into consideration when evaluating networks.

Similarly, our analysis also relates to another topic in organizational analysis: wrong choice. The choice of operating methods is crucial for system effectiveness, and the best choice at one time may not be the best at other times. Further, there are external pressures that may push network members away from their optimal choices. Given the difficulty of coordinating networks that do not have a central authority, as do organizational hierarchies, this should not be surprising.

In a seminal work on organizational coordination, Lawrence and Lorsch (1967) suggested that a failure in evolution explains why business organizations are not as effective as they could be. Their theory was that as structural differentiation increases, there should be more integration; if systems fail to integrate, then poor performance occurs. We propose to apply this thesis to interorganizational networks. The failure in evolution is a lack of evolutionary development toward more complex forms of coordination. But unlike the work of Lawrence and Lorsch, we attempt to indicate the reasons for failure. We believe one answer lies in resource dependency theory, which provides an explanation of why interorganizational networks are pushed away from their optimal form of collaboration. Our perspective allows population-ecology theory and resource dependency theory to be combined to explain failed evolution and the choice of incorrect forms and methods (for a different synthesis, see Aldrich & Pfeffer, 1976).

A NORMATIVE THEORY OF SYSTEMIC NETWORKS

We need a parsimonious way of categorizing our 15 variables and summarizing our theoretical arguments if we are to extract principles for the design and operation of systemic networks. Two of the most useful variables for this purpose are resource dependency and task scope. These two—one an external control and one a technology variable—were related to the largest number of structural variables in our study and were important in explaining the choice of coordination and integration methods. We believe, however, that with better measures for some of our concepts, we might have obtained more variance. Then, too, our sample is only 15 networks, located in the same two-state metropolitan area. Larger samples will undoubtedly produce more variation. Resource dependency and task scope, however, appear to be the best organizing concepts we have at this time for building a typology.

A Typology of Networks

The cross-classification of resource dependency and task scope generates four cells that summarize the various combinations of the structural variables, the coordination methods, and the outcomes of conflict and performance gap. Together, the typology contains four normative types of networks. It could be made more complex by adding task volume and/or task duration. Interestingly, these task variables involve many of the same assumptions about efficiency as does vertical dependency. Because of our small sample size, however, we cannot increase the number of categories at this stage in the development of the theory. This is an important area for future investigation.

Types of Network Structures. We began Chapter Five by suggesting there is a need to move beyond the concept of centrality in describing networks and network systems. We suggested that other concepts, such as size, structural complexity, structural differentiation, and connectedness, are useful additions to network analysis. To manage this task conceptually, however, we need a means of identifying and clustering structural dimensions. We used vertical dependency and task scope for this purpose and found that among our 15 network systems in Fulton and Farnam counties, there appeared to be four basic types of network structures. The resulting four structural models are described in Figure 7.1. The central assumptions are that as increasing amounts of resources outside the network have to be relied upon, the task scale of the network becomes larger, and a larger number of organizations become involved. By contrast, as the technology becomes more sophisticated, such as when community networks must service multiple-problem clients, then the structure becomes more complex and differentiated. Together, these two trends provide the two axes of the typology shown in Figure 7.1.

Type 1 describes the simplest pattern of interorganizational network structure. It does not have to rely on vertically channeled resources nor does it use broad task scope. This is a small, long-linked association of organizations or units that is highly decentralized, independent, and unsophisticated. Financial resources are generated locally from various sources, caseloads or production volume are small, and tasks are relatively simple. The large amount of autonomy and small size encourage low centrality. From this form, evolution can occur in two ways. The success of this network may lead to a rapid increase in demand for its products or services that will require infusions of external resources and support. Type 2 is the result of this eventuality.

Type 2 is dependent on outside sources of resources, but does not require broad task scope. It is somewhat centralized and fairly large in size, yet because the level of task scope is low, there is little specialization of function and role and little complexity in terms of service or product. Because of these features, it is easy for network members to remain well connected. The Type 2 pattern is undifferentiated (as compared to Type 4) and, as the graphic shows, there are few specialized work flows or communication channels. One of the more unusual features of these networks is that although they are large and thus receive significant amounts of external funding, there is a moderate amount of connectivity.

Although we do not have the network structure data, we suspect that the extended example of the supply networks in the electronics industry (Sako, in press) reflects this kind of structure. The funds come from the *kieretsu* and thus there is a

	Narrow Task Scope	**Broad Task Scope**
	Type 1	Type 3
Low Vertical Dependency	Low Centrality Small Size Low Complexity Low Differentiation	High Centrality Small Size High Complexity High Differentiation
	Type 2	Type 4
High Vertical Dependency	Moderate Centrality Large Size Low Complexity Low Differentiation	High Centrality Moderate Size High Complexity High Differentiation

Figure 7.1 Typology of External Control and Task Characteristics as Antecedent to Four Basic Forms of Systemic Networks

vertical dependency. However, the task scope of printed circuit boards is relatively simple, compared to other parts needed in consumer electronics. The structure is therefore moderately centralized, low in complexity, and differentiated. Reports indicate considerable emphasis on personal methods of coordination but not much teamwork or joint problem solving. As with reliance upon public funds in the United States, we assume that there is considerable emphasis on quality.

If there is innovation of technology in a Type 1 network, then Type 3 emerges. Type 3, like Type 2, is mixed, having a low level of dependency but utilizing highly sophisticated technologies. These are contradictory influences that have opposing effects. Type 3 is small, but has centralized client flows and is also highly complex and differentiated because of its high-tech nature. The graphics for Type 1 and Type 3 are intended to illustrate the effect of increasing levels of technology—a visual depiction of low complexity and differentiation versus high complexity and differentiation and their associated affect on connectivity. We speculate that as the level of technology increases, there is an increasing need for a core organization to manage the information and work flow that have become much more specialized. In turn, the very high centrality of these networks reduces the connectivity.

Again, in the absence of data, we can only speculate that research consortia might fit this pattern. Although technically not systemic networks, they are promotional networks characterized by high complexity and high differentiation. Indeed, it is these two variables that tend to make them unstable. The funds for these consortia are provided primarily by the participating firms themselves, thus there is low vertical dependency. However, if government funded, then the structure would probably shift to Type 4.

Type 4, by contrast, is large and complex, where units have specialized roles and perform specialized tasks and where, in order to maintain operations and avoid chaos, there is a high level of centrality. Often there will be a highly centralized core ("single point of entry" in service systems), which distributes the work into specialized work flows. Because Type 4 systems are dependent and at the same time utilize sophisticated technologies, there has to be a high level of organization to rationalize the system, assign work in predetermined ways, and provide efficiency of communication.

The best example of this systemic form is the automotive supply network described in Chapter One. The source of funding is the *kieretsu*, thus there is vertical dependency. There are multiple stages, but there is also tight centralization, with all parts flowing into the assembly plant. There is considerable differentiation and the system is quite complex. Team methods are used to solve problems.

These four patterns are ideal types, a way of integrating what we have learned about network structures. They derive from our understanding of how systemic networks are pushed and pulled by environmental forces. When the demand for a service or product increases, this usually necessitates the involvement of additional units or organizations and usually requires external resources—all of which push the network to add members.

When the desire or demand for quality of service or product increases, it usually means there must be a division of labor among members to allow them to develop specialized skills. This specialization, in turn, pushes the network into more centralized configurations that can better manage the resulting fragmentation. The push toward a highly centralized network comes from two directions in the Type 4 network—the network's own desire to produce a high quality and effective outcome, and external funding organization(s) wanting cost or quality control.

Any specific systemic network, of course, may not fit exactly one of these four models, which is the reason why we provided a number of illustrations in preceding chapters. Our normative framework, however, provides a way of organizing knowledge about the structure of networks that, in turn, provides a way of summarizing our understanding of how they operate.

Methods of Coordination and Integration by Network Type. If environmental influences shape structure, then structure influences internal operations and the choice of coordination methods. Figure 7.2 shows the choice of coordination and task integration methods that should result from the relationship between vertical dependency and task scope in the four ideal types of networks. As in the typology above, there are two themes in Figure 7.2. First, we assume that vertical dependency derives from multiple external sources of funding and their concern about management of cost, and perhaps about the quality of outcomes. Second, we assume that more complex problems necessitate a more complex choice of administrative coordination and task integration methods. The integration of a variety of skills and perspectives is presumedly best achieved with group and team methods, because of the need for a considerable amount of feedback and mutual adjustment (Hage, 1980; Lawrence & Lorsch, 1967; March & Simon, 1958; Mintzberg, 1979; Perrow, 1967).

The typology in Figure 7.2 can also be summarized by saying that effective network operations depend on there being a balance between environmental demands (the technology in use and the degree of dependency) and internal coordination. Our theory, described in more detail below, stipulates that as one moves from low vertical dependency and narrow task scope (Type 1) to broad task scope and high vertical depen-

		Narrow Task Scope	Broad Task Scope
		Type 1	Type 3
		Administrative <u>Coordination</u>	Administrative <u>Coordination</u>
	Impersonal	High	Low
Low Vertical	Personal	Moderate	Moderate
Dependency	Group	Low	Moderate
		<u>Task Integration</u>	<u>Task Integration</u>
	Sequential	High	Low
	Reciprocal	Moderate	Moderate
	Team	Low	Moderate
		Type 2	Type 4
		Administrative <u>Coordination</u>	Administrative <u>Coordination</u>
	Impersonal	Moderate	Low
High Vertical	Personal	Moderate	Moderate
Dependency	Group	Low	High
		<u>Task Integration</u>	<u>Task Integration</u>
	Sequential	Moderate	Low
	Reciprocal	Moderate	Moderate
	Team	Low	High

Figure 7.2 Typology of External Control and Task Scope as Determinants of Good Choices Between Methods of Coordination and Task Integration in Four Types of Systemic Networks

dency (Type 4), administrators in systemic networks must shift their coordination methods from an emphasis on impersonal methods to personal methods and then to group methods. We make the same argument at the task integration level: As vertical dependency increases and task scope broadens, workers should change their choice of methods from sequential client handling to reciprocal to team methods.

This theoretical argument about vertical dependency is complicated. Originally we had expected that as vertical dependency increased, there would be less emphasis on personal methods of coordination and more utilization of formal contracts and agreements. We found, however, the opposite to be the case; in certain systems vertical dependency tended to be associated with more coordination and integration. We speculated that this finding was due to the fact that in the nonprofit sector, government agencies are increasingly the source of funding rather than local voluntary organizations, and that they sometimes have sufficient power to mandate, or sufficient funds to purchase, higher levels of coordination to improve the quality of care for their populations of clients (the elderly, the chronic mentally ill, and abused children are three examples). In Figure 7.2 we are assuming that high vertical dependency means multiple state or federal funding sources who have greater concerns about the quality of care, even though our data do not allow us to determine if this is in fact the case. If, by contrast, vertical dependency meant single source funding and concerns about efficiency, the opposite argument about choice of coordination methods would have to be made.

The typology also argues, as we did in Chapter Four, that as tasks become more difficult, administrators and workers must have more knowledge in order to complete their jobs. To be effective, they cannot be directed by rules and plans because preprogramming cannot anticipate all the alternatives that are available, but must rely increasingly on feedback from their colleagues. This feedback is obtained via coordination that takes the form of decision-making groups and teams who focus on tasks and intervention methods.

Given this set of theoretical arguments, the Type 1 and Type 4 models represent the beginning and end points of an evolutionary process of internal network operations. As vertical dependency increases and task scope broadens, there should be corresponding movement toward greater group and team methods of coordination. There are two models that represent mixed types, where there are opposing influences from vertical dependency and technology. In Type 2 we expect to see moderate levels of both impersonal and personal administrative coordination, and sequential and reciprocal integration. In Type 3 we expect to see moderate levels of personal and group administrative coordination, and reciprocal and team integration.

Table 7.1 Principles for Operating Systemic Networks Based on Four
Distinct Structural Types

When dependency is low and scope is narrow . . .	then impersonal coordination and sequential task integration should be high and are quite adequate for the collaborative needs of the system.
When dependency is high but scope is narrow . . .	then equal amounts of impersonal and personal coordination as well as sequential and reciprocal task integration should be used to satisfy the requirements of external controls.
When dependency is low but scope is broad . . .	then personal and group coordination as well as reciprocal and team task integration should be used to accommodate the demands of high technology.
When dependency is high and scope is broad . . .	then group decision making and team task integration must be employed to satisfy requirements imposed by both sophisticated technologies and multiple funding sources.

Using this set of arguments encompassed by our typology, we can derive a set of principles that should help managers make effective choices of coordination and integration methods. Operations internal to the four types of network systems can be summarized by the multivariate hypotheses shown in Table 7.1.

An Evaluation of the Typology

Our position throughout the previous analysis has been that, consistent with open systems theory (Alexander & Randolph, 1985; Hage, 1980; Katz & Kahn, 1966), the environment of a network determines to a large extent its structure and operations. We focused on two environmental themes: the old concept of technology, or task environment, and the more recent concept of resource dependency (Pfeffer & Salancik, 1978). At this point in the analysis we want to know whether our empirical data supports the typology. In addition, we want to know, if we were to add a third dimension what would be. To answer these questions we did a factor analysis. Because our sample is small, the resulting factors must be considered to be purely speculative and exploratory. The results shown in Table 7.2 are orthogonal and use the Varimax Solution.

The analysis in Table 7.2 indicates that although the results are certainly inflated due to small sample size, future research may show there is theoretical justification for the addition of a third dimension to reflect the scale of the operation. In Chapter Four we found that task scale did not always work as expected. We suggested that our measures of scale were not as robust as they should have been and that there was less variation in the duration of client treatment than one would expect. Thus the next logical step for extending the typology in future research is to add task scale, and to find better measures for it.

When we use just vertical dependency and task scope as the organizing variables, the 15 systemic networks are categorized as follows:

Type 1:   2 Networks for Special Needs Adoption
2 Networks for Victims of Rape/Domestic Violence
2 Networks for Maternal-Child Health Care

Type 2:   1 Network for the Chronic Mentally Ill
1 Network for the Frail Elderly
1 Juvenile Justice System

Type 3:   2 Networks Providing Hospice Care

Type 4:   1 Network for the Frail Elderly
1 Juvenile Justice System
2 Child Protection Systems

We come, then, to the reason for the classification: Is there more conflict and performance gap in one or some of these types of networks than in others? This question was answered by looking at the levels of conflict and performance gap for each type of network in our typology. This we do in Table 7.3.

As can be seen in Table 7.3, the mean conflict score was high in Type 2 networks and higher still in Type 4. Based on the

Table 7.2 Factor Loading for Eight External Variables Associated With Network Systems

	Factor 1	Factor 2	Factor 3
Vertical Dependency	.74		
Involuntary Client Status	.87		
Task Intensity	.74		
Regulation	.93		
Task Scope		.70	
Task Uncertainty		.85	
Task Volume			.85
Task Duration			.85

Eigenvalues and Proportion of Original Variance

	Magnitude	Variance
Value 1	3.04	.38
Value 2	1.60	.20
Value 3	1.39	.17
Total Variance	.75	

classification, it appeared that the more a systemic network relied upon vertical funding—whether or not from multiple sources—the more conflict increased within the network, and high task scope appeared to make things worse. The networks with the most conflict were the Fulton Juvenile Justice system and the two Children Protection systems—all were Type 4 networks. Next came the Farnam Juvenile Justice system and the Farnam Chronic Mentally Ill system, which were Type 2 networks. Of these, the Chronic Mentally Ill system was the newest and was highly dependent on state agencies for funds, but at the same time dependent on the state hospital and the local mental health center for clients, a situation that made developing a smoothly functioning system very difficult. The Farnam Juvenile Justice system did not have as much conflict as did the Fulton system, primarily, we think, because a large proportion of the juvenile workers in Farnam were paraprofessionals and volunteers. Their expectations were not as high as those of professionals, and they worked directly with individual children and adolescents and were not concerned with systemic problems. The point is, however, that if (or when) the

Table 7.3 Analysis of Variance of Standardized Scores Measuring Conflict and Performance Gap in Four Types of Systemic Networks in Fulton and Farnam Counties ($N = 15$)

	Conflict Std. Mean	Performance Gap Std. Mean
Type 1 ($N = 6$)	−.67	−.83
Type 2 ($N = 3$)	.63	.28
Type 3 ($N = 2$)	−.42	.09
Type 4 ($N = 4$)	.78	.99
$F =$	3.12	5.34
$p <$	.06	.02

Juvenile system begins to employ more highly trained staff (which they were doing as we concluded our study), then we would expect this network to move into the Type 4 cell. Likewise, we predict that the Farnam Chronic Mentally Ill system will also become a Type 4—become larger, more complex and differentiated, and conflicted—as it matures over time.

The second column in Table 7.3 shows that performance gap was low when dependency was low, and high when it was high, a relationship accentuated when task scope was also high. Further, the range of mean scores was extreme. Workers in the Special Needs Adoption systems and Rape/Domestic Violence systems, for example, were highly satisfied with the systems and believed that all members were contributing on an equal basis to their smooth functioning. By contrast, the workers in the Juvenile Justice and Child Protection systems were extremely critical of each other and of their systems.

Based on these results, we believe this typology helps identify what types of networks are likely to have the most severe problems. Clearly, it is networks that are complex and must rely on external resources. As we have seen, it is not in the simple networks that conflict arises, but in the large and complex ones. We can appreciate Killing's observation that managers prefer simple systems (1988). This observation leads to our next question: Why should this be the case?

CONCEPTUALIZING FAILED NETWORK EVOLUTION

Why do certain types of interorganizational networks tend toward chronic and severe conflict and performance gap? Our general answer in Chapter One was that post-industrial society has seen a steady movement toward more complex institutional arrangements and complex coordinative mechanisms. In Chapter Four we discussed the fact that growth of knowledge in the social sciences has meant that society's concepts of dysfunction and pathology are becoming more complex. During the past decade, many new social, psychological, and medical problems have been discovered. Four of the eight client populations in the Fulton and Farnam study, for example, were not recognized as populations needing service or treatment until a decade ago. Many years ago Lawrence and Lorsch (1967) hypothesized that organizations' environments can change, and then new and different demands are created. When environments are changing rapidly—demanding higher quality of products and services and/or a broader range or mix of products and services—then organizations must become more complex and differentiated in their internal structure and processes in order to meet these expectations.

We propose that this thesis has application today to interorganizational networks. The central idea, that structural differentiation and integration must increase in tandem for organizations to be effective, is as true today of networks as it was for single organizations in the 1960s. But this does not mean that the "right" choice is always selected by managers, or that systemic networks evolve smoothly toward complex coordination as more and complicated kinds of problems are handled.

In applying the thesis of Lawrence and Lorsch, however, it is important to make a critical distinction. Our concept of structural differentiation is not the same as their concept of task complexity. Within the framework we presented in Chapter Five (Table 5.3), differentiation measures the degree to which there is functional specialization among the organizations in the network, while by structural complexity we mean the number of different service or product sectors represented by the member organizations. We stress this distinction here because we believe that the key insight of Lawrence and Lorsch is that managing people (or in our case, organizations) with different views of the world is the major interorganizational problem of our day. In systemic networks, the application of this insight means administrators must manage professionals who have very different paradigms of client treatment or production processes and use very different methods.

A Theory of Network Imbalance

As we got to know the networks in Fulton and Farnam counties, we slowly became aware that they had evolved, and were continuing to evolve, into very different institutional forms. What struck us as being the most distinguishing feature was the level of conflict and the negative attitudes of some workers. Some networks were absolutely riddled with strife, while others were placid and self-confident. Why such contrasts? And why didn't someone do something?

People who plan and manage multiorganizational efforts know it is a difficult job. They know it is much harder to get a set of diverse agencies to work together than it is to manage a set of similar organizations where there is agreement on objectives and methods. In highly differentiated systems, technology is segmented, and staffs operate with different norms, values, and specialized knowledge bases. The tendency is for these organizations to reduce the potential for interagency conflict by reducing communication to a minimum and replacing it with impersonal methods, which in turn reinforce the distance and differences (Hall et al., 1977; Katz & Kahn, 1966). Thus, structural differentiation and complexity do not encourage integration, they discourage it. Handling different kinds of environmental demands and working with different technologies inevitably generate internal conflict, and these differences are magnified when people from different organizations must work together.

When we apply this thesis to the study of systemic networks, and combine it with the work of Van de Ven et al. (1976), we extrapolate that as differentiation and complexity increase, the natural tendency is for systems to reduce their use of groups and team coordination and rely on impersonal and sequential methods, rather than the reverse. Here we have an explanation for why coordination and task interdependency may not evolve appropriately as functional and task complexity increases. Figure 7.3 summarizes these hypotheses concerning structural and operational imbalances and allows us to operationalize the concept of disequilibrium.

Figure 7.3 summarizes the characteristics of systemic networks that are in balance because they have an appropriate level of coordination and task integration, given specified levels of differentiation and complexity. It also hypothesizes negative consequences when, for whatever reason, the amount of coordination and integration does not keep pace with structural development, and the network slides into disequilibrium.

As Figure 7.3 demonstrates, we believe that networks can fail to develop as effective operating units, and two outcomes of this failure are internal conflict and performance gap that go beyond the bounds of being functional. There are a number of explanations why systemic networks evolve toward this type of imbalance, rather than toward a balance between structure and operational coordination. The most obvious to us, as we studied the systems in Fulton and Farnam counties, was that mandated systems (Hall et al., 1977), those serving involuntary clients that had to be operated according to state law, were, by definition, highly impersonal and had not compensated with equally high levels of coordination. The same is true of those systems that were required to cope with large numbers of clients. They had to rationalize the handling of many clients by using many rules and regulations, and did not balance their rule-driven systems with appropriately integrative methods. This provides some insight into why evolution fails and why there may be more conflict and performance gap in those networks classified as Type 2 and 4.

An Evaluation of the Theory of Network Imbalance.

The results in Table 7.3 show that highly dependent networks (Types 2 and 4) can be problematic and that, when their task scope is also high, they may have to operate with very conflictual interorganizational relationships. Juvenile Justice and Child Protection networks are, unfortunately, good examples. Although

Systemic Networks in Equilibrium

Differentiation & Complexity	Administrative Coordination Methods	Task Integration Methods	Conflict & Performance Gap
low	impersonal	sequential	low
moderate	personal	reciprocal	low
high	group	collective	low

Systemic Networks in Disequilibrium

Differentiation & Complexity	Administrative Coordination Methods	Task Integration Methods	Conflict & Performance Gap
low	impersonal	sequential	low
moderate	impersonal	sequential	moderate
high	impersonal *	sequential	high

Figure 7.3 Hypothesized Explanation for Imbalance Between Complexity, Differentiation, and Coordination Methods and Its Consequences

*Lawrence and Lorsch (1967) did not hypothesize that too much integration can be employed relative to the amount of differentiation, so this logical possibility has not been included. It will be seen below, however, that this is an empirical possibility.

they have high levels of staff interaction via personal communication and interagency teams, they tend to be administered by impersonal administrative procedures. This suggests that even though staff have what may be ample opportunity for peer consultation and feedback, the source of problems may lie with the amount and kind of administrative coordination.

To test the theory of network imbalance, we constructed an index representing the *amount of administrative coordination* and the *amount of task integration*. On the assumption that personal methods represent more coordination than do impersonal methods, and group methods represent more than personal methods, we weighted the scores for each methods (the proportion of clients handled via each method) and summed them. The weights used were:

Amount of Coordination = (Impersonal * 1) + (Personal * 1.5) + (Group * 3.0)
Amount of Task Integration = (Sequential * 1) + (Reciprocal * 1.5) + (Team * 3.0)

The resulting indexes are a measures of coordination and task integration effort, since group and team methods provide more feedback, mutual adjustment and, hypothetically, less conflict.

To summarize our previous empirical findings and the relationships between these single indexes of coordination and task integration, their correlations with the 13 external control and structural variables are shown in Table 7.4.

One of our central theses has been that high levels of external control as well as high task scope should result in more administrative coordination and task integration. As can be observed in Table 7.4, this does indeed occur. High levels of resource dependency are associated with task integration ($r = .51$), but not with coordination. Task scope in particular has a strong association with task integration ($r = .83$), and a lesser association with administrative coordination ($r = .61$). Task uncertainty is related to administrative coordination ($r = .56$), but not task integration. In sum, we find general support for our thesis that increases in resource dependency and task scope mean that systems will evolve toward more complexly coordinated systems.

The relationship between the structural variables and the indexes is interesting. Centrality was highly associated with task integration; team work seemed to necessitate a highly centralized referral system, with a powerful core organization to pull teams together. Structural differentiation, on the other hand, had a weak negative relationship. In these 15 systems, highly structured structures did not use large amounts of administrative coordination, but in those that were centralized there was a liberal use of task integration in the form of interagency teams.

In an attempt to determine if these findings generally supported our theory of network balance, the indexes were grouped by the theoretical categories of the typology. The resulting group means for the four types of networks are shown in Table 7.5.

Table 7.5 identifies Fulton and Farnam networks that were operated with more or less of these two operating methods. The results showed that the amount of coordination and task integration increased steadily from Type 1 to Type 3, but decreased from Type 3 to Type 4. It should be noted, especially, that there was significantly less administration coordination in Type 4, when compared to Type 3. Here is some evidence that there were networks that failed to balance their coordinating and integrative mechanisms with the demands made on them by

Table 7.4 Correlations Between Environmental Conditions, Structural Properties, and the Amount of Administrative Coordination and Task Integration in Systemic Networks in Fulton and Farnam Counties ($N = 15$)

	Amount of Coordination	Amount of Task Integration
Environmental Conditions		
Resource Dependency	.24	.51
Regulation	.04	.41
Involuntary Status	−.24	.29
Task Scope	.61*	.83**
Task Uncertainty	.56*	.24
Task Intensity	−.02	.49
Task Duration	.09	.00
Task Volume	.03	−.34
Structure		
Centrality	.37	.75**
Size	.02	.22
Complexity	−.18	.24
Differentiation	−.34	−.27
Connectedness	−.21	−.42

*$p < .05$ **$p < .01$

their external and structural determinants, and, clearly, they are the Type 4 networks.

Even though the correlations listed in Table 7.4 did not show significant negative relationships between the structural characteristics of complexity and differentiation and our indexes for coordination and task integration, we suspected they were related. Applying the Lawrence and Lorsch thesis, we thought that rather than these characteristics per se causing network failure, it might be that the discrepancy between the level of structural complexity and the amount of coordination is responsible for imbalance. By the theory shown in Figure 7.3, the equation for this hypothesis is:

Complexity − Coordination = Conflict (or Performance Gap)
Complexity − Task Integration = Conflict (or Performance Gap)
Differentiation − Coordination = Conflict (or Performance Gap)
Differentiatiov − Task Integration = Conflict (or Performance Gap)

Table 7.5 Analysis of Variance of Mean Scores for Indexes Representing Amount of Coordination and Amount of Task Integration in Four Types of Systemic Networks

	Amount of Coordination	Amount of Task Integration
	Mean	Mean
Type 1 (N = 6)	.87	1.02
Type 2 (N = 3)	1.22	1.27
Type 3 (N = 2)	1.83	1.93
Type 4 (N = 4)	1.04	1.63
F =	11.76	14.77
p <	.00	.00

In other words, it might be that networks become increasingly unbalanced as the levels of complexity and/or differentiation increase and coordination methods fail to keep pace. There should, therefore, be a positive association between the discrepancy scores and the levels of conflict and performance gap.

There is, however, another possible explanation for network failure. Perhaps conflict and performance gap are merely transitory and reflect a lack of opportunity to develop the necessary operating methods. To explore this possibility, we introduced the age of the network as an independent variable into our analysis at this point, because it seemed a plausible explanation for part of the variance in conflict and performance gap. The failure to use appropriate amounts of administrative coordination might occur only in young networks, for example, rather than independently of the age. We then had three scenarios for explaining conflict and performance gap; imbalance, age, or a combination of both. They are explored in Table 7.6 and Table 7.7. In the regression models shown in those Tables, we combined the structural variable with the discrepancy score as a control in order to test the idea of failed evolution. It should be remembered, however, that this is exploratory work and that the small sample size undoubtedly leads to inflated results. When the relative size of the resulting regression coefficients and the pattern of their signs are compared, however, these exploratory results do provide some potentially useful findings.

It can be seen in Table 7.6 that Model 1 generally supports our thesis regarding the results of a discrepancy between complexity and the amount of coordination in the system, although the variance accounted for is not particularly high. The standardized βs for complexity minus the amount of coordination (β = .61) is higher than the coefficient for complexity (β = .05). Here is preliminary evidence that imbalance is the culprit. When age is added to the equation in Model 2, the pattern of the signs does not change and, although the β for age has a negative sign, the β for discrepancy is considerably stronger. The same results involving the discrepancy between complexity and the amount of task integration can be seen in Models 3 and 4. We believe that this does constitute preliminary confirmation for the imbalance hypothesis, although it might be that with increasing age, the levels of conflict and performance gap may decrease.

In Table 7.7 it can be seen that differentiation, as opposed to complexity, by itself has a powerful and direct influence that was not mitigated by the levels of coordination and task integration in these networks. The βs for differentiation are positive and considerably higher than the βs for the discrepancy score. Further, the βs for age, although negative, are relatively weak.

There is another major difference, however. The results shown in Models 3 and 4 and Models 7 and 8 are not as we predicted—the βs for the discrepancy score for task integration are negative. With workers, it appeared that high levels of integration matching high levels of complexity and differentiation did not operate to reduce performance gap. When discrepancy was down, the perceptions of performance gap were high! With performance gap, what was true for administrative coordination was not true for task integration.

This was an unexpected and puzzling finding, one we felt we had to explore further in order to decide on the best explanation for network failure. The question we wanted to answer was whether age really played a significant role that we were not understanding, or whether there was a fundamental difference between administrative coordination and task integration in our 15 systemic networks, or whether another factor was more significant.

Table 7.6 Standardized βs for Environmental, Technological, and Structural Variables Regressed on Conflict ($N = 15$)

Model	1	2	3	4	5	6	7	8
Complexity—Amount Coordination	.61							
Complexity—Amount Task Integration		1.24	1.22	2.02				
Complexity	.05	-.25	-.55	-.89				
Differentiation—Amount Coordination					-.25	-.25	-.28	-.34
Differentiation—Amount Task Integration					.94	1.03	.93	1.10
Differentiation						-.15		-.24
Age		-.44		-.58				
$R^2 =$	.33	.35	.38	.47	.59	.57	.61	.62
$F =$	4.14	3.29	5.00	4.80	10.46	6.77	11.30	8.10
$p <$	.05	.06	.03	.03	.00	.01	.00	.01

Table 7.7 Standardized βs for Environmental, Technological, and Structural Variables Regressed on Performance Gap ($N = 15$)

Model	1	2	3	4	5	6	7	8
Complexity—Amount Coordination	2.11		-1.79	-1.12				
Complexity—Amount Task Integration		2.66						
Complexity	1.38	1.55	1.49	1.10				
Differentiation—Amount Coordination					.17	.18		
Differentiation—Amount Task Integration					.66	.63	-.48	-.55
Differentiation						.08	.59	.65
Age		-.52		-.39				-.18
$R^2 =$	.49	.60	.46	.48	.35	.28	.59	.57
$F =$	6.76	6.96	6.05	4.73	4.19	2.57	9.49	6.31
$p <$	.01	.01	.02	.03	.05	.12	.00	.01

FAILED EVOLUTION AND NETWORK
DEVELOPMENT

The ideal research design would study the evolution of systemic networks across time. Unfortunately, our study was cross-sectional. To explain some of our unusual and unexpected findings, we had to make some inferences.

Developmental histories of the 15 service systems we studied in Fulton and Farnam counties showed that they were created when community attitudes identified a new client population. For example, the Women's Movement changed attitudes about the nature of sexual assault and domestic violence. These new public attitudes resulted in cooperative relationships between clusters of hospitals, law enforcement agencies, and counseling organizations. Likewise, changes in the abortion law and in community standards regarding single parents have required adoption agencies to define their clients not as childless parents but as special needs infants and children—a change requiring these agencies to join together in regional and national campaigns to recruit homes and place children.

Responding to newly perceived needs, service delivery systems had to acquire resources. Funding and technology were obtained horizontally (from the community), or vertically (from state or federal sources), or from a combination of the two. All of the early Rape Counseling and Domestic Violence systems, for example, were initiated by local effort, while Special Needs Adoption systems have often utilized a combination of federal, state, and local funding.

Newly Created Systems. In Fulton and Farnam counties, there were five systems classified as newly created systems. Their ages ranged from 1 to 5 years. There were two Hospice Care systems (Alter, 1988a), two Victim Service systems, and one system serving the young mentally ill. Not all of these systems may survive their first 5 years: one of the Hospice systems, for example, is struggling financially and may be forced to change its structure dramatically if it is to survive at all.

These new systems can be described as disorganized. They were large and sprawling, and their referral patterns were often very complex. Specialization among the member organizations was very low; that is, these agencies did their own intake and assessment, rather than agree on a division of labor where members are assigned specific functional roles. Each agency was a generalist in regard to the functional requirements of the system. The system was, therefore, very decentralized; there was usually no core organization through which a large proportion of clients flowed.

Young Systems. There were five systems categorized as young: they were started more than 5 five but less 10 years ago. In this group were two systems providing prenatal medical care and social/educational services to pregnant teens, two systems providing adoption services, and one in-home health care system for elderly patients (Alter, 1988b). A number of trends could be observed. In general, the structure of the system was more easily identified and its properties had become more intensified. There was a tendency for the systems to become more centralized and differentiated, to serve larger volumes of clients and/or provide service for a longer duration, and to grow in the number of participating organizations.

Established Systems. There were five systems in the sample that were 10 years old or older: two Juvenile Justice systems (Alter, 1988c), one Well Elderly system (Alter, 1988b), and two Child Protection systems. Although these systems were the largest in term of scale of service—they consumed the most resources because of number of clients and duration of service—they were smaller in size than their younger counterparts (having fewer participating agencies). It appeared that a point had been reached in the developmental process at which further increase in number of participating organizations was seen to be dysfunctional: In order to gain incremental efficiencies, the network size was reduced. This shrinkage in size, which occurred toward the end of the first decade, was accomplished because these systems had become highly centralized and controlled by state agencies.

As we hypothesized in Chapter Two, we observed that the older networks—ones that had progressed from exchange to joint action to systemic operation procedures—had captured external funding in order to maintain the system. As increased support was obtained, the state agencies that provided the funds demanded accountability, which was imposed by means of increasing the formality of operating procedures. In other words, as the networks developed, vertical control increased and decision-making authority for system operations was transferred from community organizations to state governmental units.

This relationship is tested by grouping the 15 Fulton and Farnam networks by age and comparing the group means for the resource dependency scores. The results are shown in Table 7.8.

Table 7.8 shows that those networks that were between 10 and 20 years of age were perceived by local administrators as relying to a significantly greater extent on state or federal authorities than were the younger networks. This is a strong relationship. When we regressed resource dependency on age of network as a continuous variable, there was also a strong positive relationship and the variance accounted for was large (Adj. $R^2 = .72$; $F = 17.94$; $p < .0003$; df = 14.) It is possible, of course, that there is another environmental variable that is an intervener; however, at this point in the research, it appears that this is a theoretically important relationship.

By itself this finding is not new or startling. It is common sense to say that as networks develop and grow, they must rely increasingly on external, usually vertical, resources. What makes this fact important to us is the impact this has on choice of coordination and integration methods. For example, when we categorize service delivery systems by increasing levels of resource dependency and look at the administrative coordination processes being used, striking differences appear. Specifically, systems with the greatest reliance on outside resources tended to rely on impersonal coordinating methods to a greater extent and personal coordinating methods to a lesser extent. These relationships are illustrated in Figure 7.4.

The plot in Figure 7.4 compares the mean scores for each method of coordination across increasing levels of resource dependency in Fulton and Farnam counties. As illustrated, when resource dependency was low, the networks functioned on personal interaction between administrators: sharing of resources, reciprocal referrals arrangements, planning and maintenance of the system handled across organizational boundaries through relationships based on friendship (Galaskiewicz & Shatin, 1981). Conversely, when resource dependency was high—as when law enforcement agencies were involved—systems were operated increasingly by means of impersonal controlling

Table 7.8 Increasing Levels of Resource Dependency Categorized
          by Age of Service Delivery System

Age of System	Level of Resource Dependency (Mean Score)	Schefe (F-test)
New Systems (< 5 Yrs.)	3.40	.019
Young Systems (6 < 10 Yrs.)	3.45	13.461 *
Established Systems (10 < 20 Yrs.)	7.20	12.929 **

95% Sig. *New vs. Established **Young vs. Established

mechanisms (Hall et al., 1977). Furthermore, these were linear relationships. When resource dependency was regressed on methods of coordination, βs and variance accounted for were high and were not improved by using a polynomial equation. This was not true for task integration.

The relationship between resource dependency and methods of task integration was quite different. In this sample of networks, as resource dependency increased, reliance on reciprocal and team methods of task integration increased, while the use of sequential methods decreased. To generalize, we can say that as resource dependency increased, the amount of task integration within the system also tended to increase. These relationships are illustrated in Figure 7.5.

Figure 7.5 compares the mean scores for each type of task integration across increasing levels of resource dependency. The trend lines demonstrate that regardless of the level of resource dependency, reciprocal client flow was the predominant method of integrating and sharing tasks across organizational boundaries. An interesting finding was that increasing resource dependency was associated with increases in teaming and decreases in sequential client flows. This supports the proposition that as resource dependency increases, the amount of task integration increases. Furthermore, the trend lines demonstrate clearly that these are curvilinear trends. In fact, there are no linear relationships; good explanation requires the use of polynomials.

In summary, these results suggest that increasing levels of resource dependency (and thus state control) were associated with the decreasing capacity of administrators to coordinate

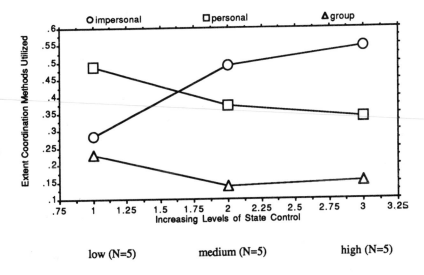

Figure 7.4 Profile of Coordination Methods on Increasing Levels of State Control

their service systems. We now have still another explanation for failed evolution—external control imposed because of reliance on outside resources. Networks' ability to adjust to changing needs and conditions of clients and consumers, to modify interagency programs, and to innovate in service delivery appeared to be therefore diminished because of outside control. Simultaneously, however, it appeared that opportunities for workers to interact and to share tasks were increased in networks that were dependent on outside resources. Important ramifications are to be found in these *opposing* trends. They suggest that task integration may compensate for the lack of administrative coordination. Put another way, the networks we studied failed to evolve at the administrative level, but not at the client or task level. In this context, we should remember that the original work of Lawrence and Lorsch examined only the managerial level; they did not attempt to explore what might be happening at the production level.

The development of contingency theory in organizational studies established that different organizational structures re-

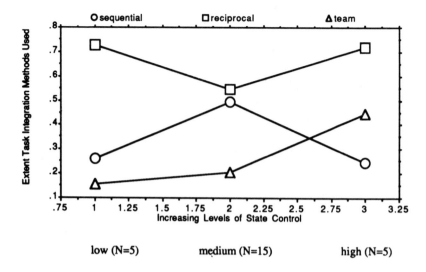

Figure 7.5 Profile of Task Integration Methods on Increasing Levels of State Control

quire differing amounts of integration. When quality is the performance objective, as is usually the case in human service delivery, work systems are highly complex and require highly integrative mechanisms (Hage, 1980; Lawrence & Lorsch, 1967). The explanation for this finding lies in understanding that when diverse units must work together to achieve a mutual objective, there is a necessity for mechanisms that will engage the disparate parts in joint planning and management processes. When the work process is highly complex, there is a necessity for mechanisms that will mesh dissimilar interventions and work tasks (Miles, 1980). In other words, as human service delivery develops, it requires highly complex technologies which, in turn, necessitate a high level of collaboration between working units and individuals.

Does this principle, obtained from the theory of organizational behavior, also hold for interorganizational work processes? In general, we think the answer is yes. There is a tendency over time for the amount of coordination to fall below what is needed and for the system to overcompensate with task integration. This hypothesis can be tested by using the discrepancy scores—the numeric difference between a complexity score and the amount of coordination and the amount of task integration found in the system. The results of this analysis are shown in Figure 7.6.

The trend lines in Figure 7.6 show clearly that in Fulton and Farnam counties, administrative coordination discrepancy grew over time while task integration discrepancy shrank. Coordination discrepancy occurred because state authorities imposed formalized and programmed operational procedures, leaving little discretion to local administrators. Task integration, on the other hand, tended to keep pace with complexity because it was perceived by workers as necessary for quality and was somewhat more difficult for state authorities to regulate. It is true that task integration is costly, that its full cost is difficult to build into unit costs and purchase of service agreements; nevertheless, among the systems studied in this project, there was a surprisingly large amount of task integration occurring as compared to coordination of management processes.

These data have allowed us to address the idea of failed evolution, the inability of a systemic network to evolve in all areas. The data also allowed us to understand the concept of imbalance—the combination of technology, structure, and coordination that do not develop in tandem. Specifically, high task, complex or highly differentiated structure, combined with impersonal coordination, we found to be ineffective. To our knowledge, this is the first time in population-ecology thinking that both effective and ineffective forms have been postulated and tested.

In addition to imbalance as a reason for failed evolution, we have shown that developmental processes have a built-in failure track when heavy reliance must be placed on external and vertically provided resources. External controls with an emphasis on regulation and structural differentiation may be used by state and federal authorities as a means of avoiding conflict and perceptions of poor performance, but they only make them worse.

The large amount of task integration occurring in these service systems was not anticipated, although perhaps it should have been. In 1971 Mathiesen published an excellent account of this dynamic in a phenomenological study titled *Across the Boundaries of Organizations*. In rich detail he described boundary work: workers who establish personal ties with workers in other organizations in order to get the resources needed by their

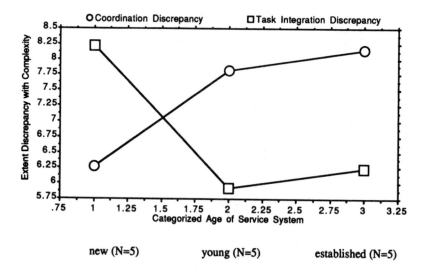

Figure 7.6 Profile of Discrepancies Between Service Complexity and Amounts of Administrative Coordination and Task Integration Categorized by Increasing Age of Service Systems

clients. The finding is simple but very important. It is much easier to establish interorganizational direct service teams than administrative decision-making groups. It is far easier to share work tasks than power.

The reason that large amounts of task integration contributed to perceptions of performance gap is also easy to understand. Workers and administrators who have little control over the operations of their work systems, and who have close relationships with others in the same situation, develop negative attitudes, which they share. These perceptions escalate and have serious negative impact on morale. If there is a lesson here, it lies in the concept of balance—or *good fit*, as some term it (Alexander & Randolph, 1985). Those responsible for interorganizational systemic networks—both state authorities and local administrators—should strive to find a good balance between these collaborative processes.

EIGHT

Theoretical Implications, Practical Recommendations, and Global Applications

The startling explosion in the number of symbiotic joint ventures, systemic networks, research consortia, and other forms of interorganizational collaboration (Hergert & Morris, 1988; Nielsen, 1988; Pollack, 1992a; Powell & Brantley, in press; Zuckerman & Kaluzny, 1990) in just one decade is truly remarkable. This is not to say these institutional forms never existed prior to the 1980s, but only that they are rapidly becoming a common method of producing goods and services. These various forms of interorganizational collaboration are replacing the giant conglomerates with multidivisional forms (Aldrich & Mueller, 1982; Chandler, 1962; Hage, 1980; Mintzberg, 1979), which dominated during the middle of this century, as well as the vertically integrated organizations (Chandler, 1977), which were recently our most successful institutional arrangement.

Rapid transformation always begs for both an explicit theory to explain it and research to verify and understand it. Obviously, this book is only one in what is proving to be a stream of theoretical and research works, starting with the large amount of work on joint ventures that has already been published (Berg, Duncan, & Friedman, 1982; Contractor & Lorange, 1988; Grandori & Soda, 1991, for a review; Kogut & Singh, 1988; Laage-Hellman, 1989; Powell, 1990; Powell & Brantley, in press). Our reading of this literature is that systemic production networks, as we defined them in Chapter Two, have not received much scrutiny, even in the literature that we cited as examples—most notably the Womack et al. (1990) description of automotive supplier networks. Indeed, we believe this is perhaps our most useful contribution—to call attention to this complex form of coordination that has remained largely invisible or ignored, despite the rapid changes of the last decade.

Evolutionary theory has been out of vogue for some time (see Collins, 1988, for a review). Its nineteenth-century assumptions of universal and singular progress based on the Western model fell into disrepute during the twentieth century. When a theoretical perspective has been ignored for several decades, it reappears in an altered state. The most dramatic example of this resurgence of nineteenth-century evolutionary ideas is Fukuyama's thesis about the end of history, which essentially argues the inevitable triumph of liberal democracy. We also see a reappearance of evolutionary thinking in institutional economics (Nelson & Winter, 1982; North, 1990; Williamson, 1975, 1985) and in political sociology (most notably Campbell et al., 1991; but also Aldrich & Mueller, 1982; Burns & Dietz, 1991a, 1991b; Hage, 1988; Hage & Powers, 1992). This literature has concentrated on what is for us the major issue: the form of governance. Much of this work started with transaction cost analysis, which proved to be a fruitful springboard for the understanding of the emergence of vertically and horizontally integrated firms, but appears less applicable for understanding the many new kinds of institutional forms that we have described. Surprisingly, population-ecology theory (Carroll, 1988; Hannan & Freeman, 1989), which is perhaps the most relevant to this topic, has largely ignored the question of interorganizational forms.

Our theoretical synthesis attempts to avoid the previous pitfalls of evolutionary theory. Rather than perceiving this evolution as both inevitable and necessary, we have tried to indicate that it does not develop automatically—much to the detriment of American competitiveness and the performance of our heath and welfare systems. Rather than argue that the end state of the evolutionary process is a utopia where all problems are solved, we observe a number of dilemmas associated with different kinds of interorganizational collaboration—most notably the management of conflict, the difficulty of maintaining collaboration (Pollack, 1992b), and the pitfalls related to trying to achieve effectiveness. In the previous chapter, we argued that in some of the 15 delivery systems we studied, evolution failed or had been incomplete because of these barriers.

Our theory of institutional evolution should assess at least four basic questions for it to be useful:

1. What pushes organizations towards collaboration in spite of the difficulties?
2. What are the forms of collaboration and how do they differ?
3. What influences the way in which systemic networks are structured and operate?
4. What influences the choice of partners and insures compliance?

Evolutionary theory typically focuses on only the first question and therefore fails to evaluate all of the false starts and dead ends associated with the evolutionary process. The errors of evolution are the focus of the first section of this chapter. In the second section, we address the ramifications of these ideas for population-ecology theory. Then as we consider how the theory in this book impacts on rational choice theory, we consider the question of compliance.

Evolutionary theory has usually emphasized both a single end point and a single pathway to this end (Collins, 1988, provides a good critique of evolutionary theory). Our theory is quite different. We suggest a taxonomy of 12 forms of interorganizational collaboration and then elaborate subtypes within a particular end state, such as the systemic production network. The choice of a systemic network does not guarantee effectiveness, of course. New institutional arrangements can be badly constructed as well as wisely arranged, as we have seen in the previous chapter. The evidence points to the former as being much more common. We need to understand why.

Our answers to these theoretical questions have implications for a number of contemporary theories in both sociology and economics. Besides the theories about joint programs and joint ventures, our theory of collaboration is relevant for population-ecology models (Aldrich, 1979; Carroll, 1988; Hannan & Freeman, 1989), rational choice theory (Coleman, 1990; Hechter, 1987), transaction cost analysis (Williamson, 1975, 1985), and more generally institutional theory (Scott, 1987; Zurcher, 1987).

Each of these frameworks, we believe, is considerably augmented when integrated with our proposed theory. In particular, we believe our synthesis of the concept of adaptive efficiencies with transaction cost analysis, population-ecology theory, and rational choice theory represents a major theoretical integration that goes far beyond the concerns of this book. We believe we have developed a general model of interest to both sociologists and economists, one that has a number of practical implications.

These practical implications are the subject of the third section of this chapter. We perceive that correctly managed systemic networks provide viable solutions to the problems of American competitiveness, as well as the difficulties of achieving highly individualized but low-cost services in the public sector. For these advantages to be realized, a number of questions must be answered.

The advantages of systemic networks apply far beyond the borders of the United States, however. One of the most distinctive characteristics of the new world order is the large number of global problems that require nations to work together in systemic networks. A large number of environmental, scientific, political, and economic problems require national collaboration if there is to be a new world order. The end of the Cold War means that developing nations can no longer play the United States and Russia off against each other, and that international progress requires decision making and problem solving from a much larger group of nations. To effectively solve global problems in the future, the United States must work within the collective framework of the United Nations. Rather than see liberal democracy as the end of history, we should be focusing on the need for networks of nations working together to solve specific problems—ethnic conflicts, the ozone layer, global warming, population, and so on.

AN EVOLUTIONARY THEORY OF COLLABORATION

Collaboration has always been a part of human existence. Theories of organization and the relationships between them, however, have been dominated by the model of competition.

The assumption that individuals and organizations strive only to maximize profit makes cooperation difficult to understand, especially when it requires the sharing of profits, as in the Japanese model. Obviously, long-term views about how best to gain profits can be quite different from short-term perspectives, hence the concept of enlightened self-interest. But enlightened self-interest is not enough to explain the changes occurring in the organizational world, especially in advanced capitalist societies. This change, this discontinuity we term a social revolution, requires a more complicated explanation.

Throughout our discussion, there is one major theme that unifies a number of the arguments, and that is the impact of the growth in knowledge on development. To date, most evolutionary theories have viewed wealth and power as the most important antecedents of development, and have not considered the critical influence of knowledge. Recently economists have argued that it is only knowledge that can explain the differential growth of nations (Roemer, 1986, 1990). Classical economic theories predict convergence and gradual decline in growth rates ("Economic Growth," 1992). Instead, we have observed accelerated rates of growth and divergence. But these new ideas leave unexplained how growth in knowledge works its way through the institutional framework of societies and how it can lead to economic growth and improvement in efficiencies. This is our central theoretical task.

The Dynamics of Institutional Evolution

Before organizations surrender their autonomy and are willing to share in decision making across organizational boundaries, a number of conditions have to be met, as described in Figure 8.1, where many of the ideas presented in Chapter One are combined in a single diagram.

The four necessary but not sufficient preexisting conditions for collaboration are a willingness to collaborate, a need for expertise, a need for financial resources, and a need for adaptive efficiencies. When all four conditions are met, then collaboration in the form of a joint venture or a systemic network is likely. When only three conditions exist—such as a need for expertise and funds in combination with a willingness to collaborate—then one of the partial forms of collaboration described in Chapter Two is likely, for example, promotional linkages and networks involved in technological development or federations for fund-raising. If a willingness to collaborate does not exist, then the development of any advanced form of institutional arrangement cannot occur. Thus, in some respects, it is the most important precondition.

A willingness to collaborate is a necessary but not sufficient condition, because it produces preferred exchanges or obligational linkages of one kind or another. The accompanying need for complementary expertise and/or the sharing of risk and resources can then move organizations to accept a more complex form of promotional linkage or even a network. It is the need for speed, flexibility, and adaptive efficiencies that pushes organizations to advance to a higher level of collaboration, namely joint ventures and systemic production networks. Which option is more appropriate at a particular point in time depends upon the complexity of the task and thus, the number of organizations that must be involved.

One of the critical problems in evolutionary theory is understanding how a new discontinuous stage of development is achieved. We believe the explanation is the interaction effect between these four variables. Perceptions about the need for collaboration, for expertise, for economic resources, and for adaptive efficiencies occur singly in degrees, but when they occur together, their interaction creates pressure that can lead managers and administrators to take the giant step toward either a joint venture or a systemic network. The requirement that all four of these antecedents of collaboration be present before systemic production networks emerge explains why evolution does not occur automatically.

A Culture of Trust. Although Williamson (1975) overemphasized the problem of distrust in transaction cost analysis, the question of willingness to collaborate is certainly anything but unproblematic (Litwak & Hylton, 1962). Our explanation of a differential willingness is dependent on whether a climate of trust exists. As we previously suggested in Chapter One, various parts of the world—northern Italy, western Denmark, Taiwan, Japan—have higher levels of interpersonal and interorganizatio-

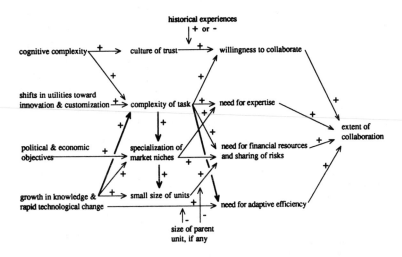

Figure 8.1 Evolutionary Trend Toward Interorganizational Collaboration

nal trust than do many parts of the United States. Rice growing, fishing, lumbering, and other kinds of agricultural endeavors require collaborative behavior, and over the centuries a climate of trust has developed in the areas where these occupations predominated. The provision of welfare and health services at the community level in the United States has had a similar result during the past several decades. Here, professional associations and friendship networks create institutional networks of weak ties (Granovetter, 1973), which facilitate the development of complex delivery systems of services. A similar phenomenon has been observed in Silicon Valley (Delbecq & Weiss, 1988)—technical experts rotating between companies, generating a network of obligations. Currently, in response to the health care crisis, units of state and federal government are trying to create "managed health care systems"; it remains to be seen if effective and efficient service delivery systems can be forged in the absence of a preexisting willingness to work together.

In the United States, especially in the private sector, a different ethos prevails, one of considerable distrust and self-aggrandizement. The myth of Horatio Alger, the self-made man, and the supremacy of the competitive model have made the exceptions we cite above especially interesting because the United States, more than most countries, has fostered a climate of distrust—explaining why so many of our psychological, social psychological, microeconomic, and political theories start with rational men and women calculating their costs and benefits (for reviews, see Collins, 1988; Ritzer, 1992; Turner, 1991).

The trend toward greater cognitive complexity is independent of prior historical circumstances. The immediate antecedents are higher levels of education and occupational specialization, which make individuals more able to perceive the long-term benefits of collaboration, as opposed to the long-term costs of competition. This does not mean we do not do cost-benefit analysis, but only that we employ longer temporal horizons. With more complex cognitive ability, individuals are more careful about calculating their self-interest and more competent about how to make collaboration work.

The Complexity of Task. The critical determinant of greater interorganizational collaboration is the fact that tasks are increasingly more complex; this factor increases our willingness to collaborate, our need for expertise, and our need for funds and the sharing of risks. Complex tasks are necessary for technological development, product innovation and customization, as well as the development of services for multiple-problem clients, which has been our focus in the past four chapters. Throughout this book we have emphasized that complex methods—ones radically different from those of prior decades—allow organizations to develop the adaptive efficiencies needed for success today.

The complexity of the task impacts on two dimensions in our typology reported in Chapter Two: the number of organizations involved and the likelihood that these organizations lie in different niches, and even different sectors. Given our examples in Chapters Four and Five, it would seem obvious that task complexity is strongly associated with both the number of organizations in the systemic networks and the diversity or variety of them as well as their differentiation. Although the relationships between task complexity and the specific kind of choice are not depicted in Figure 8.1, these are important aspects of any evolutionary theory of interorganizational forms.

Specialization of Market Niches. Cognitive complexity makes new demands of organizations, whether in the private or the public sectors, and increases the complexity of tasks that organizations must manage. If consumers did not demand innovative products and individualized services, then firms and agencies would have far fewer management problems and could rely on simpler institutional arrangements (Hage, 1988). We stress this trend because it lies at the heart of any evolutionary theory that purports to predict discontinuous change. Few theorists have attempted to explain why customers are increasingly more interested in quality, more concerned about the environment, and have more complex political and economic attitudes (for a fuller explanation of this thesis, see Hage & Powers, 1992). The industrial age was dominated by concerns about the resource allocation efficiencies associated with mass production; our new epoch is controlled by the utilities of innovation, customization, flexibility, and the speed with which new products and services can be developed and new market niches opened. Achieving this kind of adaptive efficiency is difficult. Indeed, a famous article in population-ecology argues against change because it can produce less efficiency (Hannan & Freeman, 1984), and argues that stability has adaptive advantages for this reason. We agree that the argument holds for the industrial age, but not for our post-industrial age, where successful competition is dependent on the capacity to innovate quickly.

It is not just consumer demand that drives task complexity. Equally important is the increasing recognition, especially by governments, that competition between nations is as important as it is between firms, making national industrial policy a critical economic and political objective (see examples in Hollingsworth et al., in press). The term *Japan, Inc.,* has been coined to describe the close collaboration between MITI and industrial enterprises within Japan, and a number of studies describe how the Japanese government controls economic development, not only for itself but in Western Europe (Cawson, in press; Sako, in press; Strath, in press). Further, economic and political objectives are difficult to separate as governments attempt to nurture sunrise industries or protect sunset industries in order to reduce unemployment and increase standards of living. Likewise, public unhappiness with taxes makes the public sector increasingly focused on achieving efficiencies at the same time that there is a demand for quality of services. And the current debate about the costs of welfare and health care in the United States is both political and economic in nature. There is a stated interest in successful means of increasing investments in basic research, which translates over time into increasingly complex applications and processes.

Small Size of Units. One of the central ideas in population-ecology theory is the concept of niche specialization—that the growth in knowledge increases the number of small niches, which in turn makes collaboration more necessary and more possible. Just as the solution of one problem creates two new ones, so the development of new products tends to divide markets into specialized niches. The customization of the automotive industry has generated a large number of specialized product niches in the past decade, which increases the need for both expertise and funds. This entire process, which favors small high-tech firms and loosely coupled decentralized small units of large firms, has several ramifications. The small size of firms means that capitalization and cash flow are far more problematic than for large organizations. Therefore, there must be an external source of funds, as with the Japanese *kieretsu* or the American venture capital networks, or the small unit must be part of a parent agency or firm that has sufficient capital for funding joint ventures and other forms of collaboration.

Collaboration as Opportunities for Learning

Our theory about the evolutionary trend toward interorganizational collaboration makes explicit many of the factors that are creating such dramatic changes in the ecology of organizations. There is one consideration that is implicit in our model and of special benefit. It is the opportunity for learning. The business literature has emphasized the importance of sharing risks (see many references in Contractor & Lorange, 1988), and as the costs of product development have skyrocketed, even the most centralized business organizations have been forced into partnerships (Pollack, 1992a). But even more fundamental than the costs of development is the need to learn new technologies so that firms can continue to innovate. The opportunities to expand tacit knowledge far outweigh the risks and costs of having technology stolen, especially when technologies, products, and services are changing so rapidly. In a number of industrial sectors, there is little patenting of product ideas today because the process takes longer than their useful life.

Most discussions of rational choice do not include the problems of technological development and innovation, and thus have not anticipated the evolution toward collaboration. By sharing information and know-how, the stage is set for more learning than a single organization could achieve by itself. This process ensures compliance in the partnership or network and builds a basis for further collaboration in other development efforts. This is an important point. We assume that success encourages organizations to evolve toward the next form of collaboration, but this is not always the case. Once a new product is developed, there may not be need for marketing or production skills, because the partners have them; or, once a new product is developed, enough learning may have occurred so there no longer is a need for sharing expertise. The variables in Figure 8.1 are dynamic.

Joint learning occurs because group problem solving leads to better solutions. As boundary spanners from different organizations engage in joint problem solving, they are learning flexibility and adaptive efficiencies. This is the real secret of the Japanese production networks. As their organizations problem solve together, they reduce the time it takes to put a new product on the market. If the product fails, they may have time to correct their mistakes.

Working in a small niche means one is unlikely to have the necessary expertise, especially in a global economy. But at the same time, the creation of new products and services for limited markets provides a zero-plus sum game, encouraging collaboration. Thus, the growth in knowledge is lessening the forces of competition, via the process of niche specialization, and reducing the costs and risks of collaboration, even in such very complex forms as the systemic production network.

Differential Evolution

Although these five contingent factors—cognitive complexity, shifts in utilities, the combination of political and economic objectives, the culture of trust, and the growth of knowledge—tend to covary as we have indicated in Figure 8.1, they are not perfectly correlated. The culture of trust can have historical antecedents, as we have seen. Furthermore, these variables themselves vary within society, across both industrial sectors in the economy and its equivalent in the public sector (education, health, welfare, and the like). Any society finds that it has mixtures of the new and old institutional forms—systemic networks in some businesses, and giant vertically integrated firms in other sectors. Our arguments about cognitive complexity primarily apply to the middle class that has received a college education, and not to other social classes. Therefore, we expect uneven and differential evolution.

Paradoxically, and assuming that our theory is correct, in general the evolutionary process of moving toward more complex tasks has proceeded farther in the United States than perhaps it has in Europe or Japan. By this we mean that there are higher levels of education, especially university level, and larger amounts of knowledge creation (National Science Foundation, 1989), especially in defense and health, and perhaps a greater preference for the new utilities requiring adaptive efficiencies. Yet we find the United States has large trade deficits and is not able to compete in many industrial sectors: signs of the inability of many business forms to evolve. The network of production appears to be more common in Japanese business firms than in American ones. Furthermore, many of the common examples of collaboration cited in Europe would appear to have their origins in special ecological situations. This suggests the special and fundamental role of the mediating force of the culture of trust. Although we believe that this too is evolving across time, that trust is generally growing, as a consequence of greater cognitive complexity that rejects reasoning à la the prisoner's dilemma, the prior cultural history of the United States and its emphasis on individualism and personal success have slowed down considerably the movement toward greater collaboration. This, then, becomes a critical contingency in our evolutionary theory.

We have explained that in the United States there has been a long history that prevented competition in welfare services, which has required welfare agencies to established quite specialized niches. It is somewhat ironic that quite opposite processes are producing similar effects in the two major sectors of advanced post-industrial societies. Both competition, when it is based on quick development of new technologies and products, and the lack of competition because of the concern about cost containment, are generating a different calculation of the costs and benefits of interorganizational cooperation in the private and public sectors.

In the case of the human service delivery systems that are the focus of our research, though, the benefits are remarkably similar to those discussed in the business literature on joint ventures (Contractor & Lorange, 1988). By collaborating, private agencies have opportunities of gaining access to expertise and resources that they would not otherwise have, the same advantages that accrue to the firms studied in Sweden (Laage-Hellman, 1989).

The failed evolutions that we have examined in the previous chapter in local welfare services, the areas of the United States where they would appear to be easiest, indicate that just because there is an evolutionary process, it does not occur automatically. Indeed, we would suggest that this problem of differential evolution and failure should be the focus of research in population-ecology theory, because it could help us understand what might be done to make the evolution work more smoothly. Our analysis in the previous chapter is one example of what could be done. The Lawrence and Lorsch (1967) model is another.

Failure in the process of evolution is not the only issue in understanding alternative patterns of evolution. In Chapter Two, we indicated that there were a number of different scenarios of how forms of interorganizational collaboration might evolve across time. In particular, we suggested that the movement toward joint ventures and the movement toward systemic networks were quite different because they have different starting points; that is, it is easier for several organizations to become involved in an exchange than an entire field. The government is more likely to be involved in the creation of promotional networks, as we have seen, but this does not mean that they evolve into systemic networks. Evolution stalls at particular moments because it does not have clear adaptive advantages for the partners involved. Above, we suggested that one explanation for this is that these needs shift, depending upon the particular management task, whether production, marketing, or development. This problem of the process of evolution or the pathway or scenario needs much more research attention than it has received. In this regard, the study of the evolution of Community Clinical Oncology Programs (see McKinney, 1990) is a model of what can be done.

IMPLICATIONS FOR SOCIOLOGICAL THEORY

As we suggested in the first chapter, our theory of the process of evolution toward more interorganizational collaboration has implications not only for interorganizational relations and the new developing literature on joint ventures but also for population-ecology theory, rational choice theory, and transaction cost analysis. Although these implications are perhaps obvious, they are worth at least a brief summary.

Population-Ecology Theory

The general model of population-ecology is quite vague (see Aldrich, 1979). Variations in the environment produce new populations of organizations. As population-ecology theory has done little research on the emergence of new organizational forms, let alone any research on new interorganizational forms, an explicit theory of evolution has not been developed (for one exception, see Aldrich & Mueller, 1982, but one that emphasizes the emergence of the multidivisional form). We have attempted to be specific about the sources of variation, the variety of interorganizational forms, and then within is the most important and complex—systemic production networks—the variety of basic types.

Sources of Variation. This has been the focus of the previous section. To explain these environmental variations, we have relied upon five variables: the shift in consumer preferences requiring a new kind of efficiency; the increasing involvement of the central governments in interorganizational collaborations of all kinds; the importance of a culture of trust; increasing levels of education and cognitive complexity; and finally and most importantly, the growth of knowledge and the shift to sophisticated technologies.

One might ask why our argument should be so complex, but we believe that it is only when a number of factors are operating simultaneously that there is a multiplier effect, a new historical epoch, which requires new organizational forms (see Hage, 1988, for a discussion of these) and interorganizational ones. Population-ecology theory has not emphasized as yet the concept of historical epochs, but as with so many other ideas that have been borrowed from biology, there is little reason not to recognize that different eras can be described on the basis of their dominant organizational forms (see Aldrich & Mueller, 1982; Hage, 1980). We suggest there is a new historical era that we can label the post-industrial society (see Hage & Powers, 1992). What is distinctive about post-industrial society is that it is the interorganizational forms that are replacing organizational ones. This requires a new way of thinking, of managing, and of educating.

Despite this complexity, there is one underlying social force that accounts for much of the explanation: the growth in knowledge. This affects the level of education and thus cognitive complexity and by extension, the culture of trust. Knowledge has increased global competition by reducing the costs of communication and transportation, and thus by extension, interdependencies and governmental involvement in industrial policy. Finally, knowledge has led to rapid technological and product/service change. All of these conditions have altered the rules of competition, forcing collaboration as the best way of sharing risks, gaining technical competencies, and becoming efficient in adaptiveness (Hage, 1988). Population-ecology theory has emphasized the importance of resources, which generally do not include ideas such as human capital or research. Therefore, the focus on knowledge is distinctive and, we believe, one of the defining elements of post-industrial society. It is also interesting that economics (Roemer, 1986, 1990) has begun to emphasize the importance of knowledge for economic growth.

The Basis of Selection. One of the most important hypotheses in population-ecology theory (Aldrich, 1979) is that organizational forms, and by extension, interorganizational forms, are selected on the basis of their fitness. Furthermore, rather than suggest that there are variations in the environment, we have attempted to be quite specific about what is causing the birth of not just one new kind of interorganizational form, such as the joint venture, but a variety of these, particularly the six symbiotic ones that we have stressed most in our discussion in Chapter Two.

Population-ecology theory, like economics, has placed too much emphasis on the problem of efficiencies associated with long runs of production in mass quantities for standardized tastes (Hannan & Freeman, 1984). Now firms have to be concerned with a new kind of efficiency, namely adaptive efficiency, that is, the ability to change rapidly and at the same time provide customized services or products, and at low cost.

Although we are not able to measure all of the components of adaptive efficiency, there are three quite separate aspects to it: reaction time, design or problem-solving time, and implementation time. Each of these aspects is associated with different factors in the mentality of the managers and the organizational structure. For example, we believe that a slow reaction time is likely to be a consequence of the models that managers use to analyze problems. Certainly the absence of a measure of adaptive efficiency increases the amount of reaction time. One study that does bear on this aspect is *Top Decisions* (Hickson, Butler, Cray, Mallory, & Wilson, 1986), which attempted to measure the cause of selecting some radical decision and then tracing how much time it took to make it. The time to market typically measures the design time and the implementation time, but does not include reaction time.

One argument is that American manufacturers have been very good at developing innovative products, but these are seldom implemented, or else are not implemented very rapidly. If so, and not everyone agrees, then measuring the separate components of adaptive efficiency would be necessary to determine the source of slowness.

What is producing this need for adaptive efficiency is the shift in consumer preferences, or what economists refer to as *tastes*. As we have already suggested, the origin of these shifts lies in the growing cognitive complexity that is a result of the rising levels of mass college education. Elsewhere Hage and Powers (1992) have argued that this growing ability to perceive the world in more complicated terms leads to the appreciation of the long-term consequences of particular actions, along with a much better understanding of the interdependencies of the world. As a consequence, we predict that the problem of a short-term emphasis on profits, a frequent criticism of American managers, will gradually disappear. The emergence of strategy studies in business schools is just one reflection of this growing tendency to think about the long term.

But complex cognitive structures not only change the way we perceive the world, they also influence the kind of theoretical models or sets of social beliefs, what cognitive psychologists would label *schema*, that we bring to bear when analyzing problems. We believe that one of the most important insights of a complex cognitive structure is an appreciation that the assumptions of classical microeconomics are too simpleminded; for example, that collaboration over time produces gains, and the world is a not a zero-sum game. Furthermore, the free-rider effect (Olson, 1965) is less of a problem than is realized. There are many opportunities for mutual benefit (Nielsen, 1988), as we have suggested in our analysis of the opportunities for learning in the previous section. Thus, the models that we bring to bear also influence the choice of forms. We suggest that this is one of the reasons why the Society for the Advancement of Socio-Economics has had such a strong following since the publication of Etzioni's *The Moral Dimension* (1988), which argues the need for more complex models of social science than are to be found in microeconomics.

The Forms of Collaboration. Another central idea in population-ecology theory is the concept of form. The concept of form (Aldrich & Mueller, 1982) has stressed three distinct ideas: the nature of the technology, the kind of organizational structure, and the mechanisms of control. In the previous chapter, we used task scope and vertical dependency to generate a typology of four kinds of systemic networks that combines the technology, structure, and kinds of coordination. Essentially, we argued that as task scope of the technology increases, impersonal methods of administrative coordination and of routinization of the task become less and less viable. Instead, there is a need to rely more and more upon group decision making and team task integration.

Not only has population-ecology theory generally ignored interorganizational forms (one exception is the discussion of strategy in Astley & Fombrun, 1983) but it also has not attempted to develop a systemic taxonomy. Although McKelvey (1982, and also McKelvey & Aldrich, 1983) called for a taxonomy of organizations similar to the biological classification of plants and animals, to our knowledge none has been proposed. In striking contrast to the population-ecologists, the transaction cost analysts (Campbell et al., 1991; Grandori & Soda, 1991; Williamson, 1975, 1985) have been attempting to develop these taxonomies. However, we believe that these attempts suffer precisely because they are not informed by population-ecology thinking, and also that they have ignored one of the most fundamental forms, namely the systemic production network.

We have attempted to be quite specific in the definition of interorganizational forms by carefully defining the 12 kinds of interorganizational forms of collaboration with three concepts: whether the relationship involved competitors or organizations that stood in some symbiotic relationship; the number of organizations involved; and the extent of cooperation. Of these three dimensions, the symbiotic versus competitive nature of the participating organizations is a concept that is central to population-ecology theory, but one that has not been used in recent research (see Carroll, 1988; Hannan & Freeman, 1989).

We believe that our periodic table of 12 kinds of interorganizational forms of collaboration is a superior formulation because it is being used to describe the future rather than the past; it moves beyond transaction costs and the problem of contracts (Campbell et al., 1991; Grandori & Soda, 1991; Williamson, 1985) to include production costs, and it focuses more on adaptive efficiencies (North, 1981) than the efficiencies of resource allocation. Furthermore, it has as one of its dimensions a key concept in population-ecology theory, namely the idea of symbiotic relationships, a concept missing from the other taxonomies.

What discussions there are of evolution of forms in population-ecology theory (see Aldrich, 1979; Aldrich & Mueller, 1982) have emphasized the movement toward one particular form, whether this be large-scale bureaucratic enterprise or the multidivisional conglomerate. Rather than stress one single kind of inter-organizational collaboration, we have suggested that at minimum there are 12 basic forms (Figures 2.1 and 2.2).

Not only have we delineated 12 basic forms of interorganizational collaboration and stressed the importance of the systemic production network, but we also furthered our attempt at a taxonomy of interorganizational forms by observing that there are four distinct types of systemic production networks.

In Chapters Four and Five, we examined the relationship between resource dependency, task scope, the structure of the network, and the kind of coordination style. In Chapter Seven we summarized a large amount of our analysis by suggesting that there are four basic forms of systemic production networks. Given our small sample size, we suspect that we could find more variations than this. What is unusual about our typology is that, like Aldrich and Mueller (1982), we have attempted to combine not just technology but also resource dependency. Furthermore, we examined five structural properties, ones that have wide applicability to many other kinds of networks.

There are two promising lines of expansion in our attempt to discern alternative kinds of systemic production networks. First, we believe much more could be done with the concept of resource dependency. Such variables as the number and relative importance of funders or resource controllers should be explicitly measured. Second, we were unable to obtain enough variation in our measures of the volume or scale of work processed in the production network. We continue to believe that this is an important dimension for defining subtypes.

Perhaps the best test of some of our normative theories is our concern with forms that fail. Our measures of failure are very high levels of conflict (moderate levels are not undesirable) and perceived performance gaps. Rising levels of task scope, structural specialization, and differentiation without corresponding increases in the amount of coordination and, specifically, a movement toward group coordination appears to be a nonviable form—not in the sense of existence but in the sense of performance. To our knowledge, no one has attempted to specify which form fails or appears to be less likely to survive. Obviously, there is a need for much more research on this topic, and our work can only be considered to be suggestive. But this would appear to be a strategic arena for research because of its implications for improving the performance of systemic networks.

Today, there is a lot of research on the different kinds of joint ventures. We can anticipate that eventually there will be some taxonomy that satisfies everyone. Certainly there are a number of attempts to define the different kinds of joint ventures, usually on the basis of either the number of managerial functions involved or the kind of contract (Contractor & Lorange, 1988; Grandori & Soda, 1991).

What is really needed is more research on the different kinds of production networks in the private sector, and especially with adaptive efficiency used as the criterion of performance. This has been our argument throughout the entire book, but it has not been directly tested.

Historical Epochs and Failed Evolution

Rather than perceive evolution as an ever onward and upward movement toward more successful forms of institutional arrangements, we must recognize that there are moments when a new historical epoch occurs, and in the process, a large and wide number of institutional failures occur. At various points we have suggested that we are entering a post-industrial society and era (for the development of this thesis, see Hage & Powers, 1992) with new rules of competition.

The implication of our argument about interorganizational collaboration is that organizations that remain vertically integrated will fail, especially as task complexity increases. As yet, population-ecology has not considered the idea of failed evolution, but it should focus more attention on this problem. Most of the studies in population-ecology have focused on the past century (see Carroll, 1988; Hannan & Freeman, 1989) and therefore may be quite irrelevant to the next hundred years. If our thesis about post-industrial society is correct—and not all would agree—then we are in a new historical epoch where the dinosaurs of the past will quickly disappear.

At this point in time, the issue of why organizations fail to adapt and enter into collaborative relationships should become an important topic. Certainly there is growing literature on this, under the name of organizational decline. But we believe this only substantiates our general argument about the emergence of a new historical epoch.

Rational Choice Theory

Consistent with the emphasis in the United States on individualism and personal success, we have developed a number of micro theories that consider why individuals engage in relationships with each other, whether called social exchange theory, rational choice theory, behaviorism or neoclassical market theory (for reviews of these various theories, see Collins, 1988; Ritzer, 1990; Turner, 1991). All of these theories postulate individuals calculating their costs and benefits, entering into relationships primarily when the benefits or rewards outweigh the costs or losses. Given this tradition, and given our arguments that there is this long-term trend toward collaboration, it becomes important to explain why individuals, firms or agencies, or significant actors within them would be more willing to engage in joint ventures, promotional networks, and systemic networks in the 1980s and the 1990s than they were in the 1950s and 1960s. It is not enough just to argue that there are long-term trends toward greater collaboration; we also need to think through the costs and benefits of collaboration. The application of rational choice theory to the problem of interorganizational collaboration requires that we develop some specific theory of the costs and benefits associated with interorganizational collaboration—as distinct from the cooperation between individuals.

The New Cost-Benefit Calculus. In Table 1.2 we listed the costs and benefits of interorganizational collaboration. What is distinctive about this particular list, besides its length, is that as we suggested, there is an evolutionary bias built into it. When competition emphasizes adaptive efficiencies, then organizations need to become flexible, and there is learning and adaptation in this process.

Our argument about the new costs and benefits of inter-organizational collaboration centers on three essential arguments. First, that the perception of costs and benefits has changed, even if the actual benefits/cost relationship has not, an argument that is increasingly common in the game literature as well (Axelrod, 1984). For example, if we take a long time horizon rather than a short one, we are more likely to perceive the long-term benefits of collaboration.

Second, that in fact there are some new benefits, which are remarkably different from those most typically considered in rational choice theory. For example, we have stressed the advantages of joint product development because it allows for the sharing of risk; generally it generates a positive-sum game; and failure to engage in joint product development is likely to lead to competitive disadvantages, given the pace of technological change. In particular, we have suggested that the opportunity for learning is a critical advantage, and one not stressed enough in the literature (for an exception, see Powell & Brantley, in press).

Third, the problem of how to ensure compliance has also changed because there are new social processes and new sets of skills that lessen the likelihood of noncompliance or noncooperation. In a recent book, Hage and Powers (1992) argue that cognitive complexity allows individuals to understand symbolic communication more effectively, and this in turn leads to better negotiations about rights and responsibilities in relationships, and a greater capacity to ensure compliance.

The Perception of Benefits and Costs. In our discussion of the dynamics of evolution, we stressed task complexity and, antecedent to this, the growth in knowledge as being the most critical factors among the ones that we have identified. Here much of our argument focuses more on cognitive complexity as explaining why the calculus of rational choice is altering. The main point about cognitive complexity is that it leads to a much longer view of the world and provides more skills for handling the difficulties—of which there are many—involved in joint ventures and systemic networks.

Having long time spans changes one's perception dramatically. Increasingly, businesses are providing bonuses on the basis of performance over the previous 5 years, as a way of ensuring that top management takes a longer view. In our discussion in Chapter One, we also stressed how more complex views of the world lead us to appreciate the interrelatedness of life, and thus, appreciate that if our neighbor suffers, in the long run we do as well. This appreciation of interdependencies also teaches us that maximization of profits or of personal gain is essentially a "beggar thy neighbor" approach to the world. Many well-educated people are now acutely aware that we are living on one planet and we need each other.

But these more complex visions are not the only source of change in our rational thought processes; there are also changes in the nature of the costs and benefits that are being calculated. Typically, the literature has emphasized the importance of resources and ignored the very special problem of information, especially technical information, a theme in the population-ecology literature (Aldrich, 1979). Understanding the particular importance of the need for this also helps explain why particular partners are selected: presumably because they help maximize our benefits and minimize our loses. Still another advantage of our focusing on the actual costs and benefits, whether perceived or not, is that it helps us to understand how strong the "glue" holding the relationship together is, and whether the relationship is likely to evolve across time toward some more complex form of collaboration.

The Special Benefit of Learning. We have already discussed how the benefit of learning increases the probability of firms or agencies engaging in collaborative relationships, and thus tilts evolution in a particular direction. But we have not also indicated how the dynamics of mutual learning alter the typical rational choice model and its emphasis on the calculation of costs and benefits.

The problem with rational choice theory, and more generally exchange theory (Cook, 1977), is its emphasis on money, power, prestige, and beyond this, joint goods of one kind or another. We believe that opportunities to learn reflect a very different kind of interorganizational (and interpersonal) dynamic. With exchanges of information and joint problem solving emerges a special reward, a sense of self-competence or group efficacy. As we solve problems together, we are personally rewarded because we feel self-actualized. Joint product development provides this opportunity; but to perceive the joint effort as being only as good as the joint product misses an important aspect of the benefits for the two organizations involved in the relationship. Furthermore, we argue that group efficacy also increases trust.

The Variables Predicting Costs and Benefits. The advantage of Figure 8.1 is that it allows us to predict in which sectors of society the benefits of collaboration—the needs for expertise, the sharing of risk, and the importance of adaptive efficiency— are the greatest. Usually these variables, the predictors of the costs and benefits, are not included, especially in a format that allows for the prediction of evolution. We need not repeat all of the arguments again, but only note how we are synthesizing population-ecology theory and rational choice theory.

The Problem of Compliance. A very special kind of cost is the problem of compliance, that is, ensuring that each partner does its share. The rational choice framework (Hechter, 1987) and transaction cost analysis (Williamson, 1975, 1985) have emphasized this problem of compliance, and we believe correctly so. However, compliance must also be understood in the context of trust. Several Swedish studies that we have referenced (Johanson & Mattsson, 1987; Laage-Hellman, 1989) have demonstrated that the sharing of information leads to adaptation, and when this occurs, trust is built. Adaptation is stressed by them for three reasons: It strengthens the bonds because, after adaptation, the parties are more dependent upon each other; it increases the willingness to negotiate difficulties when they arise; and it increases the sharedness of attitudes and behaviors and a common language.

Certainly, the Japanese example of the automotive product network (Womack, et al., 1990), given in Chapter One, indicates how the sharing of information, joint problem solving, and the like lead to mutual adaptation. Although the study did not stress the concept of trust, we would suggest that this is a covariate.

The sharing of information, the mutual adaptation that occurs with this, and the building of trust all impact on the problem of compliance, which becomes less of an issue because self-control is operating. Given interdependencies created by the adaptations, the costs of cheating are greater.

Another factor that ensures compliance is the capacity of the other firm to withdraw needed resources, especially technical competencies. We have stressed the opportunities for learning as a special inducement to engage in symbiotic relationships (in competitive relationships they are less likely to occur, although they still can). Furthermore, it is in the context of collaborative technological development that the withdrawal of expertise is most likely to be acutely felt as a cost.

Buckley and Casson (1988) have suggested that when one partner cheats, the other cheats as well, and both quickly learn the folly of this kind of behavior. However, they observe that this is more likely to occur in joint ventures involving marketing than when the purpose of the collaboration is joint product development. In other words, joint product development forces the sharing of information, and thus the train of events described in the Swedish research.

Finally, cognitive complexity alters the capacity to solve problems of noncompliance, an issue not considered in the rational choice framework. We suggest that both individuals and, by extension, organizations are becoming adept at solving noncompliance difficulties. In a recent book, Hage and Powers (1992) argue that cognitive complexity has led to a greater ability to read symbolic messages involving emotions, negotiate expectations and manage conflict, problem solve, and tolerate informal and ambiguous situations. These skills decrease the risks associated with interorganizational collaboration. They also explain the remarkable growth in the number of relationships that are not covered by contracts. If transaction cost analysis (Williamson, 1975) were the most appropriate method of understanding these situations, then we would not expect to see them flourish.

Transaction Cost Analysis

The central argument in a transaction cost framework is that if there is a high frequency of interaction and a great deal of asset specificity, then vertical integration will occur. All of the service delivery systems that we studied have these characteristics, as do the Japanese networks producing automobiles and printed circuit boards. Although the transaction cost framework is useful for explaining the movement toward vertical integration, it is not helpful in understanding the movement away from vertical integration under precisely the same set of conditions.

In a recent and provocative article, Johanson and Mattsson (1987) suggest that a transaction cost analysis should be replaced by a network analysis of the relationships between organizations. The central theoretical ideas in their definition of network analysis originate with a social exchange perspective (Cook & Emerson, 1984) and a resource dependency perspective (Pfeffer & Salancik, 1978). To this we would add a population-ecology perspective, which stresses the idea of symbiotic relationships. Together, these perspectives provide a way of understanding how organizations might be able to build trust over time, so that the solution of vertical integration is unnecessary.

Johanson and Mattsson focus much of their criticism of the transaction cost analysis on asset specificity, because they suggest that via mutual adaptation, firms become more dependent or interdependent and naturally increase their asset specificity vis-à-vis each other. This process of social bonding is not allowed for in the transaction cost analysis framework. Furthermore, Johanson and Mattsson observe that if it is the case with asset specificity that the strategy is to absorb needed external assets, then firms would be placed in an impossible growth situation, especially if they are in an heterogeneous environment, or what we would call a diverse ecological niche. Here is an important insight. Vertical integration and horizontal integration worked well as strategies during the nineteenth century (Chandler, 1977) because products were highly standardized, demand was stable, and therefore there was a limited need for different kinds of exchanges. Under these circumstances, absorption of firms providing the needed assets was quite easy and allowed for greater profits. But as the needed assets increase in diversity, this strategy becomes less viable.

Furthermore, as asset specificity increases both in the firm and in the environment—and the two tend to be related—then it is more difficult for managers to coordinate across the diverse kinds of assets or skills or competencies (Chandler, 1962). Again, the movement is toward small profit centers, especially in high-tech organizations, because it is difficult to manage different kinds of products or services well. The growth in knowledge generates asset diverse environments, requiring organizations to interact with larger numbers of different kinds of organizations. In another major criticism of transaction cost analysis, Johanson and Mattsson (1987, p. 15) argue that industrial markets are characterized by lasting relationships between firms because such relationships can reduce costs of exchange and production and can promote knowledge, development, and change. Although this is a starting point for us as well, our main focus suggests that production costs are more critical than transaction costs, and they produce the movement toward systemic production networks and symbiotic and even competitive joint ventures.

Johanson and Mattsson (1987) are quite correct to argue that these enduring relationships produce knowledge, development, and change, issues that are not part of the transaction cost analysis. But we can push the logic of their position further and suggest that the major kind of efficiency is now adaptive efficiency, which is different from the resource allocation efficiency that lies at the heart of transaction cost analysis. Our analytical emphasis has been on the movement away from vertical and horizontal integration, because these strategies are not efficient in their adaptiveness.

Although Johanson and Mattsson (1987) are not interested in developing the theory of institutional governance, namely the choice of a market or hierarchy, this has been an explicit focus of our work. We believe that systemic production networks represent a new kind of governance structure, one much more complex than a market, a hierarchy, or even an obligational or promotional network (Williamson, 1985). Hollingsworth (1991) and others tend to locate these latter kinds of networks as in between markets and hierarchies, yet we believe it is an incorrect placement and reflects the bias or concern with transaction cost analysis rather than production costs. The key to our definition is that prices, production, and other issues are coordinated jointly by two or more organizations. There is joint problem solving and, where it is appropriate, a sharing of profits. These reflect quite new forms of governance, but they are the wave of the future.

At various places in this book we have argued that transaction cost analysis assumes people want to maximize profits and therefore, when there are small numbers and dependency, there is opportunism. The development of interorganizational relationships with partners in highly specialized niches is a movement toward dependency upon small numbers, the pattern of evolution that we observe presently. Furthermore, in Chapter One, we tried to present a large amount of data that indicates there is a movement in organizational behavior away from a maximization of profit and toward greater trust, even when only small numbers are involved. Rather than sole reliance upon formal contracts, there is now much more reliance upon social contracts, especially in product development.

Although Williamson (1975) qualifies his analysis of opportunism with the concept of trust, he does not analyze the various factors that build trust, a focus of this book. In particular, the Swedish work (Johanson & Mattsson, 1987) cited above provides a number of insights about how organizations evolve toward greater collaboration.

In sum, we have suggested some fundamental alterations in transaction cost analysis. Specifically, we have argued that it is important to examine production costs as well as transaction costs, to look for a number of variables that create a climate of trust, and to understand that adaptive efficiencies make the movement away from vertical integration and toward systemic production networks logical. The opportunities for learning overcome fears of opportunism. Indeed, in a world based on the growth in knowledge, the only ways in which organizations can survive is to be small and flexible and to have strong bonding with their suppliers and their customers.

RECOMMENDATIONS FOR IMPROVING AMERICAN BUSINESS AND PUBLIC SECTOR SERVICES

At a variety of different points, we have stressed the similarities in the nature of organizations in the private and the public sector. However, the extent of their evolution in the United States is quite different, for reasons that we have explicated. A number of these recommendations therefore apply more to business firms than to public agencies, in the sense that the private sector could learn a considerable amount from the experiences of the public sector, at least in this arena of how to construct and manage complicated forms of collaboration. It has become clear to us that some of the problems that American firms are having reflect their lack of experience in managing across interorganizational boundaries. When we make recommendations, however, we attempt to maintain the parallel between the private and public sectors, even if there has been differential evolution.

Recommendation One. In those firms or agencies that are highly integrated vertically, and where there is a sizable amount of investment in research and development or their costs are quite high, the firms or agencies should divest themselves of the internal production of many of the component parts or the provision of separate services.

Consistent with our argument in Figure 8.1, not all organizations should necessarily be involved in collaborative relationships, whether obligational, promotional or systemic networks or joint ventures, whether symbiotic or not. Which sectors depends upon how far vertical integration has proceeded on the one hand, and the speed of technological change or product innovation on the other hand. The key variable in Figure 8.1, the growth in knowledge, can be estimated by the amount of money spent on research and development, or the cost of new product development. In the private sector, there are a number of industrial sectors, such as automobiles, computers, and the like, that should be much less vertically integrated than they are and, of course, this varies even across firms within each sector. The public sector, as we noted in Chapter One, is largely horizontally decentralized, most notably in the area of mental illness where this process has been called deinstitutionalization. How much more should occur in large public welfare agencies in the major cities is unclear.

Recommendation Two. In large high-tech firms and in universities and other public agencies that involve a number of different departments and divisions, power should be decentralized to those units that occupy separate niches relative to technology and customers.

Organizations not only have to downsize by eliminating various stages of the production process, but they must also then allow their separate product lines or service departments considerable autonomy, so that it is possible for them to build the new collaborative relationships that are to replace vertical integration. Loose coupling (Weick, 1976) is the watchword. The movement toward profit centers is quite strong in the United States. The only point is that we need more and not less.

As the departments of American universities, in particular, become more involved in various kinds of research consortia with business firms, they need to have considerable flexibility. This kind of joint product development offers a number of rich opportunities for American universities, as well as some obvious risks. To achieve the benefits and to handle some of the risks, there must be considerable decentralization.

Recommendation Three. If there is a large volume of trade with a particular supplier or customer, or exchanges of clients between agencies, then it is worth creating a boundary spanner to facilitate the movement of these relationships toward joint product or service development.

Here is one of the areas where the private sector could probably learn a great deal from the public sector. Boundary spanners have been common in public agencies for at least two decades (see Aldrich, 1979). The model of how boundary spanners can facilitate a relationship is provided in Chapter Two, where there is a discussion of the pattern in the printed circuit boards example, again in Japan.

Recommendation Four. When product development involves a complex task, then it is better to search for partners with complementary competencies and jointly develop the product.

The Swedish research (reviewed in Laage-Hellman, 1989) has found many examples of joint product development in Sweden. We are unsure of how frequently it occurs in the United States. The studies by Hergert and Morris (1988), Powell and Brantley (in press), Pollack (1992a), and others suggest that joint product development is quite common, both across national boundaries and within the United States. We do not know how common it is but believe that it should be tried frequently more than it is presently.

Here is one arena where the public sector might learn from the private sector. In our research, we have not focused on the frequency of joint development of new services, but we suspect that more is occurring than we are aware of. Regardless of how much is occurring, much more could. Here the public sector could learn from the private sector. It is important to be pro-active about service development in the same way the more successful business firms are proactive about research and development.

Recommendation Five. In both promotional linkages and net-works, it is better if all of the organizations have approximately the same personnel and operating revenue size.

The United States is presently attempting to create research consortia that involve organizations of different sizes, but their interests are not the same. It would be better to create multiple research consortia so that they can focus on different issues. The large firms tend to want to find mass products and are less concern with specialized niches.

If the large high-tech firms did destructure themselves into small profit centers, then some of these differences of interests might disappear. We suspect, but do not know, that the prob-lems stem from large companies still resisting the movement toward the creation of small units.

This is not a pattern in the large number of joint ventures in the bio-tech industry, where the typical pattern is for small bio-tech firms to be in joint ventures with large pharmaceutical com-panies. The issue here is whether the latter have decentralized their profit centers so that small units within them can relate flexibly with the bio-tech companies. We do not have data on this trend, but believe it provides an interesting avenue for future research.

Recommendation Six. When production networks are established, it is desirable that supplier associations be created at the same time, so that there are social bonds as well as instrumental or task bonds.

These associations already have some precursors in the United States, in the associations for car dealers or for brokers who sell particular products. The pattern needs to be extended to in-clude those who produce parts for the particular product being produced or the service being provided in the systemic net-work. They become an excellent and informal way of sharing information and learning collectively, something that is missing from many industrial sectors in the United States. We are unfamiliar with any parallel in the public sector side, but again feel that this would be desirable. Perhaps the closest equivalent are the support networks that we described in Chapter Two, but these are not exactly the same as associations of *all* the professionals involved in some service delivery system, such as a hospice service or a service network for the chronic mentally ill.

Trust is fundamentally a question of feelings. It is important that socioemotional forms of association be created to parallel interorganizational networks, so that more trust is built via the exchanges of information and the interdependencies that this creates. This also helps speak to the problem of compliance. If there are social bonds, then the self-control over exploitive behavior is greater. This is, of course, exactly why the Japanese are interested only in long-term relationships and want to establish a firm social basis for this relationship before they become involved in a business relationship.

Recommendation Seven. Within promotional networks and systemic production networks, as the task grows in complexity, it is critical that coordination be performed by all the member organizations.

In our analysis of service delivery systems, we stressed the importance of task scope or complexity as the key variable defining whether coordination could be programmed. As yet, we have not related this analysis to the consideration of production networks, such as those of the Japanese described in Chapters One and Two. In the private sector, it is the design of products that signals the need for teamwork, the kind of teamwork found in the Japanese automobile production networks. When problems arise, problem solving should be jointly accomplished as well. These two examples—team research and team problem solving—are illustrations of task integration in the private sector. In other words, there should be teamwork across organizational boundaries whenever creative solutions are necessary.

But not all production networks need this. Those involving simple products are quite different. These production networks can be programmed as they were in vertically integrated organizations of the nineteenth century.

Recommendation Eight. With promotional linkages and production ventures, it is critical that boundary spanners keep the participating organizations informed of the various developments that are occurring and aware of difficulties as they are encountered.

Although these are relatively simple forms of collaboration, it does not mean that they do not have problems of communication and coordination. Here the task is to keep a steady flow of information about the progress occurring and reports of any problems that are encountered. Once problems are detected, it would be better if they were jointly solved.

Recommendation Nine. Within systemic production networks and joint ventures, it is critical that profits and praise, losses and criticism be shared.

Co-prosperity is the operative word. Maximizing profit is the surest way of preventing the development of trust. Collaboration can only be built upon the sharing of risk and of gains. The joint problem solving, which is such a critical component of systemic networks and joint ventures, will occur only if the benefits are continually shared. This is a lesson that American business has yet to learn.

Recommendation Ten. Within systemic production networks and even joint ventures, it is important that there be coordinating councils, both at the production level and at the administrative level.

Again, we have an idea that is borrowed from the public sector, but one that would help the private sector as well. It is not only that boundary spanners are useful as channels of information, but also that coordination requires the active participation of the various participants. In joint ventures this appears to be a simple problem when only two companies are involved, but in fact, much more attention should be paid to the problem of ensuring joint problem solving. Typically, American business firms establish the joint venture as another stand-alone company. When they do, they lose many of the benefits that can be derived from collaboration.

Recommendation Eleven. In collaborative efforts, whether obligational networks, promotion networks, symbiotic joint ventures, or systemic production networks, it is important to transfer personnel so that there develops a common definition of the problem. In our analysis of conflict in the public sector delivery systems, it is clear that one of the major causes is the structural differentiation that has occurred. There is little redundancy in the public sector, with the consequence that there is not necessarily a common frame of reference. This we consider to be an existential problem. The only way in which differentiation can be overcome is by having people from different firms or agencies spend time working in other firms or agencies. We must learn to understand the other organizational culture or occupational model of thinking. Specifically, within juvenile delivery systems, it is important to appreciate both the police officer's perspective and that of the social worker. Rotation through organizational cultures can increase the complexity of the chosen solutions.

Not unexpectedly, the major management difficulties are at the administrative coordination level, the same probable source of difficulties in American business. Typically workers are blamed, when the real inadequacies are with the administrators and the managers. Therefore, it follows that it would be important to transfer managers so that they develop a much more complex cognitive structure than they presently have.

Recommendation Twelve. Both firms and the federal government need to measure adaptive efficiency, that is, the time to market and the time cost of development.

One of the reasons managers do not respond rapidly is simply because they are unaware of adaptive efficiency as the new competitive standard. These managers are still concentrating on productive efficiencies. Just as the federal government measures the productivity of the economy by determining the productivity of individual firms, we propose using the same approach for measuring adaptive efficiency. This should become a national goal.

Flowing from these recommendations are ways of improving the competitiveness of the United States. The logic of our comparison of Japanese industries and American industries is that we have not moved far enough toward production networks. American companies need to divest themselves of a number of their component parts and then build systemic networks.

GLOBAL APPLICATIONS

Recently, Fukuyama (1992) has caused a stir with his thesis about the end of history. His major point is that all people desire recognition, and it is liberal democracy that provides it. With the collapse of the Soviet Union and other authoritarian forms of government, he believes the last stage of history has been reached in many countries. Without agreeing or disagreeing with the major tenets of this thesis, we want to acknowledge that we are in a new stage of history, characterized by networks of nations working together to solve global problems. Consistent with our argument advanced at the beginning of this chapter, the increasing complexity of the earth's problems is forcing nations both to work together to find solutions and to share the costs of those solutions. Some of these international networks are already in place, at least in embryonic form, and many more need to be established. We will touch upon four problems where international collaboration is badly needed: collective security, environmental health, social and economic development, and the production of global knowledge.

The Gulf War was an unusual example of nations working together on a common objective that none could have achieved on its own. The United States dominated a network of armies from many nations that worked together on very short notice, and it was supported and financed by a number of other countries. It remains to be seen whether this police action marks a new world order. This is an important question because currently there are many regional disputes that have become regional wars. With the collapse of the economic and social structure of the former Soviet Union, there is a resurgence of the ethnic and religious hatreds and national disputes that historically dominated the region. In some cases, networks of armies under the central control of the United Nations may be the only alternative to mass killing and destruction.

An enduring example of international network collaboration is the Group of Seven (United States, United Kingdom, France, Germany, Italy, Japan, and Canada), which meets yearly to coordinate monetary policy and discuss common problems. The representatives have had great trouble at times in agreeing upon common policies, but at other times have been able to coordinate the operations of their respective national banks in order to contain speculation against various currencies. Slowly, over time, these nations may align their policies more closely to control social and economic development, and this benefits all concerned.

Equally important is the emerging integration of Europe via the Common Market. This is still a network, as are all confederations, because each nation must agree before action can be taken. Newspapers and magazines have carefully reported all the different kinds of negotiations that have been necessary before there has been agreement on a common policy. While there are still a considerable number of issues on which these nations have trouble in achieving consensus, especially in the area of foreign policy, they have also moved much further toward economic and political integration than many would have thought possible some 10 years ago. Presently, they are coordinating their social welfare and educational policies and discussing the creation of a common monetary unit. Certainly, the success of the Common Market and its evolution indicate how even a few cooperative relationships can gradually evolve over time into a network of nations that actively coordinates a number of policies. Here is an example of what can be done.

There are many problems, however, which have not yet been the target of inter-nation collaboration. Perhaps the most critical in terms of our survival are those problems of environmental degradation—global warming, the ozone hole, and acid rain—which are destroying the quality of life and posing significant health threats in various parts of the world. Despite a considerable amount of discussion and debate, the nations of the world have not yet begun to plan, much less coordinate, interventions that will ameliorate these problems. The dilemma, of course, is that economic development has produced these negative side-effects, and individual nations, especially the developing ones, do not want to lose the benefits of economic growth. If the Group of Seven were to establish policies to reduce the production of harmful gases and pollutants, then a start would be made. This will take leadership, and unlike the Gulf War, the United States has a poor record in this area.

Another closely related environmental problem is how to protect the earth's forests and seas so that we protect endangered animal species. Success in this direction to date has also been very minimal and is unlikely as long as there are free markets in ivory, whale oil, and hardwood timber, and unless there is a collaborative plan for helping the developing nations to advance their economies without putting undue stress on their environments. We believe that increasing levels of education will ultimately produce changes in values as well as greater recognition of the interdependencies in our world. Already we see the growth of Green parties in many parts of the world, which cut across the traditional political ideologies of left and right, and which identify new issues and the need for new forms of political alliances. It remains to be seen how great a force they will become worldwide.

The United Nations can be thought of as a network composed of all nations of at least one million population. Global problems such as collective security, controlled social and economic development, and environmental degradation are best solved in this large network. But consistent with our theories discussed earlier, it is the very size of this network, the presence of very large and powerful nations, and the complexity of interests and motivations that reduce the effectiveness of the United Nations. Since the success of the Gulf war, there has been an increasing interest and willingness by many nations to use this international structure as a means for handling global issues.

Increasing the effectiveness of the United Nations as a network of nations probably requires both a change in its political structure to more accurately reflect present-day realities and a change in the nature of its funding to reduce imbalances and its level of resource dependency. For example, the Security Council should be reconstituted to include representatives of large, developing nations, such as India and Brazil, as well as small, already developed nations, such as Germany and Japan. Change in this direction has recently been attempted with the push to more closely involve Japan in the funding of the International Monetary Fund (IMF).

There are many political and economic impediments to achieving collaborative international relationships. The United States, for example, opposes an expanded role for Japan in the United Nations and the International Monetary Fund. France and Britain are interested in keeping both Japan and Germany excluded from the Security Council and are concerned about their relative rank in the hierarchy of funding for the IMF. The developing countries, in turn, have every reason to want to limit the power and control of the wealthier nations.

The great economic disparities among nations, and thus the hierarchical control over international networks, certainly form the greatest barrier to better international relations. The problem is how to create a democracy of nations with more egalitarian decision making. One solution, but one that may not be acceptable to anyone, is a tax on international trade. A 1% tax would generate more than enough revenue to delimit the contributions presently made by the major sponsors, pay for the various peacekeeping efforts, fund the World Bank, IMF, UNESCO, and the rest of the United Nations. The problem, of course, is that the most powerful nations will oppose the creation of a new source of revenue they do not control.

So far, at the international level, we probably have more network failures than successes, despite the obvious need for nations to work together. Is there a potential solution to this problem? The Swedish research we reviewed earlier suggests that the best starting place is the joint development of global knowledge, the sharing of resources and information that will accomplish extraordinarily difficult tasks such as mapping the human gene, exploring the ocean floors, and exploring Mars, as well as other major and costly science projects. A logical basis for this kind of global research consortium would be the Group of Seven, to which Russia should be added because of her historical efforts in a number of these areas. Knowledge generation can begin to build the trust between nations that is needed. If nations start working together on major scientific projects, then there are is an opportunity for a division of labor that would help resolve some of the potential areas of conflict.

Other opportunities for cooperation and the development of trust will present themselves as violence breaks out. The Gulf War is certainly not likely to be the last opportunity for international cooperation in response to aggression. But of the four goals—collective security, social and economic development, environmental health, and the production of knowledge—it is the least promising basis for the evolution of nation states into an international network. Instead, by concentrating attention on a discrete problem, such as global warming, acid rain, or the ozone layer, the world can move into a new stage of history. In this stage, the importance of single nations declines just as the importance of single corporations and agencies has declined as networks become the dominant institutional arrangement for producing products and providing services. Just as we have suggested that the evolution of organizations is producing multiple forms of network coordination and control, we would expect a considerable variety of international forms as well.

Sample Selection Process: Bounded Subsystems in a Metropolitan Area

In 1986 the authors completed an exploratory study of a two-state metropolitan area in the Midwest. The total population of this Metropolitan Statistical Area was 365,000 and it encompassed two contiguous urban counties—Farnam, population 154,968, and Fulton, population 160,022—as well as two federal Department of Human Service (DHS) regions, three rural counties, four cities, and many small towns.

Sample Selection

Researchers wanting to study interorganizational relationships at the community level have many problems when confronted with myriad political subdivisions and jurisdictional boundaries. The issue is one of inclusion/exclusion: how, within a densely populated interorganizational field, to identify a subpopulation of similar organizations and then select a sample of interorganizational systems that meet a priori operating criteria. This problem may seem straightforward, but in reality it is often complex. As in any study of units that are simultaneously vertically and horizontally ordered, where you enter the analysis is crucial.

The logic of network analysis requires identification of all organizations that participate together by exchange, action, or production. There are various methods for identifying structurally equivalent interorganizational structures; they can be broadly classified as either macrostructural or microstructural methods. The macro approach starts by identifying all pairwise relationships between all organizations within a geographic area, using one medium or more of exchange (or type of relationship) as the inclusion criteria. By using sociometric or multivariate procedures (Burt, 1980), structurally equivalent clusters are detected within this total network. This is the approach that has been used in many network analysis studies (for example, Galaskiewicz, 1978, 1979; Galaskiewicz & Shatin, 1981; Morrissey et al., 1982; Morrissey, Steadman, et al., 1984; Morrissey, Tausig, et al., 1984). Microstructural methods take a different approach (Laumann & Marsden, 1982). Here the inclusion criteria are set more narrowly, thereby narrowing the field at the outset. This approach allows us to locate network patterns that fit a priori criteria, detect similar subsystems, and thereby compare their structures and operations. In this approach we first collect information from the target organizations in order to set the boundaries of all subsystems within a selected groups of organizations (without ever describing the entire network), and then set exclusion criteria in order to decrease the number of subsystems to be studies.

The study of Fulton and Farnam counties utilized microstructural methods of bounding and selecting a sample. This process followed a four-step process, which is listed below and illustrated in Figure A.1.

a. At the first inclusion step, it was decided to study only human service delivery systems. All organizations in Fulton and Farnam counties that were listed in the *Voluntary Action Center Directory* were included in this first step. This yielded 126 organizations in Fulton County and 152 in Farnam County (Figure A.1 a).

b. Exclusion criteria were established for selection of organizations from this population of organizations. To remain in the study, organizations had to: (1) be formally organized, (2) be providers of human services, and (3) make referrals to and/or accept clients from other organizations. By these criteria, 144 of the 278 organizations listed in the directories were excluded from consideration (some examples of those excluded were animal shelters, arts councils, fund-raising organizations, and Scouts) (Figure A.1 b).

c. In order to bound all subsystems operating within the two counties, a survey was mailed to all organizations that had survived step b. The survey requested the following information: (1) *type(s) of clients* for which referrals are made and/or accepted by the responding organization, (2) *organizations* to which the responding organization makes referrals or from whom referrals are accepted for each type of client, (3) *number of referrals* made to each of these organizations and number of referrals accepted from each of these organizations for each type of client. These data were then used to identify the number and boundaries of existing service delivery systems as follows:

A list was made of all reported client types and from this list client categories were established. The number of client categories represented the number of service delivery systems within the total community network.

Within client categories, a list was made of all organizations in each county that reported having at least one asymmetrical referral relationship (of at least 12 referrals per year) with another organization in the county. Organizations that did not meet this criteria were dropped from the analysis.

In Fulton County this procedure yielded a population of 13 systems having a total organizational membership of 72, and in Farnam County there were 19 systems with 80 organizations (Figure A.1 c).

d. Criteria were then established for selection of service delivery systems for study. For inclusion a system had to: (1) be a twin (similar systems had to exist in both counties), and (2) appear to maximize variation in the study's independent variables. Application of the criteria yielded 7 service systems in each county. A 15th system was included at a later date. These 15 systems included 152 organizational members. There were multiservice organizations that had membership in more than one service system, however, so the total unduplicated count of organizations was 92 (41 in Fulton and 51 in Farnam) (Figure A.1 d).

Figure A.1 is only a heuristic, but it graphically illustrates that this metropolitan area had an expansive network of human

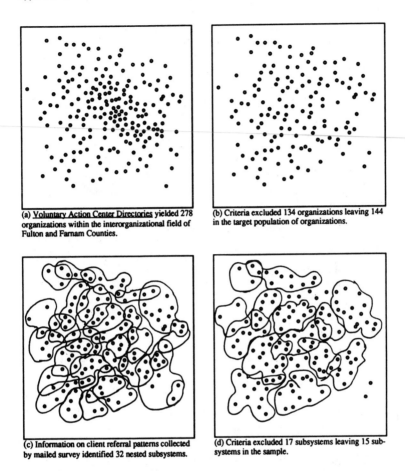

(a) <u>Voluntary Action Center Directories</u> yielded 278 organizations within the interorganizational field of Fulton and Farnam Counties.

(b) Criteria excluded 134 organizations leaving 144 in the target population of organizations.

(c) Information on client referral patterns collected by mailed survey identified 32 nested subsystems.

(d) Criteria excluded 17 subsystems leaving 15 subsystems in the sample.

Figure A.1 Four Steps in Bounding and Selecting a Sample of Network Subsystems Within an Interorganizational Field

service organizations. The outcome of the sample selection process is summarized in Table A.1.

When client flow is the medium of analysis, then organizations serving the same clients cluster together because they are tied together by these exchange channels. When channels are separated by client type, these patterns become visible. In addition, as organizations are excluded in the sampling process,

Table A.1 Sample Selection Process Summary

	Fulton County	Farnam County	Total
Total number of human service organizations in the two counties	126	152	278
Number of organizations that provided direct service	74	84	144
Total number of IO service delivery systems in the two counties	13	19	32
Number of IO service delivery systems selected for study	7	8	15
Number of organizational members of the selected service systems			
Duplicated Count	72	80	152
Unduplicated Count	41	51	92
Number of individual respondents			
Administrators	61	70	131
Workers	141	156	297

and the interorganizational field becomes less dense, it is easier to "see" the patterns of intertwining relationships. There was, in fact, a good deal of overlapping of systems in Fulton and Farnam, as indicated by the fact that the total duplicated count of organizational memberships was 152, yet the unduplicated count was only 92. This happens because it is necessary for large multiservice organizations (such as hospitals, mental health centers, and state departments of human services) to disaggregate their functionally autonomous units when they must be linked to different systemic networks.

Figure A.1 (d) shows the 15 service delivery systems that became the sample of systems that we studied in Fulton and Farnam counties. They are listed again in Table A.2 to show that they represent a broad cross-section of human services:

- 4 systems provided special medical care—hospice care to terminally ill cancer patients and prenatal care to pregnant adolescents;

- 2 were child welfare systems—adoption services for special needs children who are minorities or handicapped, and child protection for children who are physically or sexually abuse, and/or neglected;
- 2 were law enforcement systems—juvenile justice systems and services for victims of rape and domestic violence; and
- 3 provided community care as an alternative to institutionalization—chronic mentally ill persons and frail elderly.

Even though we classified these 15 systemic networks in four service categories, they were all complex, multiservice, and interdisciplinary service systems that provided social, medical, emotional, educational, and physical support and treatment to those in need.

Table A2 The Size, Location, and Purpose of the 15 Sample Interorganizational Service Delivery Systems

Type of Service	Size	Location	Goal of System
1. Special Needs Adoption	5	Fulton Co.	Achieve successful adoptions for special needs and handicapped children.
2. Special Needs Adoption	6	Farnam Co.	Same as #1.
3. Hospice Care	6	Farnam Co.	Provide alternatives to hospital care for terminally ill; improve quality of dying.
4. Hospice Care	7	Fulton Co.	Same as #3.
5. Maternal Health Care	9	Farnam Co.	Reduce health risks for babies of teenage mothers; reduce welfare dependency.
6. Rape/Domestic Violence	9	Farnam Co.	Reduce victim trauma; successful prosecution of offender.
7. Rape/Domestic Violence	9	Fulton Co.	Same as #6.
8. Chronic Mentally Ill Support	10	Farnam Co.	Maintenance of chronically mentally ill in the community; prevention of institutional placement.
9. Maternal Health Care	11	Fulton Co.	Same as #5.
10. Juvenile Justice	11	Fulton Co.	Rehabilitation of juvenile offenders; protection of life and property.
11. Frail Elderly In-Home Care	12	Farnam Co.	Prevention of nursing home placement.

12. Juvenile Justice	13	Farnam Co.	Divert status offenders from court; rehabilitation; public protection.
13. Frail Elderly In-Home Care	14	Fulton Co.	Same as #11.
14. Child Protection Services	15	Farnam Co.	Prevention and treatment of child abuse.
15. Child Protection Services	15	Fulton Co.	Same as #14.

Data Collection and Instrumentation

Qualitative information about the 15 interorganizational service delivery systems we described in this book were collected in personal interviews with administrators and community informants. The purpose of the interviews was to gain a full understanding of why the network developed, how it has been maintained, and current pressures for change. Topics included: the developmental history of the network; the governance structure; characteristics of the client population, service philosophy and service approach; and past and current financing strategies. Case studies were written for each network from this data (Alter, 1988a, 1988b, 1988c).

In addition, two instruments for collecting quantitative data were developed. Questionnaire 1 was completed by 131 administrators, and Questionnaire 2 was completed by 297 workers. In all cases the questionnaires were administered face-to-face during interviews or staff meetings. When administering the questionnaires, we always gave our subjects a verbal explanation of the research project and definitions of the terms used.

There were 32 unique items on the two questionnaires. Fifteen of these items were used to compute scores utilized for the analysis in this book. In addition, we constructed three indexes from the items by summing. These 18 variables, their conceptual and operational definitions, and directions for computation are reported in Table B.1.

Analysis of Data

   Problems are encountered when the network is taken as the unit of analysis. Foremost are problems associated with collecting data at one level for analysis at another (Blalock, 1979). Although there were more than 400 individual respondents in this study ($N = 428$), these responses had to be aggregated to the organization level ($N = 158$), and the organizational scores aggregated to the network level ($N = 15$). This procedure introduced the possibility of regression to the mean (Morrissey et al., 1982, 1984). Further, small sample size limited the range of statistical procedures used. This study relies on correlation analysis and regression with only one or two independent variables.

   Because of these problems, microstructural analysis has usually not aggregated data twice, but has left it at the organizational level (for example, see Hall et al., 1977). The approach taken in this study, however, is to explore data analysis at the network level in spite of associated problems. A sample size of 15 is not large, but neither is it very small. Until this data set can be expanded, the result of its analysis must be considered to be preliminary and exploratory. Findings must be considered to be tentative, and should not be generalized.

Table B.1
Environmental Characteristics

Resource Dependency (1)	Degree to which a network of organizations relies on external resources.	Proportion of an organization's total budget derived from state or federal agency as opposed to client fees.	Organizational responses averaged to network level.
Network Autonomy (1)	Degree to which a network is constrained in its ability to be self-governing as opposed to being autonomous.	Administrators' perception regarding how much freedom they have in assessing, planning, and delivering needed services within the network.	Organizational responses averaged to network level.
Work Status (2)	Degree to which clients receive services voluntarily/involuntarily.	Percent of clients in workers' caseloads under court order to receive service	Organizational responses averaged to network level.

Technological Characteristics

Task Scope (2)	Breadth of task paradigm: extent to which service is narrow or holistic.	Number of categories used in diagnosis; number of intervention roles used during service delivery.	The numbers of diagnostic categories and intervention roles indicated by each worker were taken as a percentage of the six categories given in the item; the two scores were summed for the individuals' score and averaged to the organization; organizations' scores were averaged to the network.
Task Intensity (2)	Degree to which client services are concentrated.	Average number of minutes workers spend with or on behalf of each client.	Responses were averaged to the organization level; organizations' scores were averaged to the network.
Task Duration (2)	Degree to which client services are long lasting.	Average number of months workers' cases remain open. Average number of cases workers have on caseload at one time.	Responses were averaged to the organization level; organizations' scores were averaged to the network.
Task Volume (2)	Size of work stream.	Average number of years before workers know the outcome of their intervention.	Responses were averaged to the organization level; organizations' scores were averaged to the network.
Task Uncertainty (2)	Extent to which task processes or interventions have knowable outcomes.	Responses were averaged to the organization level; organizations' scores were averaged to the network.	Responses were averaged to the organization level; organizations' scores were averaged to the network

continued

Structural Characteristics

Size (1)	Size of network.	The number of organizations identified as participating in a network using procedure described in Appendix A.
Centrality (1)	Extent to which one or a small number of organizations dominates a network.	Degree to which all clients flow through the core of a network.	Symmetrical matrices were created from client referral data; centralization index was computed using Mackenzie (1978) algorithm.
Complexity (1)	Extent to which a variety of services are available to clients within a network.	Number of different types of service sectors represented in a network.	Index is the average number of different services provided by each organization in the network.
Differentiation (1)	Extent to which there is a division of function among organizations in a network.	Ratio of actual functional specializations to the highest degree of specialization possible in a network.	Index is the ratio of the number of organizations within a system performing a single function to the number of organizations in the network performing multiple functions.
Communication Connectivity (1)	Number of communication linkages between organizations in a network.	Average number of verbal interactions between a worker and workers in other organizations in network per week.	Responses were averaged to the organization level; organizations' scores were averaged to the network.

Operational Processes

Administrative Coordination (1) *	Extent to which administrators make decisions jointly and rely on mutual adjustment and feedback.	Percentage of time administrators perceive that they use impersonal, personal, or collective methods for decision making.	Three percentages for the three types of coordination were averaged to the organizational level and weighted as follows: impersonal * .75; personal * 1.5; group * 3.0; weighted scores were summed for each organization; organizations' scores were averaged to the network.
Task Integration (2) *	Extent to which staff members work together interdependently across organizational boundaries.	Percentage of time workers perceive that they use sequential, reciprocal, or team methods of task accomplishment across organizational boundaries.	Three percentages for the three types of task integration were averaged to the organizational level and weighted as follows: sequential * .75; reciprocal * 1.5; collective * 3.0; weighted scores were summed for each organization; organizations' scores were averaged to the network.

Network Outcomes

Conflict (1, 2) *	Amount of disharmony and strife between organizations in a network.	Administrators' and workers' perceptions of the severity of conflict within a system, measured by frustration, verbal disputes, and acts, both overt and covert.	Individuals' responses were averaged with equal weight to obtain an organization's score; organizations' scores were averaged to the network.

311

References

Agranoff, R., & Pattakos, A. (1979). *Dimensions of services integration: Service delivery, program linkages, policy, management, organizational structure.* Human Service Monograph Series Project Share, Government Printing Office.

Aiken, M., Dewar, R., DiTomaso, N., Hage, J., & Zeitz, G. (1975). *Coordinating human services.* San Francisco: Jossey-Bass.

Aiken, M., & Hage, J. (1968). Organizational interdependence and intra-organizational structure. *American Sociological Review, 33*(6), 912-930.

Aldrich, H. (1979). *Organizations and environments.* Englewood Cliffs, NJ: Prentice-Hall.

Aldrich, H., & Mueller, S. (1982). The evolution of organizational forms: Technology, coordination and control. *Research in Organizational Behavior, 4,* 33-87.

Aldrich, H., & Pfeffer, J. (1976). Environments of organizations. In A. Inkeles, J. Coleman, & N. Smelser (Eds.), *Annual review of sociology, Vol. 2* (pp. 79-105). Palo Alto, CA: Annual Review.

Alexander, J., & Randolph, W. A. (1985). The fit between technology and structure as a predictor of performance in nursing subunits. *Academy of Management Journal, 28*(4), 844-859.

Alinsky, S. D. (1971). *Rules for radicals: A practical primer for realistic radicals.* New York: Random House.

Alter, C. (1988a). The changing structure of elderly service delivery systems. *The Gerontologist, 28,* 91-98.

Alter, C. (1988b). Function, form and change of juvenile justice systems. *Children and Youth Services Review, 10*(2), 71-99.

Alter, C. (1988c). Integration in interorganizational hospice care systems. *The Hospice Journal, 3,* 11-32.

Alter, C. (1990). An exploratory study of conflict and coordination in interorganizational service delivery systems. *Academy of Management Journal, 33*(3), 478-501.

Alter, C., Deutelbaum, W., Dodd, T. E., Else, J., & Raheim, S. (1992, March). *Integrating three strategies of family empowerment: Family, community, and economic development.* Paper presented at the annual program meeting of the Council on Social Work Education, Kansas City, Missouri.

Aoki, M. (1988). *Bargaining in the Japanese economy.* New York: Cambridge University Press.

Ashar, H., & Shapiro, J. Z. (1988). Measuring centrality: A note on Hackman's resource-allocation theory. *Administrative Science Quarterly, 33,* 275-283.

Assael, G. (1969). Constructive role for interorganizational conflict. *Administrative Science Quarterly, 14,* 573-581.

Astley, W. G., & Fombrun, C. J. (1983). Collective strategy: Social ecology of organizational environments. *Academy of Management Review, 8,* 576-587.

Axelrod, R. (1984). *The evolution of cooperation.* New York: Basic Books.

Axelrod, R., & Hamilton, W. D. (1984). The evolution of cooperation. *Science, 211*(4489), 1390-1396.

Azumi, K., & Hage, J. (1972). *Organizational systems.* Lexington, MA: D. C. Health.

Bachrach, R. H. (1983). *Theories of social change: A critical appraisal.* New York: Haworth.

Bavalas, A. (1948). Mathematical model for group structures. *Applied Anthropology, 7*(3), 16-30.

Beder, H. (1984). *Realizing the potential of interorganizational cooperation.* San Francisco: Jossey-Bass.

Benjamin, A. E., Lindeman, D. A., Budetti, P. P., & Newacheck, P. W. (1984). Shifting commitments to long term care: The role of coordination. *The Gerontologist, 24,* 598-603.

Benson, J. (1975). The interorganizational network as a political economy. *Administrative Science Quarterly, 20*(2), 229-249.

Benson, J., Kunce, J., Thompson, C., & Allen, D. (1973). *Coordinating human services.* Columbia: University of Missouri Regional Rehabilitation Research Institute.

Berg, S., & Hoekman, J. (1988). Entrepreneurship over the product life cycle: Joint venture strategies in the Netherlands. In F. Contractor & P. Lorange (Eds.), *Cooperative strategies in international business* (pp. 145-167). Lexington, MA: Lexington Books.

Berg, S. V., Duncan, H. J., & Friedman, P. (1982). *Joint venture strategies and corporate innovation.* Cambridge, MA: Oelgeschalger, Gunn & Hain.

Biddle, B. J. (1986). *Recent developments in role theory.* Palo Alto, CA: Annual Reviews.

Birnbaum, H., Burke, R., Swearingen, C., & Dunlop, B. (1984). Implementing community-based long-term care: Experience of New York's long-term home health care program. *The Gerontologist, 24,* 380-386.

Blalock, W. M. (1979). Measurement and conceptualization problems: Major obstacles to integrating theory and research. *American Sociological Review, 44*(6), 881-894.

Blau, P. M. (1970). A formal theory of differentiation in organizations. *American Sociological Review, 35,* 210-218.

Blau, P. M. (1972). Interdependence and hierarchy in organizations. *Social Science Research, 1,* 1-24.

Blau, P. M. (1973). *The organization of academic work.* New York: Wiley-Interscience.

Blau, S., & Scott, W. R. (1962). *Formal organizations: A comparative approach.* San Francisco: Chandler.

Boje, D., & Whetten, D. A. (1981). Effects of organizational strategies and contextual constraints on centrality and attributions of influence in interorganizational networks. *Administrative Science Quarterly, 26*, 378-395.

Boudon, R. (1986). *Theories of social change: A critical appraisal.* Cambridge, UK: Polity Press.

Bradach, J., & Eccles, R. (1989). Price, authority, and trust: From ideal types to plural forms. *Annual Review of Sociology, 15*, 97-118.

Broskowski, A. (1981). *Linking health and mental health.* Beverly Hills, CA: Sage.

Buckley, P. J., & Casson, M. (1988). A theory of cooperation in international business. In F. Contractor & P. Lorange (Eds.), *Cooperative strategies in international business* (pp. 31-53). Lexington, MA: Lexington Books.

Burns, M., & Mauet, A. (1984). Administrative freedom for interorganizational action: A life-cycle interpretation. *Administration & Society, 16*(3), 289-305.

Burns, T., & Dietz, T. (1991a). Cultural evolution: Social rule system, selection, and human agency. Paper presented at the conference "Technology at the Outset," Wissenschaftszentrum, Berlin.

Burns, T., & Dietz, T. (1991b). *Institutional dynamics: An evolutionary perspective.* Paper presented at the XVth World Congress of the International Political Science Association.

Burns, T., & Stalker, G. M. (1961). *The management of innovation.* London: Tavistock.

Burt, R. (1980). Models of network structure. *Annual Review of Sociology, 6*, 79-91.

Cameron, K. (1981). *The enigma of organizational effectiveness.* San Francisco: Jossey-Bass.

Campbell, J. L., Hollingsworth, J. R., & Lindberg, L. N. (Eds.). (1991). *The governance of the American economy.* New York: Cambridge University Press.

Carroll, G. R. (1984). Organizational ecology. *Annual Review of Sociology, 10*, 71-93.

Carroll, G. R. (1985). Concentration and specialization: Dynamics of niche width in populations of organizations. *American Journal of Sociology, 85*, 1261-1283.

Carroll, G. R. (Ed.). (1988). *Ecological models of organizations.* Cambridge, MA: Ballinger.

Carroll, G. R., & Delacroix, J. (1982, June). Organizational mortality in the newspaper industries of Argentina and Ireland: An ecological approach. *Administrative Science Quarterly, 27*, 169-98.

Cawson, A. (in press). Sectoral governance in consumer electronics in Britain and France. In J. R. Hollingsworth, P. C. Schmitter, & W. Streeck (Eds.), *Comparing capitalist economies: Variations in the governance of sectors.*

Chandler, A. D. (1962). *Strategy and structure: Chapters in the history of industrial enterprise.* Cambridge, MA: MIT Press.

Chandler, A. D. (1977). *The visible hand: The managerial revolution in American business.* Cambridge, MA: MIT Press.

Clark, K. B., Fujimoto, T., & Chew, W. B. (1987). Product development in the world auto industry. In *Brookings papers on economic activity* (No. 3, p. 741). Washington, DC: Brookings Institution.

Coase, R. (1937). The nature of the firm. *Economica, 4*, 386-405.

Cohn, A. H. (1979). Effective treatment of child abuse and neglect. *Social Work, 24*(6), 513-519.

Coleman, J. S. (1990). *Foundations of social theory.* Cambridge, MA: Belknap Press of Harvard.

Coleman, W. D. (in press). Keeping the shotgun behind the door: Governing the securities industry in Canada, the United Kingdom and the United States. In J. R. Hollingsworth, P. C. Schmitter, & W. Streeck (Eds.), *Comparing capitalist economies: Variations in the governance of sectors.*

Collins, P. D., Hage, J., & Hull, F. M. (1988). Organizational and technological predictors of change in automaticity. *Academy of Management Journal, 31*(3), 512-543.

Collins, R. (1988). *Theoretical sociology.* San Diego, CA: Harcourt Brace Jovanovich.

Contractor, F., & Lorange, P. (Eds.). (1988). *Cooperative strategies in international business.* Lexington, MA: Lexington Books.

Cook, K. S. (1977). Exchange and power in networks of interorganizational relations. *Sociological Quarterly, 18*(1), 62-82.

Cook, K. S., & Emerson, R. M. (1984). Exchange networks and the analysis of complex organizations. *Research in the Sociology of Organizations, 3,* 1-30.

Corwin, R. G. (1969, December). Patterns of organizational conflict. *Administrative Science Quarterly, 14,* 507-521.

Coser, L. (1956). *The functions of social conflict.* Glencoe, IL: Free Press.

Dawes, R. M. (1991). Social dilemmas, economic self-interest, and evolutionary theory. In R. M. Coughlin (Ed.), *Morality, rationality, and efficiency: Perspectives on socio-economics 1990* (pp. 17-40). New York: M. E. Sharpe.

Delacroix, J., Swaminathan, A., & Solt, M. (1989). Density dependence versus population dynamics: An ecological study of the failings in the California wine industry. *American Sociological Review, 54,* 245-262.

Delbecq, A., & Weiss, J. (1988). The business culture of Silicon Valley: Is it a model for the future? In J. Hage (Ed.), *The futures of organizations* (pp. 123-142). Lexington, MA: D. C. Heath.

De Swaan, A. (1988). *In care of the state.* New York: Oxford University Press.

Dewar, R., & Hage, J. (1978). Size, technology, complexity, and structural differentiation: Toward a theoretical synthesis. *Administrative Science Quarterly, 23,* 111-136.

DeWitt, J. (1977). *Managing the human service "system": What we have learned from services integration.* Human Service Monograph Series Project Share, Government Printing Office.

DiStefano, T. (1984). Interorganizational conflict: A review of an emerging field. *Human Relations, 37*(5), 351-366.

Dryfoos, J. D. (1991). *Adolescents at risk: Prevalence and prevention.* New York: Oxford University Press.

Duncan, R. B. (1972). Characteristics of organizational environments and perceived environmental uncertainty. *Administrative Science Quarterly, 17,* 313-327.

Durkheim, E. (1964). *The division of labor in society.* Glencoe, IL: Free Press.

Eccles, R., & White, H. (1988). Price and authority in inter-profit center transactions. *American Journal of Sociology Supplement, 94,* S17-S51.

Economic growth: Explaining the mystery. (1992, January 4). *The Economist,* pp. 15-18.

Etzioni, A. (1988). *The moral dimension: Toward a new economics.* New York: Free Press.

Evan, W. (1966). The organization-set: Toward a theory of interorganizational relations. In J. Thompson (Ed.), *Approaches to Organizational Design* (pp. 173-192). Pittsburgh, PA: University of Pittsburgh Press.

Evashwick, C. (1985). Home health care: Current trends and future opportunities. *Journal of Ambulatory Care Management, 8,* 4-17.

Frank, G. (1983). Policy is one thing, implementation is another: A comparison of community agencies in a juvenile justice referral network. *American Journal of Community Psychology, 9,* 581-604.

Frazier, G. (1983). Interorganizational exchange behavior in marketing channels: A broadened perspective. *Journal of Marketing, 47,* 68-78.

Freeman, L. (1978/1979). Centrality in social network: Conceptual clarification. *Social Network, 1*(1), 215-239.

Freund, D. A. (1986). The private delivery of Medicaid services: Lessons for administrators, providers, and policy makers. *Journal of Ambulatory Care Management, 9,* 54-65.

Fujimoto, T. (1989). *Organizations for effective product development: The case of the global motor industry.* Doctoral dissertation, Harvard University, Cambridge, MA.

Fukuyama, F. (1992). *The end of history and the last man.* New York: Free Press.

Galaskiewicz, J. (1978). The structure of community organizational networks. *Social Forces, 57*(3), 1346-1364.

Galaskiewicz, J. (1979). *Exchange networks and community politics.* Beverly Hills, CA: Sage.

Galaskiewicz, J. (1985, October). Professional networks and the institutionalization of a single mind-set. *American Sociological Review, 50,* 639-658.

Galaskiewicz, J., & Shatin, D. (1981). Leadership and networking among neighborhood human service organizations. *Administrative Science Quarterly, 26*(3), 434-448.

Galtung, J. (1967). *Theory and methods of social research.* New York: Columbia University Press.

Garnier, M. A., Hage, J., & Fuller, B. (1989). The strong state, social class and controlled school expansion in France, 1881-1975. *American Journal of Sociology, 95,* 279-306.

Gawthrop, L. C. (1984). *Public sector management, systems, and ethics.* Bloomington: Indiana University Press.

Georgopoulos, B. S., & Mann, F. C. (1962). *The community general hospital.* New York: Macmillan.

Gillespie, D., & Mileti, D. (1979). *Technostructures and interorganizational behavior.* Lexington, MA: Lexington Books.

Goodman, P., & Pennings, J. J. (1977). *New perspectives on organizational effectiveness.* San Francisco: Jossey-Bass.

Gouldner, A. (1960). The norm of reciprocity. *American Sociological Review, 25*(2), 161-178.

Gouldner, A. W. (1959). Organizational analysis. In R. K. Merton, L. Broom, & L. S. Cottrell, Jr. (Eds.), *Sociology today* (pp. 400-428). New York: Basic Books.

Grandori, A., & Soda, G. (1991). *Inter-firm networks: A state of art.* Unpublished paper, Universitat Commerciale, Milano, Italy.

Granovetter, M. S. (1973). The strength of weak ties. *American Journal of Sociology, 78*(6), 1360-1380.

Granovetter, M. S. (1985). Economic action and social structure: The problem of embeddedness. *American Journal of Sociology, 91*(3), 481-510.

Gray, B. (1985). Conditions facilitating interorganizational collaboration. *Human Relations, 39*(10), 911-936.

Gray, B. (1989a). The art of collaborating. *Association Management, 41*(50).

Gray, B. (1989b). *Collaborating: Finding common ground for multiparty problems.* San Francisco: Jossey-Bass.

Gray, B., & Hay, T. (1986). Political limits to interorganizational consenses and change. *The Journal of Applied Behavioral Science, 22*(2), 95-112.

Guetzkow, H. (1966). Relations among organizations. In R. V. Bowers (Ed.), *Studies in behavior in organizations* (pp. 13-44). Athens: University of Georgia Press.

Hackman, J. R. (1985). Power and centrality in the allocation of resources in colleges and universities. *Administrative Science Quarterly, 30*, 61-77.

Hage, J. (1965, December). An axiomatic theory of organizations. *Administrative Science Quarterly, 10*, 289-320.

Hage, J. (1974). *Communication and organizational control: Cybernetics in health and welfare organizations.* New York: John Wiley.

Hage, J. (1980). *Theories of organizations: Form, process, and transformation.* New York: John Wiley.

Hage, J. (1984). Organizational theory and the concept of productivity. In A. P. Brief (Ed.), *Productivity research in the behavioral and social sciences* (pp. 91-126). New York: Praeger.

Hage, J. (Ed.). (1988). *Futures of organizations: Innovating to adapt strategy and human resources to rapid technological change.* Lexington, MA: Lexington Books.

Hage, J., & Aiken, M. (1967, March). Program change and organizational properties: A comparative analysis. *American Journal of Sociology, 72*, 503-519.

Hage, J., Collins, P., Hull, F., & Teachman, J. (1991). *Organization form and the survival of American manufacturing plants from 1973 to 1987: An extension of Aldrich and Muller's theory of the evolution of organizational form.* Unpublished manuscript. College Park, MD: University of Maryland Center for Innovation.

Hage, J., Garnier, M. A., & Fuller, B. (1988). The active state, investment in human capital and economic growth. *American Sociological Review, 53*(6), 824-837.

Hage, J., Hanneman, R., & Gargan, E. T. (1989). *State responsiveness and state activism.* London: Unwin Hyman.

Hage, J., & Powers, C. (1992). *Post-industrial lives.* Newbury Park, CA: Sage.

Hakansson, H. (1990). Technological collaboration in industrial networks. *European Management Journal, 8*(3), 371-379.

Hakansson, H., & Johanson, J. (1988). Formal and informal cooperation strategies in international industrial networks. In F. Contractor & P. Lorange (Eds.), *Cooperative strategies in international business* (pp. 369-379). Lexington, MA: Lexington Books.

Hall, R. H. (1990). *Organizations: Structure and process* (5th ed.). Englewood Cliffs, NJ: Prentice-Hall.

Hall, R. H., Clark, J. P., Giordano, P. C., Johnson, P. V., & Van Roekel, M. (1977). Patterns of interorganizational relationships. *Administrative Science Quarterly, 22*(3), 457-474.

Hallen, L., Johanson, J., & Mohamed, N. (1987). Relationship strength and stability in international and domestic industrial marketing. *Industrial Marketing and Purchasing, 2*(3), 22-37.

Hanf, K., & Scharpf, F. (1978). *Interorganizational policy making: Limits to coordination.* Beverly Hills, CA: Sage.

Hannan, M. T., & Freeman, J. (1977). The population ecology of organizations. *American Journal of Sociology, 82,* 929-964.

Hannan, M. T., & Freeman, J. (1984, April). Structural inertia and organizational change. *American Sociological Review, 49,* 149-164.

Hannan, M. T., & Freeman, J. (1989). *Organizational ecology.* Cambridge, MA: Harvard University Press.

Harrigan, K. R. (1986). *Managing for joint venture success.* Lexington, MA: Lexington Books.

Harrigan, K. R. (1988). Strategic alliances and partner asymmetries. In F. Contractor & P. Lorange (Eds.), *Cooperative strategies in international business* (pp. 205-226). Lexington, MA: Lexington Books.

Hawley, A. (1950). *Human ecology.* New York: Ronald.

Hawley, A. (1968). Human ecology. In D. Sills (Ed.), *International encyclopaedia of the social sciences* (pp. 328-337). New York: Macmillan.

Hechter, M. (1987). *Principles of group solidarity.* Berkeley: University of California Press.

Hechter, M. (1989). Rational choice foundations of social order. In J. H. Turner (Ed.), *Theory building in sociology: Assessing theoretical cumulation* (pp. 46-72). Newbury Park, CA: Sage.

Helfer, R., & Kemp, C. H. (1968). *The battered child.* Chicago: University of Chicago Press.

Hergert, M., & Morris, D. (1988). Trends in international collaborative agreements. In F. Contractor & P. Lorange (Eds.), *Cooperative strategies in international business* (pp. 99-109). Lexington, MA: Lexington Books.

Hickson, D. J., Butler, R. J., Cray, D., Mallory, G. R., & Wilson, D. C. (1986). *Top decisions: Strategic decision-making in organizations.* Oxford: Basil Blackwell.

Hickson, D. J., Pugh, D. S., & Pheysey, D. C. (1969). Operations technology and organizational structure: An empirical reappraisal. *Administrative Science Quarterly, 14,* 370-397.

Hilts, P. J. (1989, May 24). U.S. consortium is formed to commercialize superconductors. *Washington Post,* p. A1.

Hladik, K. (1988). R&D and international joint ventures. In F. Contractor & P. Lorange (Eds.), *Cooperative strategies in international business* (pp. 187-204). Lexington, MA: Lexington Books.

Hollingsworth, J. R. (1991). The logic of coordinating American manufacturing sectors. In J. L. Campbell, J. R. Hollingsworth, & L. N. Lindberg, *The governance of the American economy* (pp. 35-74). New York: Cambridge University Press.

Hollingsworth, J. R., Hage, J., & Hanneman, R. A. (1990). *State intervention in medical care: Consequences for Britain, France, Sweden, and the United States.* Ithaca, NY: Cornell University Press.

Hollingsworth, J. R., & Hollingsworth, E. J. (1987). *Controversy about American hospitals: Funding, ownership, and performance.* Washington, DC: American Enterprise Institute.

Hollingsworth, J. R., Schmitter, P. C., & Streeck, W. (Eds.). (in press). *Comparing capitalist economies.* New York: Oxford University Press.

Houghton, J. R. (1989, September 24). The age of the hierarchy is over. *The New York Times*, p. 3.

Hyman, R., & Streeck, W. (Eds.). (1988). *New technology and industrial relations.* New York: Basil Blackwell.

Jarillo, J. C. (1988). On strategic networks. *Strategic Management Journal, 9,* 31-41.

Johanson, J., & Mattsson, L. (1987). Interorganizational relations in industrial systems: A network approach compared with the transaction cost approach. *Working Paper Series* (#7), Department of Business Adminstration, University of Uppasala, Sweden.

Johns Hopkins University. (1989). *Entrepreneurial training.* Pamphlet advertising a training program provided by JHU staff. Baltimore, MD.

Kaluzny, A. D., Morrissey, J. P., & McKinney, M. M. (1990). Emerging organizational networks: The case of community clinical oncology programs. In S. S. Mick & Associates (Eds.), *Innovations in the organization of health care: New insights into organizational theory* (pp. 86-115). San Francisco: Jossey-Bass.

Kanter, R. M. (1989, August). Becoming PALS: Pooling, allying and linking across companies. *Academy of Management Executives, 3,* 183-193.

Katz, P., & Kahn, R. (1966). *The social psychology of organizations.* New York: John Wiley.

Kidder, T. (1981). *The soul of the new machine.* Boston: Little, Brown.

Killing, J. P. (1988). Understanding alliances: The role of task and organizational complexity. In F. Contractor & P. Lorange (Eds.), *Cooperative strategies in international business* (pp. 55-67). Lexington, MA: Lexington Books.

Knoke, D. (1988, June). Incentives in collective action organizations. *American Sociological Review, 53,* 311-329.

Kogut, B., Shan, W., & Walker, G. (1990). *The structuring of an industry: Cooperation and embeddedness among biotechnology firms.* Unpublished manuscript. Philadelphia: University of Pennsylvania, Wharton School.

Kogut, B., & Singh, H. (1988). Entering the United States by joint venture: Competitive rivalry and industrial structure. In F. Contractor & P. Lorange (Eds.), *Cooperative strategies in international business* (pp. 241-251). Lexington, MA: Lexington Books.

Kraar, L. (1989, March 27). Your rivals can be your allies. *Fortune*, pp. 66-76.

Kramer, R., & Grossman, B. (1987). Contracting for social services: Process management and resource dependences. *Social Service Review, 61,* 33-55.

Kübler-Ross, E. (1969). *On death and dying.* New York: Macmillan.

Laage-Hellman, J. (1989). *Technological development in industrial networks.* Doctoral dissertation, published by the University of Uppsala, Uppsala, Sweden.

Laumann, E., Galaskiewicz, J., & Marsden, P. (1978). Community structure as interorganizational linkages. *Annual Review of Sociology, 4,* 455-484.

Laumann, E., & Marsden, P. (1982). Microstructural analysis in interorganizational systems. *Social Networks, 4,* 329-348.

Laumann, E., & Pappi, F. (1976). *Networks of collective action: A perspective on community influence systems.* New York: Academic Press.

Lawrence, P. F., & Lorsch, J. W. (1967). Differentiation and integration in complex organizations. *Administrative Science Quarterly, 12,* 1-47.

Leach, S. N. (1980). Organisational interests and interorganisational behavior. *Town Planning Review, 51*, 286-300.

Lefton, M. (1970). Client characteristics and structural outcomes. In W. Rosengren, & M. Lefton (Eds.), *Organizations and clients* (pp. 17-36). Columbus, OH: Charles E. Merrill.

Lefton, M., & Rosengren, W. (1966). Organizations and clients: Lateral and longitudinal dimensions. *American Sociological Review, 31*(6), 802-810.

Lehman, E. (1975). *Coordinating health care: Explorations in interorganizational relations.* Beverly Hills, CA: Sage.

Levine, S., & White, P. E. (1961). Exchange as a conceptual framework for the study of interorganizational relationships. *Administrative Science Quarterly, 5*, 583-601.

Likert, R. (1967). *The human organization: Its management and value.* New York: Holt, Rinehart & Winston.

Lincoln, J., & McBride, K. (1985, March). Resources, homophily and dependence: Organizational attitudes and asymmetric ties in human service networks. *Social Science Research, 14*, 1-30.

Lincoln, Y. (1985). *Organizational theory and inquiry: The paradigm revolution.* Beverly Hills, CA: Sage.

Litwak, E. (1970). Towards the theory and practice of coordination between formal organizations. In W. Rosengren, & M. Lefton (Eds.), *Organizations and clients* (pp. 137-186). Columbus, OH: Charles E. Merrill.

Litwak, E., & Hylton, L. F. (1962). Interorganizational analysis: A hypothesis on co-ordinating agencies. *Administrative Science Quarterly, 6*, 395-420.

Mackenzie, K. D. (1978). Structural centrality in communications networks. *Psychometrika, 31*(1), 17-25.

Mann, F. C., & Williams, L. K. (1960, September). Observations on the dynamics of a change to electronic data processing equipment. *Administrative Science Quarterly, 5*, 217-256.

March, J. G., & Simon, H. A. (1958). *Organizations.* New York: John Wiley.

Marwell, G., & Oliver, P. (1984). Collective action theory and social movements research. *Research in Social Movements, Conflict and Change, 7*, 1-28.

Mathiesen, T. (1971). *Across the boundaries of organizations.* Berkeley, CA: Flendessary Press.

McKelvey, B. (1982). *Organizational systematics.* Berkeley: University of California Press.

McKelvey, B., & Aldrich, H. (1983, March). Populations, natural selection, and applied organization science. *Administrative Science Quarterly, 28*, 101-128.

McKinney, M. M. (1990). *Interorganizational exchanges as performance workers in a community cancer network.* Unpublished doctoral dissertation, University of North Carolina, School of Public Health, Chapel Hill.

Merton, R. K. (1957). *Social theory and social structure.* Glencoe, IL: Free Press.

Meyer, J. W. (1978). *Environments and organizations.* San Francisco: Jossey-Bass.

Miles, R. (1980). *Macro organizational behavior.* Glenview, IL: Scott, Foresman.

Milner, M. J. (1980). *Unequal care: A case study of interorganizational relations.* New York: Columbia University Press.

Mintzberg, H. (1979). *The structuring of organizations.* Englewood Cliffs, NJ: Prentice-Hall.

MIT Commission. (1989). *Made in America.* Cambridge: MIT Press.

Mohr, L. (1971). Organizational technology and organizational structure. *Administrative Science Quarterly, 16*, 444-459.

Molnar, J., & Rogers, D. A. (1979). A comparative model of interorganizational conflict. *Administrative Science Quarterly, 24*, 405-424.

Morris, R., & Lescohier, I. M. (1978). Service integration: Real versus illusory solutions to welfare dilemmas. In R. Sarri, & Y. Hasenfeld (Eds.), *The management of human services* (pp. 21-50). New York: Columbia University Press.

Morrissey, J. P., Hall, R. H., & Lindsey, M. L. (1982). *Interorganizational relations: A sourcebook of measures for mental health programs* (Series BN No. 2 DHHS Pub. No. ADM 82-1187). National Institute of Mental Health.

Morrissey, J. P., Steadman, H. J., Kilburn, H., & Lindsey, M. L. (1984). The effectiveness of jail mental health programs: An interorganizational assessment. *Criminal Justice and Behavior, 11*, 235-256.

Morrissey, J. P., Tausig, M., & Lindsey, M. L. (1984). *Interorganizational networks in mental health systems: Assessing community support programs for the chronically mentally ill.* Washington, DC: Community Support Rehabilitation Branch, Division of Mental Health Service Programs.

Mowery, D. C. (Ed.). (1988). *International collaborative ventures in U.S. manufacturing.* Cambridge, MA: Ballinger.

Moxon, R., Roehl, T., & Truitt, J. F. (1988). International cooperative ventures in the commercial aircraft industry: Gains, sure, but what's my share? In F. Contractor & P. Lorange (Eds.), *Cooperative strategies in international business* (pp. 255-278). Lexington, MA: Lexington Books.

Mulford, C. L. (1984). *Interorganizational relations: Implications for community development.* New York: Human Science Press.

Mulford, C. L., & Rogers, D. L. (1982). Definitions and models. In D. L. Rogers, & D. A. Whetten (Eds.), *Interorganizational coordination: Theory, research and implementation* (pp. 9-31). Ames: Iowa State University Press.

National Institute of Mental Health. (1983). *Hospital & community psychiatry service.* Washington, DC: Government Printing Office.

National Science Foundation, National Science Board. (1989). *Science indicators.* Washington, DC: Government Printing Office.

Nelson, K., Landsman, M., Deutelbaum, W. (1990). Three models of family-centered placement prevention services. *Child Welfare, 69*(1), 3-21.

Nelson, R. R., & Winter, S. G. (1982). *An evolutionary theory of economic change.* Cambridge, MA: Harvard University Press.

Nielsen, R. (1988). Cooperative strategy. *Strategic Management Journal, 9*, 475-492.

Nishiguchi, T. (1989). *Strategic dualism: An alternative in industrial societies.* Doctoral dissertation, Nuffield College, Oxford, England.

Nocks, B. C., Learner, R. M., Blackman, D., & Brown, T. (1986). The effects of a community-based long term care project on nursing home utilization. *The Gerontologist, 26*, 150-156.

Nohria, N., & Eccles, R. (Eds.). (in press). *Networks and organizations.* Cambridge, MA: Harvard Business School Press.

North, D. (1981). *Structure and change in economic history.* New York: Norton.

North, D. C. (1990). *Institution, institutional change, and economic performance.* New York: Cambridge University Press.

O'Brien, P. (in press). Governance systems in steel: The American and Japanese experience. In J. R. Hollingsworth, P. C. Schmitter, and W. Streeck (Eds.), *Comparing capitalist economies: Variations in the governance of sectors.*

Olson, M. (1965). *The logic of collective action.* Cambridge, MA: Harvard University Press.

Paulson, S. K. (1985). A paradigm for the analysis of interorganizational networks. *Social Networks, 7*(2), 105-126.

Perlman, R. (1975). *Consumers and social services.* New York: John Wiley.

Perrow, C. (1967). A framework for the comparative analysis of organizations. *American Sociological Review, 32,* 194-209.

Peters, T. J. (1987). *Thriving on chaos: Handbook for a management revolution.* New York: Knopf.

Peters, T. J., & Waterman, R. H. (1982). *In search of excellence: Lessons from America's best run companies.* New York: Harper & Row.

Pfeffer, J. (1981). *Power in organizations.* Marshfield, MA: Pitman.

Pfeffer, J., & Salancik, G. R. (1978). *The external control of organizations: A resource dependence perspective.* New York: Harper & Row.

Piore, M. J., & Sabel, C. F. (1986). *The second industrial divide: Possibilities for prosperity.* New York: Basic Books.

Polanyi, K. (1944). *The great transformation: The political and economic origins of our time.* Boston: Beacon.

Pollack, A. (1992a, January 1). Technology without borders raises big questions for U.S. *The New York Times,* p. 1.

Pollack, A. (1992b, January 6). A founding member leaves Sematech chip consortium. *The New York Times,* p. D1.

Pondy, L. (1969). Varieties of organizational conflict. *Administrative Science Quarterly, 14,* 499-505.

Potuchek, J. (1986). The context of social service funding: The funding relationship. *Social Service Review, 60,* 421-436.

Powell, W. W. (1990). Neither market nor hierarchy: Network forms of organization. In L. L. Cummings & B. Staw (Eds.), *Research in organizational behavior* (pp. 295-336). Greenwich, CT: JAI Press.

Powell, W. W., & Brantley, P. (in press). Competitive cooperation in biotechnology: Learning through networks. In. N. Nohria & R. Eccles (Eds.), *Networks and organizations.* Cambridge, MA: Harvard Business School Press.

Provan, K. G. (1984a). Interorganizational cooperation and decision making autonomy in a consortium multihospital system. *Academy of Management Review, 9*(3), 494-504.

Provan, K. G. (1984b). Technological and interorganizational activity as predictors of client referrals. *Academy of Management Journal, 27*(4), 811-829.

Redekop, P. (1986). Interorganizational conflict between government and voluntary agencies in the organization of a volunteer program: A case study. *Journal of Voluntary Action Research, 15,* 32-45.

Richards, E. (1989, April 10). U.S.-Japanese venture develops new supercomputer. *Washington Post,* p. A16.

Ritzer, G. (1990). *Frontier of social theory: The new synthesis.* New York: Columbia University Press.

Ritzer, G. (1992). *Contemporary sociological theory* (3rd ed.). New York: McGraw-Hill.

Roemer, P. M. (1986). Increasing returns and long run growth. *Journal of Political Economy, 94*(5), 1002-1037.

Roemer, P. M. (1990). Are non-convexities important for understanding growth? *American Economic Review, 80*(2), 97-103.

Rogers, D. L., & Whetten, D.A. (1982). *Interorganizational coordination: Theory, research and implementation.* Ames: Iowa State University Press.

Rogers, E. M., & Larsen, J. K. (1984). *Silicon Valley fever.* New York: Basic Books.

Rosenbaum, J. E., Karija, T., Setheasten, R., & Maier, T. (1990). Market and network theories of the transition from high school to work: Their application to industrialized societies. *Annual Review of Sociology, 16*, 263-299.

Rosengren, W. (1968). Organizational age, structure, and orientations toward clients. *Social Forces, 46*(1), 1-11.

Sako, M. (in press). Neither markets nor hierarchies: A comparative study of the printed circuit board industry in Britain and Japan. In J. R. Hollingsworth, P. C. Schmitter, & W. Streeck (Eds.), *Comparing capitalist economies: Variations in the governance of sectors.*

Salamon, L. M. (1982). *The federal budget and the nonprofit sector.* Washington, DC: Urban Institute Press.

Scherer, F. M. (1980). *Industrial market structure and economic performance* (2nd ed.). Chicago, IL: Rand McNally.

Schmit, S., & Kochan, T. (1972). Conflict: Towards conceptual clarity. *Administrative Science Quarterly, 17*, 359-370.

Scott, W. R. (1987). *Organizations: Rational, natural, and open systems* (2nd ed.). Englewood Cliffs, NJ: Prentice-Hall.

Scott, W. R., & Black, B. L. (1986). *The organization of mental health services: Societal and community systems.* Beverly Hills, CA: Sage.

Simmel, G. (1968). *The conflict in modern culture.* New York: Teachers College Press.

Snehota, I. (1990). *Notes on a theory of business enterprise.* Published doctoral dissertation, Uppsala University, Department of Business Studies, Uppsala, Sweden.

Sosin, M. (1985). Social problems covered by private agencies: An application of niche theory. *Social Service Review, 59*, 75-93.

Storey, J. R. (1986). Policy changes affecting older Americans during the first Reagan administration. *The Gerontologist, 1*, 27-31.

Strath, B. (in press). Modes of governance in the shipbuilding sector in West Germany, Sweden and Japan. In J. R. Hollingsworth, P. C. Schmitter, & W. Streeck (Eds.), *Comparing capitalist economies: Variations in the governance of sectors.*

Sydow, J. (1991). *On the management of strategic networks.* Unpublished working paper #67/91. Institute fur Management, Freie Universitat, Berlin, Germany.

Terreberry, S. (1968). The evolution of organizational environments. *Administrative Science Quarterly, 12*(4), 560-613.

Thompson, J. D. (1967). *Organizations in action.* New York: McGraw-Hill.

Toffler, A. (1981). *The third wave.* New York: Bantam.

Tosi, H. L., & Carroll, S. (1986). *Management: Contingencies, structure and process* (3rd ed.). New York: John Wiley.

Trist, E. (1983). Referent organizations and the development of inter-organizational domains. *Human Relations, 36*(1), 269-284.

Turner, J. C. (1991). *The structure of sociological theory* (5th ed.). Belmont, CA: Wadsworth.

Turner, J. C., & Tenoor, W. J. (1978). NIMH community support program: Pilot approach to a needed social reform. *Schizophrenia Bulletin, 4*(3), 319-334.

U.S. *Abstract of Statistics.* (1989). Washington, DC: Government Printing Office.

Van de Ven, A. H., Delbecq, A. L., & Koenig, R. (1976). Determinants of coordination modes within organizations. *American Sociological Review, 41,* 322-338.

Van de Ven, A. H., & Ferry, D. (1980). *Measuring and assessing organizations.* New York: John Wiley.

Vickers, G. (1968). *The art of judgement.* London: Chapman and Hall.

Walker, C. R. (1950, May). The problem of the repetitive job. *Harvard Business Review, 28,* 54-58.

Walker, C. R. (1957). *Toward the automatic factory: A case study of men and machines.* New Haven, CT: Yale University Press.

Walton, R. E., & Dutton, J. N. (1969, March). The management of interdepartment conflict: A model and review. *Administrative Science Quarterly, 14,* 73-90.

Warren, R. (1973). Comprehensive planning and coordination: Some functional aspects. *Administrative Science Quarterly, 12,* 396-419.

Warren, R., Rose, S., & Bergunder, A. F. (1974). *The structure of urban reform.* Toronto: D. C. Heath.

Weber, M. (1946). Bureaucracy. In H. Gerth & C. W. Mills (Eds.), *From Max Weber: Essays in sociology* (pp. 196-244). New York: Oxford University Press.

Weick, K. (1976). Educational organizations as loosely coupled systems. *Administrative Science Quarterly, 21*(1), 1-19.

Whetten, D. A. (1981). Interorganizational relations: A review of the field. *Journal of Higher Education, 52*(1), 1-28.

Wiewel, W., & Hunter, A. (1985). The interorganizational network as a resource: A comparative case study on organizational genesis. *Administrative Science Quarterly, 30,* 482-496.

Wildavsky, A. (1979). *Speaking truth to power: The art and craft of policy analysis.* Boston: Little, Brown.

Williamson, O. E. (1975). *Markets and hierarchies—analysis and antitrust implications: A study in the economics of internal organization.* New York: Free Press.

Williamson, O. E. (1985). *The economic institutions of capitalism: Firms, markets, relational contracting.* New York: Free Press.

Williamson, O. E. (1991). *Comparative economic organizations: The analysis of discrete structural alternatives.* Working paper, University of California, Berkeley.

Womack, J., Jones, D., & Roos, D. (1990). *The machine that changed the world.* New York: Rawson Associates.

Wooldridge, R. (1981). *Evaluation of complex systems.* San Francisco: Jossey-Bass.

Work, C. (1988, June 20). Business without borders. *U.S. News and World Report,* p. 48.

Young, R. (1988). Is population ecology a usual paradigm for the study of organization? *American Journal of Sociology, 94*(1), 1-24.

Yuchtman, E., & Seashore, S. E. (1967). System resource approach to organizational effectiveness. *American Sociological Review, 32*(6), 891-903.

Zeitz, G. (1985). Interorganizational dialectics. *Administrative Science Quarterly, 25,* 72-88.

Zey-Ferrel, M. (1979). *Dimensions of organizations: Environments, context, structure, process, and performance.* Santa Monica, CA: Goodyear.

Zuckerman, H., & Kaluzny, A. (1990). Strategic alliances in health care: The challenges of cooperation. *Frontiers of Health Services Management, 7*(3), 3-35.

Zurcher, L. G. (1987). Institutional theories of organization. *Annual Review of Sociology, 13,* 443-464.

Name Index

Subject Index

Abused children. *See* Child protection networks

Accessibility, of clients, 84, 87

Action, collective, 27, 33, 34, 55, 80

Action sets, 25, 49

Adaptive efficiency, 8-9, 14, 28, 39-40, 45, 54, 76, 263-265, 266, 267, 273, 276, 279, 285
  definition of, 274

Adaptiveness, 24, 28, 36, 37, 282

Administrating coordination:
  and conflict, 204-205, 207
  as control, 93
  definition of, 98
  and external control, 115-110, 128-132, 234-237, 245-250, 254-255
  illustration of, 99-100
  and interdependence, 93
  mechanisms of, 9, 92-95
  vs. task integration, 90, 91, 99
  and task technology, 123-127, 133-136, 137, 139

Adolescent pregnancies network, 101
  strategy of, 25
  and trust, 72

Adoption service network, 58, 100, 101, 155, 156, 202, 207, 210, 238-239, 240

Aerospace industry, 2, 4-5
  joint ventures in, 4-5

Agencies, government, 2

Alliances, 51, 54, 60
  altruistic behavior, 33-34
  need for, 12
  strategic, 2, 3, 6, 23, 44, 186

Asset specificity, 284

Associations, supplier, 61-62, 289

Associations trade. *See* Trade associations

Auto industry, 2
  joint ventures in, 5, 58
  systemic networks in, 51, 61, 62, 79, 108, 233

Autonomy, 36, 69, 72, 78
  as community base, 112, 143
  and conflict, 202-205
  and decoupeing, 70-71
  of networks, 102-103, 112, 143, 166, 168-169, 179, 263
  vs. resource dependency, 112, 115, 169

Benefits of cooperation, 22, 32, 35-38, 279-283

Bio-tec industry, 2, 4, 15
  joint ventures in, 5-6, 26, 27

Boundary spinners, 25, 46, 72, 288, 291
  definition of, 46

Bureaucracy, 13, 21, 28, 114, 155

333

About the Authors

Catherine Alter is Associate Professor and Director of the School of Social Work at the University of Iowa. She has done research on a wide variety of service delivery networks during the past decade and has used network analytic techniques to do program and system evaluation. She has published her research findings in article, book, and monograph form, the most recent article being a conceptual and empirical approach to inter-organizational conflict and cooperation. She is also interested in practice assessment and has published a book on assessment methodology. Currently, she is doing research on small-scale enterprise and self-employment as one new approach to welfare reform.

Jerald Hage has published a number of articles and books on organizations, the most recent being *The Future of Organizations* (1988) and *Organizational Change as a Strategy for Development* (with Kurt Finsterbusch) (1987). Presently, he is doing research on the role of knowledge in providing survival in firms. In particular, he has a special interest in the impact of technical and vocational education on productivity and adaptive efficiency. These concerns reflect his interest in combining the theory of organizations with microeconomics. This particular book is part of a larger attempt to write a general theory of post-industrial society that integrates macro and micro levels of analysis with a theory of agency and structure.